The Nature of Adolescence

The new edition of this successful textbook provides an up-to-date introduction to all of the key features of adolescent development. While drawing on the North American literature on adolescence, it highlights European perspectives and also provides unique coverage of the topic by summarising and reviewing what is known about adolescence from a British viewpoint.

Comprehensively updated and rewritten, this edition includes material on new topics such as:

- The development of the adolescent brain;
- Sleep patterns in adolescence;
- Parenting programmes for parents of teenagers;
- Health, including sport and exercise, nutrition and obesity, and mental health;
- Education and schooling;
- Young people's use of digital technologies;
- New approaches to resilience and coping.

The book places a particular emphasis on a positive view of adolescence, and the author develops a new theoretical perspective which looks at how young people themselves construct and shape their own developmental pathways. Interview material taken from discussions with adolescents is included throughout the book. This is an essential text for anyone studying human development at undergraduate and postgraduate level, as well as on postgraduate courses for professionals including teachers, social workers, health workers, counsellors and youth workers.

John C. Coleman is Senior Research Fellow in the Department of Education at Oxford University. He is also a Visiting Professor at the University of Bedfordshire. He was the Editor of the *Journal of Adolescence* for 14 years, and is an internationally recognised expert in the field of adolescence. He was awarded an OBE for services to youth in 2001.

Adolescence and Society
Series editor: John C. Coleman
Department of Education, University of Oxford

This series has now been running for over 20 years, and during this time has published some of the key texts in the field of adolescent studies. The series has covered a very wide range of subjects, almost all of them being of central concern to students, researchers and practitioners. A mark of the success of the series is that a number of books have gone to second and third editions, illustrating the popularity and reputation of the series.

The primary aim of the series is to make accessible to the widest possible readership important and topical evidence relating to adolescent development. Much of this material is published in relatively inaccessible professional journals, and the objective of the books in this series has been to summarise, review and place in context current work in the field, so as to interest and engage both an undergraduate and a professional audience.

The intention of the authors has always been to raise the profile of adolescent studies among professionals and in institutions of higher education. By publishing relatively short, readable books on topics of current interest to do with youth and society, the series makes people more aware of the relevance of the subject of adolescence to a wide range of social concerns.

The books do not put forward any one theoretical viewpoint. The authors outline the most prominent theories in the field and include a balanced and critical assessment of each of these. Whilst some of the books may have a clinical or applied slant, the majority concentrate on normal development.

The readership rests primarily in two major areas: the undergraduate market, particularly in the fields of psychology, sociology and education; and the professional training market, with particular emphasis on social work, clinical and educational psychology, counselling, youth work, nursing and teacher training.

Also available in this series:

Adolescent Health
Patrick C.L. Heaven

The Adolescent in the Family
Patricia Noller and Victor Callan

Young People's Understanding of Society
Adrian Furnham and Barrie Stacey

Growing up with Unemployment
*Anthony H. Winefield, Marika Tiggermann,
Helen R. Winefield and Robert D. Goldney*

Young People's Leisure and Lifestyles
*Leo B. Hendry, Janey Shucksmith,
John G. Love and Anthony Glendinning*

Adolescent Gambling
Mark Griffiths

**Youth, AIDS and Sexually Transmitted
Diseases**
*Susan Moore, Doreen Rosenthal and
Anne Mitchell*

Fathers and Adolescents
Shmuel Shulman and Inge Seiffge Krenke

Young People's Involvement in Sport
*Edited by John Kremer, Karen Trew and
Shaun Ogle*

Identity in Adolescence (3rd edition)
Jane Kroger

Sexuality in Adolescence
Susan Moore and Doreen Rosenthal

**Social Networks in Youth and
Adolescence (2nd edition)**
John Cotterell

Adolescent Coping
Erica Frydenberg

Moving Out, Moving On
*Shelley Mallett, Doreen Rosenthal,
Deborah Keys and Roger Averill*

**Wired Youth: The Social World of
Adolescence in the Information Age**
Gustavo S. Mesch and Ilan Talmud

The Nature of Adolescence

Fourth Edition

John C. Coleman

Routledge
Taylor & Francis Group

LONDON AND NEW YORK

First edition published 1980 by Methuen & Co Ltd
Second edition published 1990 by Routledge

Third edition published 1999 by Routledge

Fourth edition published 2011 by Routledge

27 Church Road, Hove, East Sussex BN3 2FA

Simultaneously published in the USA and Canada
by Psychology Press
270 Madison Avenue, New York, NY 10016

Routledge is an imprint of the Taylor & Francis Group, an Informa business

Copyright © 2011 Psychology Press

Typeset in Century Old Style
by Graphicraft Limited, Hong Kong
Printed and bound in Great Britain by
TJ International Ltd, Padstow, Cornwall

British Library Cataloguing in Publication Data
A catalogue record for this book is available from the British Library

Library of Congress Cataloging in Publication Data
Coleman, John C., Ph. D.
The nature of adolescence / John Coleman.
– 4th ed.
p. cm.
Includes bibliographical references and index.

ISBN 978-0-415-56419-9 (hb) –
ISBN 978-0-415-56420-5 (soft cover)
1. Adolescence. 2. Teenagers – Great Britain. I. Title.
HQ796.C642 2010
305.235–dc22
                                        2010021808

ISBN: 978-0-415-56419-9 (hbk)
ISBN: 978-0-415-56420-5 (pbk)

Contents

CONTENTS

A word about the interviews in this book

The quotes that appear throughout the book are selected from a series of interviews carried out in England with a group of young people from many different backgrounds. The interviews were carried out specifically for the purpose of inclusion in this book. The Interview Schedule appears in Appendix 1 at the end of the book. The age range of the interviewees was from 14 to 17, and an equal number of girls and boys were included. The social circumstances of the young people varied considerably, and interviews were carried out in schools, youth clubs, church halls and community centres. No attempt was made to organise the sample in any particular way, but the guiding principle was to include young people from all walks of life who might have interesting things to say about their experiences of being an adolescent. Josephine Ramm acted as the interviewer in all cases, and she also transcribed the interviews. The author is extremely grateful for her contribution to the book.

Figures, tables and boxes

Table

Boxes

Acknowledgements

I have been greatly assisted in the development of ideas contained in this book, as well as in the writing process, by a number of people to whom I owe much gratitude. I wish to thank my colleagues at Young People in Focus (formerly the Trust for the Study of Adolescence – TSA), at the Association for Young People's Health and in the Department of Education at the University of Oxford for their support over the years in which this book was planned and completed. I would like to mention in particular Fiona Brooks, Kevin Lowe, Ingrid Lunt, Aidan Macfarlane, Anne McPherson, Debi Roker and Jane Schofield. Apart from colleagues in these settings a particular debt of gratitude is owed to Ann Hagell, Editor in Chief of the *Journal of Adolescence*, who has showed continual interest in my ideas, as well as suggesting useful leads in tracking down new research. Josephine Ramm deserves special mention for her assistance in carrying out the interviews which form an integral part of the book, and for her skill at identifying the most valuable and insightful comments by the young people. Finally I wish to thank my partner, Jenny Pearce, who has been a constant source of support and encouragement. Without her this book might never have been written!

Introduction

'I guess young people are more interested in fun whilst they are growing up, but adults have to work and get money for the family, and stuff like that.'

(14-year-old boy)

'Everyone thinks that teenagers are bad and stuff, when it's just some bunch of lunatics doing something.'

(16-year-old boy)

'Yeah, quite moody, quite a lot of the time. Like with parents and stuff, they say just do something and I'd take it a bit too far, and, like, just storm out of the room, slamming doors.'

(15-year-old girl)

Adolescence is a challenge and a delight. It is a time of life when new skills develop, and when a more complex and differentiated social life becomes possible. It is a stage when family relationships are transformed, and when there is opportunity both for greater separation from parents, as well as for more closeness and equality. It is a stage when key questions about values and attitudes come to the fore, and when the individual starts to grapple with some of the biggest questions about identity and about the future. Adolescence is a delight because there is great pleasure to be gained for adults in the idealism and enthusiasm for life apparent in this stage of a young person's development. It is a challenge, however, because there are undoubtedly many difficulties and obstacles to be overcome if adults and teenagers are to get on well with each other.

What exactly is adolescence? For many people this stage of life is a puzzle. To begin with it is far from clear when the stage starts, and when it ends. Where do the boundaries of adolescence lie? Does it start at puberty, and end at age 20? Is this too simplistic? For some, the age of 13 is a good starting point, yet what might be understood as adolescent behaviour can be seen at an earlier age, and today many believe that young adults who still live at home in their early twenties are to all intents and purposes adolescents.

Next, we know that an individual grows up in the context of social, economic and political change. So how much has the experience of adolescence altered over the past 30 years? There are many different pressures and demands on young people and their parents today, and so it will be obvious that in some important respects adolescence in the twenty-first century is different to what it was in the 1970s or 1980s.

Then there is a debate over how problematic the stage is. How challenging or anti-social are young people likely to be? Should we expect problems and difficulties, or is this a perspective that is over-emphasised by the adult world? As Anne Frank says in one of the most famous of adolescent diaries:

If I talk everyone thinks I am showing off, when I'm silent they think I'm ridiculous: rude if I answer back, sly if I get a good idea, lazy if I'm tired, selfish if I eat a mouthful more than I should, stupid, cowardly, crafty, etc., etc., etc.

(Frank, 1993, p. 57 [first published 1947])

Here Anne Frank is describing the way she thinks the adult world views her, believing that there is a fundamental misunderstanding between her and her parents. One of the great conundrums of adolescence is whether adults see young people in an excessively negative light. Some might argue that the adult world exaggerates the more problematic features of adolescence, whilst others believe that the negative perceptions of adolescence are directly caused by their own behaviour. This is one of the questions that will be explored in more detail in the course of this book.

There are also more academic questions which challenge anyone seeking to understand adolescence today. Does it make any sense at all to talk about this as a single life stage? Perhaps it is more complex than that, since adolescence lasts for ten or more years. There has been some suggestion of a new stage, called 'emerging adulthood'. Are there other stages, such as the 'pre-teen stage', that should be incorporated into our overall concept of adolescence? And then there is the question of how different theoretical perspectives can be combined. Clearly it is possible to learn something from each of the academic disciplines that study adolescence, including sociology, psychology, anthropology, the neurosciences, psychoanalysis and criminology at the very least. It is of great importance to find ways of melding these different perspectives together.

This issue links closely with another query that is often posed. Is adolescence a biological phenomenon, or is it socially constructed? In this book an attempt will be made to incorporate both approaches. It is clear that there is a lot to learn by seeking to understand the physical development of the young person, but we would be blind if we did not look too at the way in which society construes this stage of development. Here it should be added that there is a third perspective, illustrated by recent research, which will be explored. This is the idea that in some respects adolescents are constructing their own adolescence. For too long it has been assumed that young people grow up in a world constructed by adults. However, with an increasing focus on notions of agency, and a realisation that young people influence the way adults behave, there may well be an argument for saying that young people themselves play as big a part as any other factor in determining their own development.

Finally there is also a question as to how research findings and academic theories can be brought together with the actual life experiences of adolescents themselves and of their families. This of course links closely with the notion of adolescents constructing their own adolescence. If this idea is to be taken seriously more attention needs to be paid to the ways in which adolescents describe their own development. The voices of young people and their parents should never be too far away in any genuine search for an understanding of the nature of adolescence.

It will be the purpose of this book to provide some answers to these questions. Adolescent development takes place against a backdrop of changing social and political circumstances. This introductory chapter will review some of the major changes that have had an impact on the lives of adolescents. The chapter will also consider adolescence as a transition and review how this has altered over time. The chapter will conclude with an outline of three different theoretical approaches to an understanding of this stage of development.

Social change

'Today there's a massive culture of fear, so there's a lot less freedom. For example when my Mum was little she lived in London and she was allowed to take a tube and bus and go where she wanted. I would never have been allowed to do that, and I'm probably still not allowed to do that. I think there's less freedom in that respect, but with technology and stuff you can do a lot more without your parents knowing, and so there's a lot more freedom in relationships probably.'

(17-year-old girl)

For those young people growing up in the developed world at the beginning of the twenty-first century it could be argued that they have been lucky to experience relative political stability. Nonetheless a moment's thought tells us that there are a wide range of social changes that impact directly on the lives of adolescents. Indeed Mortimer and Larson wrote a book entitled *The changing adolescent experience* (2002), and much of what they had to say at that point in time remains pertinent a decade later. There are a number of topics that deserve attention under the heading of social change affecting young people. Perhaps the two most obvious areas for discussion are the family and the transition from education to work. In addition, however, attention needs to be paid to the stage of emerging adulthood, to globalisation and the greater diversity of cultures in all Western societies today, to information technologies and their influence on the lives of young people, and to changing concerns in the health field. All these topics will be reviewed here, although many will have greater coverage in their respective chapters.

Looking first at the family, a considerable number of issues should be mentioned as being relevant to this discussion. Alterations in the structure of the family have had a major influence on the way adolescents grow up today. As is well known, the divorce rate increased steadily during the 1970s and 1980s, not just in the USA but in European countries as well. Today the divorce rate has levelled out, but other changes have become apparent, in particular the growth of single parent families and the fact that more and more children are born outside marriage. It is especially among young adults that this trend is most marked, and recent evidence shows that in Britain more than three-quarters of children born to parents under the age of 20 are born outside marriage (Coleman and Brooks, 2009). The increase in families headed by a lone parent is thus not only as a result of divorce, but stems also from changes in attitudes to marriage and partnership in relation to child-bearing. The proportions of children born outside marriage are shown in Figure 1.1.

In terms of those affected by divorce, today in some European countries nearly 25 per cent of young people experience the divorce of their parents by the time they are 16. In the USA the figure is closer to 33 per cent. Changes in family structure of this sort have repercussions in a wide range of areas. In the first place a significant proportion of children and young people have to cope with family breakdown, and with the loss of one parent from the family home. This may well lead to an increase in stress levels, and the need for greater support from outside the family. There will be a fuller discussion of this in Chapter 5.

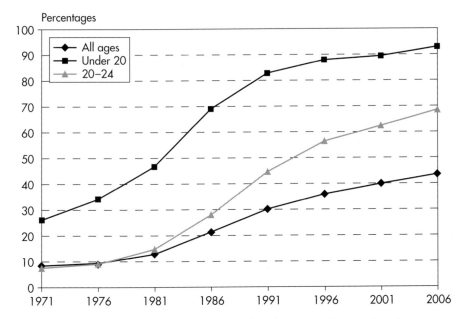

Figure 1.1 Births outside marriage, by age of mother, in England and Wales, 1971–2006.

Data from: *Population Trends* 132, Summer 2008. ONS.

A further point to consider is that a range of new family arrangements are being experienced by young people, with step-parents, live-in partners, remarriage, step-siblings and so on. Of course it is not just those adolescents whose parents divorce who are affected by this. In practice everyone is affected, because everyone has a friend, a neighbour or a relative in whose family there is a divorce or some form of reconstituted family. Attitudes to marriage are changing, and everyone's experiences encompass a much wider range of family types than was the case for previous generations.

Apart from the potential stress of family reorganisation, changing family structures have two other possible implications for young people. In the first place it is probable that values and beliefs about marriage, family and parenting are shifting as adolescents grow up in family circumstances that are, relatively speaking, less stable than was the case for their parents and grandparents. It is still not entirely clear how this will affect young people's own family histories, but at present it appears that marriage is still highly valued, but that there is more caution about this state. There is also a gradually increasing separation between marriage and parenthood, so that getting married is no longer a prerequisite for having children. Just as sex and procreation became disconnected in the 1950s and 1960s, so marriage and parenthood are becoming disconnected today.

The second implication of changing family structures is that the parenting of teenagers is more problematic. The parenting roles of lone parents, step-parents and new partners are hard to define, as is the role of the divorced or separated non-residential parent. Uncertainty about parenting practices is not good for adolescents or for parents. Adolescence is the time, more than any other in the life of the family, when parenting confidence is at a premium. Again this will be discussed in more detail in Chapter 5.

The world of employment, and the transition from education to work, is almost certainly the second major social change of significance here. Taking a historical view, youth unemployment rose dramatically in European countries in the 1980s. This was exemplified by the fact that, in Britain, unemployment rates for young men between the ages of 16 and 24 rose from 5 per cent to 25 per cent in the decade 1974–1984 (Coleman, 2000). Similar but less marked increases were also seen for young women. An even more startling trend was the decrease in the number of young people in the labour market. From the mid-1980s onwards the numbers of those under 25 in the labour market in Britain shrunk by more than a quarter. These historical shifts in the labour market have been widely discussed, and apply to all developed countries, as Mortimer (2009) indicates. The implications are numerous. In the first place more young people remain in education or training for longer periods, leading to a growth in further education for those between the ages of 16 and 18. This is true of Britain, where in the past a significant number left school at 16. However, in most countries the school-leaving age tends to be at 18, and so a second consequence of the changing labour market has been far greater numbers going on to higher education. The trend in the UK is illustrated in Figure 1.2. Government policy in Britain has been to aim for having 50 per cent of the relevant age group in higher education. In 2008 the figure was 45 per cent (Coleman and Brooks, 2009).

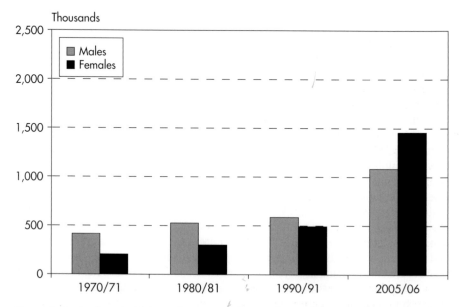

Figure 1.2 Students in higher education in the UK, by gender, 1970/71 to 2005/06. Data from: *Social Trends* 38: 2008 edition. ONS.

It is clear that entry into the labour market is more difficult for those under the age of 25 than was the case in previous generations. However, it is not only the fact that there are fewer opportunities for employment that is important. Another factor of equal significance is that the composition of the labour market is changing, with a reduction in manufacturing industry and a growth in service industries. This has opened up greater opportunities for young women, but has reduced the pool of jobs suitable for young men. It has also meant that jobs tend to be of a short-term nature, with employers unwilling to take on long-term responsibilities for their employees. As a result young people have to accept temporary contracts, and to see work as something that is less stable and dependable than was the case for their parents. These trends will be accentuated by the banking crisis of 2008 and the economic upheavals which are being experienced by all Western countries in the years following these events.

For young people without doubt the most far-reaching implication of the changing labour market is that economic independence – a tangible sign of maturity – is delayed. As a result the very nature of the adolescent transition is altered. In the years between 16 and 20, when traditionally young people were considered to be entering adulthood, they now continue to depend financially on their parents or the state. Thus adolescence lasts longer, relationships with parents and partners have to be renegotiated, independent housing is more difficult to access, and many new psychological issues have to be resolved. It is for this reason that the term 'emerging adulthood' has been coined by Arnett (Arnett, 2004; Tanner and Arnett, 2009).

The notion of a stage somewhere between adolescence and adulthood has obvious attractions, since it is evident that individuals who continue in education into their twenties, and remain living in the family home cannot be said to have reached adulthood in the sense in which that stage has been understood. For Arnett the stage of emerging adulthood is one of opportunity and freedom. Young people can explore different types of work, lifestyles and relationships. They have few responsibilities, and are therefore able to travel, and to experiment with different ways of living before settling down. However, not all writers see this as a positive stage of development. Numerous commentators note that the long transition to adulthood can be painful and challenging. Many individual young adults may experience restricted choice rather than freedom and experimentation. The postponement of economic independence can have serious consequences, leading to poor housing, fractured relationships and conflict with parents. The two different views of the stage of early adulthood may both have merit, since clearly there will be a great diversity of experiences and opportunities available at this stage. Further thought will be given to the question of diversity in the next section, which looks at transitions.

Besides family and employment there are other social changes that have significance for young people. One of these has to do with globalisation, immigration and the greater movement of ethnic groups. The numbers of adolescents from minority groups in the UK has grown substantially in recent years, and this is true of other European countries as well (Webster, 2009). There are both positive and negative features of this picture. On the one hand there is a greater awareness among young people of different cultures and lifestyles. Those from other countries and backgrounds bring a rich mix of skills and interests to the world of adolescence, with different styles of music being a good example of this. However, there are some

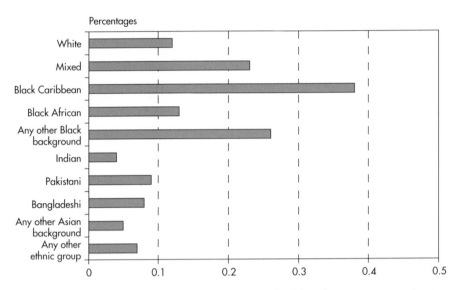

Figure 1.3 Permanent exclusions from schools in England by ethnic group, 2006/2007. Data from: Permanent and Fixed Period Exclusions from Schools in England, 2006/07. DCSF.

less happy aspects of cultural diversity, including prejudice and racial harassment, as well as manifest disadvantage suffered by those from ethnic minorities. One example of this can be seen in Figure 1.3, showing the rates of exclusion from school for different groups in England.

A further social change worth noting has been to do with health. Over the past decade or so some important trends have become apparent that bear on the development of young people into adulthood (West, 2009). Three such trends may be mentioned here. In the first place rising rates of obesity are a worrying phenomenon, and it is not yet clear how this might impact on adult health for this generation. Certainly this trend will encourage a greater focus on the place of exercise in a healthy lifestyle, as well as bringing nutrition and eating behaviour to the fore in any health promotion activities. Secondly there have been some worrying examples of poor sexual health among the adolescent age group, with a rising incidence of sexually transmitted infections becoming apparent. In Britain, for example, rates of *Chlamydia* infection doubled in the ten-year period between 1997 and 2007, and similar trends have been noted in other countries (Steinberg, 2008). Lastly there is some evidence that mental health among young people may be worsening (Collishaw *et al.*, 2004). Evidence from longitudinal studies does show increased rates of psychological disorder in the period between the 1970s and the 1990s, and this will be further discussed in Chapter 6. For all these reasons health as a topic of importance for the understanding of adolescence has become more and more significant.

The rapid and extensive growth of information technologies should also be mentioned here. As will be apparent to everyone, there has been a profound change over the past decade in the part digital technology plays in our lives, and for no group is this of more relevance than for adolescents. Again, as with all change, there are both good and bad aspects of this development, and there has been wide-ranging debate in all countries over the benefits or otherwise of new technologies for young people (e.g. Livingstone, 2009). The topic will be discussed in more detail in Chapter 9, but for the moment it may be noted that easier access to information, rapid communication with friends and family, greater opportunities for creativity, and increased control over some aspects of their lives are all obviously positive features of digital technology for adolescents. However, adult fears over the dangers of the internet, especially to do with cyber bullying, pornography and paedophile behaviour, are all of importance and not to be ignored. Perhaps of greatest significance is the fact that the internet and other media provide new avenues through which young people can develop their skills and capabilities. They need support to be able to use these avenues productively and safely, but this is surely the responsibility of the adult world.

The final topic to be noted in this section is globalisation, since it is essential to recognise that there are many ways in which global changes have impacted on young people growing up in the West. Two major factors are increased mobility of peoples across the world, and greater connectedness between those living in different countries (Brown *et al.*, 2002). As far as mobility is concerned, this has led to substantial immigration in European countries from Asia, Africa and the Middle East. Most European countries have large immigrant populations today, a situation that was unheard of twenty years ago. In addition in Britain there are significant numbers of people from Eastern Europe, so that all in all it is now common to talk of a multi-cultural society. Clearly this has an impact on adolescence, introducing young people to new cultures and norms, and creating a much more mixed society. As for greater connectedness, this can be seen in every aspect of life. Because of new technologies it is possible for adolescents in one country to share the experiences of others living thousands of miles away. Larson and Wilson (2004) argue that, across the world, there are major changes taking place which all contribute to globalisation. They point out the following as being significant:

- a demographic transition (longer lifespan, reduced birth rates and so on)
- changes in national economies (e.g. a shift away from agriculture, more consumerism)
- urbanisation (move from the country to the city in search of work)
- the spread of technology
- the development of an information society.

These are all important, but seen through the eyes of a young person in Britain, for example, probably the most obvious effects of globalisation will be a greater awareness of different cultures and a sense that other countries, previously far beyond the limits of everyday knowledge, are now close by and easy to access. As one example, following the 2010 earthquake in Haiti, young people in England were able to talk to young people who had experienced the trauma of the earthquake, and broadcast the discussion, courtesy of communication technologies and the BBC. In the past much of the study of adolescence was centred within Western societies, and there was little focus on other cultures and communities. This is no longer the case, and greater awareness of what it is like to grow up in different cultures should be celebrated and endorsed at every opportunity.

The nature of the transition

'We've got less responsibility I'd say, than adults. Like they've been there and done stuff, like jobs, careers and stuff, but we've not done stuff yet, so it's like we're a bit freer, we haven't had to do that. So in a way they're more trapped, and we're a bit, not stupider, like easy-going, sillier, like not worrying so much about things. If we went and made a mistake it wouldn't mean that we'd lose a job, or not have money for a house or something. The worst that could happen is that you'd get kicked out of school, and then you go and do something else. It's like you're freer in a way to make mistakes and I suppose to take risks.'

(17-year-old boy)

In much of the writing about adolescence, beginning with G. Stanley Hall's major work published in the first decade of the twentieth century, it has been customary to describe this stage as a transition. In many ways this has seemed the best way to encapsulate the nature of the adolescent experience, and, as will become apparent, there are many characteristics of transitions that can be ascribed to this stage of development. However, there have always been concerns over the fact that adolescence, no matter how it is described, covers a number of years. Is it realistic to describe a stage lasting nine or ten years as a transition? This problem has led some writers to talk of sub-stages, such as early, middle and late adolescence, and reference has already been made to 'emerging adulthood' as another stage. To many the attempt to identify sub-stages remains unsatisfactory, primarily because there is no agreement about the definitions of ages which apply to each sub-stage.

The situation has become even more complex in recent years, as has been outlined in the previous section. The stage of adolescence has lengthened, both at the beginning and at the end. As far as the later stages are concerned, delayed entry into the labour market and longer periods of living in the parental home have already been described here. In relation to the beginning of adolescence, it is apparent that puberty is continuing to occur earlier and earlier, and young people are maturing at a younger age. There is an earlier awareness of sexuality, dating and other adolescent behaviours commence at a younger age, and interest in clothes, music and other teenage concerns can be seen to preoccupy those who might in previous decades have been described as pre-pubertal. Thus the adolescent stage now begins for some at around 9 or 10, and continues for many until well after their twenty-first birthday. How then can this stage be best understood?

There are two ways of dealing with this dilemma. For some social scientists adolescence consists of a number of different transitions, each of which has to be researched and understood as a different event. Thus it could be that puberty should be considered in this category. It can be argued that the two years or so of biological change and maturation at the beginning of adolescence represent a major life transition, deserving attention in its own right. Many of those who have studied puberty, as for example Alsaker and Flammer (2006), would subscribe to this view. Apart from puberty one could look at other transitions in a similar way, such as the transition from one school to another (e.g. Eccles and Roeser, 2003).

However, the most popular focus for writers wishing to look at a discrete aspect of the adolescent period is to consider the transition out of adolescence and into adulthood.

In recent years there has been a stream of publications considering the changing characteristics of transition for young people as they move towards adulthood (Catan, 2004; Roche *et al.*, 2004; Furlong, 2009). Some, such as Montgomery and Cote (2003), look at the transition from school to university, whilst others focus specifically on education and training (Tucker and Walker, 2004) or the labour market (Mortimer, 2009). Many writers have considered this question from a European perspective, as for example Heinz (2009), who looks at the different pathways to be found in different countries in Western Europe. Others, such as Malmberg and Trempala (1997), compared transitions in two different contexts. They considered a country in which there was economic depression (Finland) with a country changing from socialism to a market economy (Poland). Interestingly, there were fewer differences between countries than between young men and young women, or between those at different educational levels. All the publications on this topic make the point that the stage of youth has been extended in all countries, and that the process of transition has become increasingly pluralised and fragmented.

The point that commentators make – namely that the transition to adulthood is being increasingly delayed – has concerned a wide variety of writers in the recent past. Indeed a number of years ago now Arnett and Taber (1994) wrote a paper entitled 'Adolescence terminable and interminable: when does adolescence end?' to underline the fact that there is no longer any clear or well-defined moment when an individual reaches adulthood. This has enormous implications for adolescents themselves, as well as for society as a whole. It has also led many writers to try to identify markers of the transition out of adolescence, and look at how these operate for those from different backgrounds. In the 1990s writers such as Jones (1995) and Coles (1996) noted three main status transitions:

- the school to work transition, where an individual leaves school and enters the labour market;
- the domestic transition, in which a young person attains independence from the family of origin;
- the housing transition, involving a permanent move away from the parental home.

It is striking to consider these transitions in 2010, and to recognise how much has changed. Few today move directly from school to work, with the great majority continuing in some form of training or higher education and, as already noted, having to accept temporary positions before any permanent employment may become available. Similarly the domestic and housing transitions are fraught with difficulties for many young adults (Heinz, 2009; Bois-Reymond, 2009). It will be apparent, therefore, that the transition has not only elongated, but has also become more problematic, especially for those who experience disadvantage. The discourse today is about the navigation of alternative routes through the late adolescent stage (e.g. Bois-Reymond, 2009), or about the social exclusion of

THE NATURE OF ADOLESCENCE

particular groups, including those living in poverty or deprivation, those with a disability, or those living in substitute care (MacDonald, 2007). Many writers fear that the prolonged transition and the difficulties of entering the labour market may lead to some groups becoming permanently marginalised, and thus to a generation of unemployed adults (Julkunen, 2009).

This then – to focus on one aspect of the adolescent period – is the first possible approach to understanding the adolescent transition. A second, alternative, approach is that described in a seminal paper by Graber and Brooks-Gunn (1996). In this paper the authors argue for retaining the term 'transition' to describe the adolescent period, but using the notion of turning points to refer to the key moments, such as a move from one school to another. This is helpful, although as they indicate, there remains the problem of deciding which turning points are important, and which to study:

> The premise underlying integrating notions of transitions and turning points is that transitional periods are characterised by developmental challenges that are relatively universal; that is, most individuals navigate transitional periods, and these periods require new modes of adaptation to biological, psychological, or social change. By definition, then, turning points occurring in the context of transitional periods may be particularly salient to individuals or subsets of individuals. These turning points may be more likely to result in behavioural change, or in larger or more long-lasting changes than turning points that do not occur in the context of a transitional period.
>
> (Graber and Brooks-Gunn, 1996, p. 769)

These authors then go on to identify circumstances in which turning points within transitional periods may be more problematic for particular individuals. They see these situations as being:

- when the timing of turning points within transitional periods creates additional stress, as, for example, with delayed puberty;
- when cumulative or simultaneous events occur, so that an individual has too many things to deal with all at one time;
- when mental health issues arise at the same time as the turning points are required to be negotiated;
- when there is a lack of 'goodness of fit' between context and behaviour during transition, as, for example, a poor school environment for an academic young person.

Such ideas will be especially helpful when theories of adolescence are considered in the next section of this chapter. Both the emphasis on the context of development, as well as recognition of the timing of events as a key determinant of adjustment, are particularly important in this regard. One excellent illustration of the relevance of turning points can be found in Drapeau et al. (2007). These authors consider the situation of young people brought up in foster care, and use the notion of turning points to identify those who do well and those who do badly when faced with the transition of leaving foster care.

There are many ways of looking at the concept of transition. For Graber and Brooks-Gunn the very fact that adolescence is a universal experience leads to the position that it may reasonably be called a transition. There is some strength in this argument. Transitions can be said to have a number of characteristics. They include:

- an eager anticipation of the future;
- a sense of regret for the stage that has been lost;
- a feeling of anxiety in relation to the future;
- a major psychological readjustment;
- a degree of ambiguity of status during the transition.

As will be apparent, all these characteristics are strikingly true of adolescence. Adulthood beckons, and with it freedom and opportunity, which appear very attractive. Yet there is also sadness for what has gone before – it is often said that inside every adolescent there is a child struggling to get out! Young people do worry about what is to come – more so perhaps than ever before. When jobs, housing and relationships all seem uncertain it is hardly surprising that adolescents have anxieties about the future. As will be described during the course of the book, a substantial psychological readjustment is required during the course of the adolescent years, and this is true in all spheres – in the family, with friends, with adults outside the family, and of course in relation to the individual's sense of identity. Lastly a number of themes run throughout the adolescent period, including an intensified concern with status and a realignment of roles. Thus it makes sense to consider adolescence as a transition, while at the same time acknowledging that within this stage there are many turning points which have significance for later adaptation.

Theories of adolescence

'Like you're going through that time, you don't know what you want to do, it's really indecisive, and it's like one big learning curve. And you obviously need people to bounce off and compare with, because you're never going to develop in this time if you don't interact with other people and see what's right and wrong, and sort things out. And all the crap you get into, so you need someone to go and bitch to, or like cry to, or whatever.'

(16-year-old girl)

In attempting to understand adolescence as a transition it is obvious that theory has an important part to play, and attention will now be paid to three different theoretical positions:

13

- the storm and stress viewpoint
- developmental contextualism
- the focal model.

Looking first at 'storm and stress', writers since the time of the Greeks have described adolescence as a problem period. It is often assumed that young people only began to be seen as troubled and troubling in the 1950s, when the word 'teenager' came into fashion (Savage, 2007). Different styles of clothing, musicians such as Buddy Holly and Elvis Presley, and films such as *Rebel Without a Cause*, appeared to capture a new mood among the young, and to mark the arrival of a generation that was 'all shook up'. Yet in 340 BC Aristotle wrote: 'Young men have strong desires, and tend to satisfy them indiscriminately. Of the bodily desires it is the sexual by which they are most easily swayed, and in which they show absence of self-control.' He went on to write: 'They are changeable and fickle in their desires, which are violent while they last. Their impulses are keen but not deep-rooted' (Rhetorica. In 'The basic works of Aristotle', quoted in Muuss, 1996). In later centuries a similar view prevailed. Shakespeare wrote in a number of his plays about the problems of youth, and the poet John Keats, writing in 1815, said:

> The imagination of a boy is healthy, and the mature imagination of a man is healthy, but there is a space of life between, in which the soul is in ferment; the character undecided, the way of life uncertain, the ambition thick-sighted: thence proceeds mawkishness.
>
> (Andrews, 1987, p. 3)

In modern times it was undoubtedly the publication in 1904 of G. Stanley Hall's monumental work on adolescence that set the tone for much of what was written in the subsequent half-century. Hall's two-volume, exhaustive study ushered in a new approach to the understanding of adolescence. He described it as a period of 'storm and stress', a phrase he took from the Romantic writers of the nineteeth century such as Schiller and Goethe. This was a literary movement which embraced idealism, passion and suffering, but also believed in revolution and the rejection of the old order. Hall argued that the adolescent passed through a turbulent, transitional stage, and that this was necessary for the 'higher and more completely human traits' to be accepted.

Hall's view of adolescence was given added weight by the fact that well-known psychoanalytic writers, such as Sigmund and Anna Freud, took a similar view of this stage of life. The psychoanalytic view of adolescence took as its starting point the upsurge of instincts which was believed to occur as a result of puberty. This increase in instinctual life, it was suggested, upsets the psychic balance which has been achieved by the end of childhood, and causes internal upheaval. This in turn leads to a greatly increased vulnerability of the personality (Freud, 1937).

As might be expected, later psychoanalytic writers, such as Erik Erikson (1968), have elaborated on these early theories. In so doing they have also moved beyond the notion of 'storm and stress', and have worked to explore the contribution of psychoanalysis to different aspects of adolescent development such as identity and family relationships. In addition more recent writers, such as Richard Frankel

(1998), have discussed the ways in which culture interacts with personality, and have added new perspectives to our understanding of adolescence, derived from the works of Jung and Winnicott. Nonetheless much of psychoanalytic writing does focus on the troubled and the turbulent, and there seems little doubt that such theorising has given impetus to a general view that there is somehow more upheaval in adolescence than in other stages of development.

This view began to be seriously challenged in the 1960s and 1970s when the results of empirical studies of adolescence started to appear in the scientific literature. Many writers reported findings showing the majority of young people getting on well with their parents, and coping adequately with the challenges of adolescence. Most agreed that there are a number who experience social and emotional difficulties, but that this group is a small minority of the total population of young people. Among numerous studies that have reported generally good adjustment among the majority of young people, we can consider the following as representative of many similar conclusions:

> In this study some 33.5% of the adolescents surveyed reported no symptoms of psychological distress, and another 39% reported five or fewer symptoms (a mild level of distress). On the other hand a significant 27.5% reported higher levels of psychological distress. For the majority the adolescent transition may be relatively smooth: however, for a minority it does indeed appear to be a period of stress and turmoil. . . . The large majority of adolescents appear to get on well with adults and are able to cope effectively with demands from school and peer groups. They use their resources to make adjustments with environmental stressors with hardly visible signs of psychological distress.
>
> (Siddique and D'Arcy, 1984, p. 471)

In spite of this and many other similar research findings, there still remains a powerful belief among the general public that the adolescent years bring with them trouble and strife for most families. Of all the 'popular' views of adolescence, it is undoubtedly the storm and stress model that is most familiar and most widely accepted among the general public. What are the possible reasons for this state of affairs? It could be that society has always needed a group to blame, and young people represent a useful scapegoat. The media may play their part, concentrating on the unacceptable behaviour of the few, and thereby implying that this applies to all adolescents. Teenagers themselves might contribute, as they are likely to challenge adults, and to display what seems like puzzling or even outrageous behaviour. Finally the self-fulfilling prophecy may be a factor, so that adolescents end up behaving just as adults expect them to do. Nonetheless it remains one of the puzzles about this stage of development that, in spite of clear evidence of the positive features of adolescence, the problem elements remain in the forefront of everyone's mind. The two theoretical approaches to be considered next highlight a different viewpoint, one stressing the context of development, and the other considering how young people cope with the challenges of adolescence.

The ideas outlined in the previous section relating to transitions and turning points are close to what is called the life course perspective. This implies a belief that human development can only be understood by taking into account the historical time and place of the individual's life, as well as the actual timing within any one person's life of transitions and major events (see Goossens, 2006a). The life course perspective is similar to and associated with what has come to be known as developmental contextualism, and it is to this set of theoretical beliefs that we will now turn. The key figures in the history of this viewpoint are Urie Bronfenbrenner, Paul Baltes and Richard Lerner. Each has made his own personal contribution, and here these ideas will be drawn together with the help of some recent reviews (e.g. Goossens, 2006a; Steinberg, 2008). The main elements of developmental contextualism are as follows.

The context, or ecology, of human development is essential to its understanding. The intention here is to underline the importance of the environment in the widest sense, including not only the family, but the geographical, political, social and historical context or setting in which the child or young person is situated. Elder (1998) put it like this: 'The life course of individuals is embedded in and shaped by the historical times and places they experience over their life-time' (p. 2).

Timing is critical. This principle has already been outlined as part of the Graber and Brooks-Gunn (1996) approach to transitions. In essence this implies that when events happen is as important as what these events are. Elder phrases it as follows: 'The developmental impact of a succession of life transitions or events is contingent on when they occur in a person's life' (1998, p. 3).

There is a continuity to human development. This principle is important in two respects. In the first place it draws attention to similarities and differences between stages, so that consideration of the transition of adolescence can be compared with other transitions, as for example the transition from employment to retirement. The principle is significant also in that it points up the fact that the adolescent stage does not suddenly arrive out of the blue, but is a continuation of development in childhood. Too often writers treat adolescence as a stage unconnected to other life experiences. This principle highlights the inter-relationship between childhood and adolescence.

Individuals and their families reciprocally influence each other. This principle makes reference to the fact that neither a child nor a parent is an isolated entity. Each grows, develops and changes, and most importantly, in so doing influences the others at all times. The young person's maturation produces changes in the family, but at the same time alterations in parental behaviour and family functioning have effects on the adolescent's development.

Individuals are agents of their own development. This is one of the key principles of developmental contextualism. Attention is drawn here to the part that all individuals, irrespective of age, play in shaping their own development. This innovative principle has wide-ranging implications for social science research and for translating empirical evidence into policy and practice. While it may be generally accepted that child and adolescent development results from an interplay of a variety of causes, the idea that the individual young person is an 'active agent' in shaping or determining his or her own development has not generally been part of the thinking of researchers in this field. The principle is now, however, having a significant effect on those studying human development. The idea that adolescents may in some senses construct their own adolescence has already been mentioned, and this has close links with a theoretical approach known as the focal model which will discussed further below.

When studying the interaction between person and context attention should be paid to the concept of 'goodness of fit'. The 'goodness of fit' concept takes into account the relationship between the individual and the environment in the widest sense, and asks to what extent the needs and goals of the individual are congruent with the context. Thus whether a developmental outcome is adaptive or not does not just depend on the characteristics of the individual, or on the nature of the physical or social environment. Rather, the outcome depends on whether these two systems fit together. The emphasis in research must therefore be to look at both elements and consider the extent to which they are congruent.

Numerous examples can be given of research programmes which have been conceptualized using the framework of developmental contextualism. The work of Eccles and her colleagues (Eccles and Roeser, 2003) on school transitions depends on the notion of 'goodness of fit', whilst Kerr *et al.* (2008) have drawn upon ideas of agency to show that monitoring and supervision by parents only has an effect if the young person is willing to cooperate. A recent study of parenting and mental health (Reitz *et al.*, 2006) showed the importance of reciprocity in understanding the factors that produce and maintain disturbed adolescent behaviour in the family. Developmental contextualism draws together many strands of thought. As Bronfenbrenner (1979) acknowledged, his theoretical notions were themselves based on those of earlier thinkers such as Lewin and Vygotsky. Today, however, those interested in designing high quality studies to explore various aspects of adolescent development will be remiss if they do not pay attention to the principles outlined here. No longer is it acceptable to consider only one side of the picture; the person and the context are inseparable. In addition it is no longer possible to ignore the fact that the individual adolescent shapes his or her own world, a notion that links closely to the focal model which will be explored next.

Both developmental contextualism and the focal model are rooted in the belief that it is essential for any theory to be able to take account of individual differences in development. These two approaches also give recognition to the adolescent's resources and potential for resilience. Theories of adolescence must do justice to the strengths and capacities demonstrated by young people, and must reflect the positive contribution they make both to their own development as well as to the communities in which they live. However, it is also important for a theory to identify the possible circumstances in which an individual may become vulnerable, and both approaches outlined here satisfy these criteria.

The focal model grew out of the results of a study of normal adolescent development (Coleman, 1974). Briefly, large groups of boys and girls at the ages of 11, 13, 15 and 17 were given sets of identical tests which elicited from them

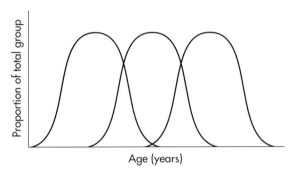

Figure 1.4 Focal theory. Each curve represents a different issue or relationship.
Source: Coleman (1974).

attitudes and opinions about a wide range of relationships. Material was included on self-image, being alone, heterosexual relationships, parental relationships, friendships and large group situations. The material was analysed in terms of the positive and negative elements present in these relationship situations and in terms of the common themes expressed by the young people involved in the study. Findings showed that attitudes to all relationships differed as a function of age, but more importantly the results also indicated that concerns about various issues reached a peak at different stages in the adolescent process.

It was this finding that led to the formulation of the focal model. The model suggests that at different ages particular sorts of relationship patterns come into focus, in the sense of being most prominent, but that no pattern is specific to one age only. Thus the patterns overlap, different issues come into focus at different times, but simply because an issue is not the most prominent feature of a specific age does not mean that it may not be critical for some individuals of that age. A symbolic representation of the model is illustrated in Figure 1.4.

In many ways such a notion is not dissimilar from any traditional stage theory. However, it carries with it a much more flexible view of development, and therefore differs from stage theory in three important respects. First, the resolution of one issue is not seen as essential for tackling the next. In fact it is clearly envisaged that a minority of individuals will find themselves facing more than one issue at the same time. Second, the model does not assume the existence of fixed boundaries between stages and, therefore, issues are not necessarily linked with a particular age or developmental level. Finally there is nothing immutable about the sequence involved. In the culture in which the research was first carried out, it appeared that individuals were more likely to face certain issues in the early stages of adolescence and different issues at other stages, but the focal model is not centred on a fixed sequence. It will be of interest to consider additional research by Kloep (1999) and Goossens and Marcoen (1999) which looks at the sequence of issues in different cultures.

In a previous publication (Coleman, 1978) the question was asked as to how it was possible for young people to face a wide range of transitions during the adolescent period and yet appear to cope without undue stress or difficulty. One possible explanation for the successful adaptation of so many young people to the developmental demands of the adolescent transition is provided by the focal model. The answer suggested by this model is that they cope by dealing with one issue at a time. They spread the process of adaptation over a span of years, attempting to deal with first one issue and then the next. Different problems, different relationship issues come into focus and are tackled at different stages, so that the various stresses resulting from the need to adapt to new modes of behaviour are rarely concentrated at one time.

It follows from this that it is precisely among those who, for whatever reason, do have more than one issue to cope with at a time that problems are most likely to occur. Thus, for example, where puberty and the growth spurt occur at the normal time individuals are able to adjust to these changes before other pressures, such as those from teachers or peers, are brought to bear. For the late maturers, however, pressures are more likely to occur simultaneously, inevitably requiring adjustments over a wider area. As Goossens (2006a, p. 21) puts it:

> Most adolescents deal with one issue at a time when working through their relationships with their parents, same-sex friends, opposite-sex friends, groups of age-mates, and authority figures. Only a small group (about 20 per cent of all adolescents) are forced by the circumstances to deal with several or all issues at the same time and evidence the signs of adolescent 'storm and stress' because they are overwhelmed by their problems.

As will be apparent the focal model draws on very similar assumptions to those implicit in the concept of 'timing' in developmental contextualism, and relates closely to Graber and Brooks-Gunn's (1996) perspective on transitions and turning points. The focal model also addresses directly the apparent contradiction between the amount of adaptation required during the transitional process and the ability of most young people to cope successfully with the pressures inherent in this process. Since the model was first proposed there has been some encouraging research which bears on the validity of this approach. Thus Kroger (1985) and Goossens and Marcoen (1999) have both studied the sequence of relationship concerns in different cultures. Kroger compared young people in New Zealand and the USA, while Goossens and Marcoen carried out their research in Belgium. Results from these studies support the notion of different issues coming to the fore at different times. As Goossens and Marcoen state:

> The general pattern of peak ages for adolescents' interpersonal concerns provided support for the focal model. Negative feelings about being alone, relationships with parents, heterosexual relationships, small groups and rejection from large groups do not all emerge all at once, but young people seem to deal with one issue at a time.
>
> (1999, p. 66)

In another study carried out in Norway (Kloep, 1999) similar results were reported, with adolescents, where possible, dealing with one interpersonal issue at a time. There has also been support for the notion of timing, with many studies indicating that adjustment is poorer where issues come all at once rather than one at a time. One well-known example is that of Simmons and Blyth (1987), whose research on school transitions illustrated clearly that the greater number of life transitions that a young person had to deal with, the greater likelihood of low self-esteem and poor academic performance. Lastly empirical support for the focal model has also come from research identifying what are known as 'arenas of comfort' (Call and Mortimer, 2001). In this research it is shown that where young people have at least one source of support they are better able to deal with stresses in other areas.

There is one further key aspect of the focal model that needs to be emphasised. This is the notion of agency, one already mentioned in the outline of developmental contextualism. The focal model argues that the young person is an agent in his or her own development, managing the adolescent transition – where possible – by dealing with one issue at a time. While at first sight this idea may be difficult to grasp, a little thought will indicate that the idea is not so far fetched as might at first appear. Consider for a moment the range of choices available to a young person in their current relationships. In any one day an adolescent may choose to confront a parent over the breakfast table, to argue with a sibling, to accept the suggestion of a good friend, to stand up to a teacher, to conform to pressure from the peer group, and so on. Every one of these situations offers the young person a choice, and all may have a bearing on the interpersonal issues with which the focal model is concerned. It is quite realistic to suggest that most young people pace themselves through the adolescent transition. Most will hold back on one issue while they are grappling with another. Most sense what they can and cannot cope with and will, in the clearest sense of the term, be an active agent in their own development.

It has to be recognised, however, that not all young people will have the same freedom to shape and manage their development. As has already been noted, when many events occur at one time it will be more difficult for the individual to manage the transitional process. In addition, those who grow up in deprived circumstances, or who face adversity because of illness, disability or family disadvantage, will inevitably experience constraints in terms of options and choices for their life course. Nonetheless the idea of an adolescent-centred perspective contains within it the belief that, no matter what circumstances surround an individual's development, there remains a sense in which it can be said that the young person is constructing their own adolescence. Imagine, in the most adverse situations, a young person talking to a youth worker, or a prison officer. Is it not the case that the adolescent is still choosing how to respond, what to disclose and what to hold back, how to shape the interaction? It is in this sense that agency plays such a key role in human development.

In the last few years a number of strands of thinking have given support to the idea of the adolescent as a constructor of his or her own development. Within studies of gene–environment interaction there have been suggestions of what is known as 'niche-picking', where individuals select the environments that best suit their developmental needs (Schaffer, 2006). In studies of family relationships researchers have looked at what is known as information management, identifying the process whereby young people actively select which information they communicate to their parents (Marshall *et al.*, 2005; Keijsers and Laird, 2010). When investigating problem behaviour researchers have shown how the behaviour of young people both predicts and moderates parental behaviour (Reitz *et al.*, 2006).

In terms of the voices of young people many of the quotes used throughout this book illustrate graphically how adolescents are actively working to organise and shape their own developmental pathways. More will be said about this process in Chapter 5 on the family and in the final chapter.

To conclude, both developmental contextualism and the focal model have contributions to make to a more realistic conceptual structure within which to understand adolescent development. A central question which faces researchers in this field has to do, not with how many young people face difficulties in adjustment, but with the process of successful and adaptive coping. Both theoretical approaches encourage an exploration of the factors that assist adolescents in the transitional process, and this is greatly to be welcomed. Throughout this book there will be a consideration of how context impacts on development, and of the various dimensions of adolescent development. Once these have been explored, the final chapter will review what is known of risk, resilience and coping.

Further reading

Graham, P (2004) *The end of adolescence*. Oxford University Press. Oxford.
In spite of the title this is a valuable book, written from a sympathetic and adolescent-centred perspective. The author is a psychiatrist, and there are good chapters on topics such as education, moods, eating behaviour, sex, alcohol and drugs.

Jackson, S and Goossens, L (Eds) (2006) *Handbook of adolescent development*. Psychology Press. Hove.
One of the few books that presents research on adolescence from a European perspective. A good chapter on theories of adolescence, followed by coverage of all the main topics concerning young people's development.

Savage, R (2007) *Teenage: the creation of youth 1875–1945*. Chatto and Windus. London.
One of the best books charting the history of our understanding of the teenage years, written by a British author who specialises in the history of music and popular culture.

Schaffer, R (2006) *Key concepts in developmental psychology*. Sage. London.
This is a useful book which discusses and defines all the key ideas relevant to an understanding of adolescence as a developmental stage. The author is one of the major figures in British child psychology.

Steinberg, L (2008) *Adolescence*, 8th edn. McGraw-Hill. New York.
One of the best of the American textbooks on adolescence. Very thorough coverage, with good examples of innovative research and boxes with interesting and challenging questions.

Physical development

'Well, last year I grew like, how much would you say that is? Half a foot? Yeah I grew so much! Because I used to be one of the shortest in the year, and now I'm at the average, which is quite amazing.'

(14-year-old girl)

'Well, yes, I did grow, sort of in Year 8. Because I was quite tall in Year 8 but now I'm sort of. . . . In Year 9 I stopped growing that much, so I slowed up quite a bit, and there's loads of people who are taller than me now. I was pretty tall. It's a bit annoying now.'

(15-year-old boy)

Of the many changes experienced by young people during adolescence, those associated with physical development can be considered to underpin much else that happens during this stage of human development. Almost every part of the body, and every bodily system, is affected by the changes that occur over a period of five or more years, usually starting at 9 or 10, and continuing until mid-adolescence. In this chapter the following topics will be considered: the development of the brain in adolescence, the growth spurt, sexual maturation and other changes associated with puberty, the psychological effects of puberty on social and emotional development, and finally recent research findings relating to sleep in adolescence.

Changes in the brain during adolescence

One of the most striking developments that have occurred since the late 1990s has been the remarkable increase in knowledge about the brain in adolescence. Detailed reviews of this topic can be found in Keating (2004) and Blakemore and Choudhury (2006). It has always been known that changes occur in the brain at the time of puberty, but new technology has made possible much more detailed knowledge of these changes. The technology has to do with advances in scanning techniques, in particular the use of what is known as fMRI, or functional magnetic resonance imaging. Scanning techniques such as fMRI have made possible new avenues of research, since they allow researchers to take pictures of the brain without being invasive. Before the advent of these scanning procedures it was necessary to inject a dye into the individual to track changes in brain function, but this is no longer necessary. Results from research using these techniques have opened a window onto a fascinating and important aspect of adolescent development.

The research has illustrated many different changes in the adolescent brain, but here we will concentrate on two main developments. In the first place it is clear that during this stage there is an elimination of unnecessary synapses or neuronal connections. This process is known as synaptic pruning. To some extent this process has been occurring since birth, but at or around puberty the process becomes much more pronounced. It might be thought that the pruning of synapses would lead to poorer functioning, but quite the opposite appears to be the case. Many more synapses are produced than is necessary for effective functioning, so the pruning process is an essential element of brain development, and allows for an improvement in information processing. Synaptic pruning occurs in various parts of the brain, but at this stage it occurs particularly in the prefrontal cortex, the area of the brain which is mainly responsible for cognitive functioning. It is also of note that research shows an increase at this time in connectivity between the prefrontal cortex and other parts of the brain, allowing for advances in thinking and reasoning.

The second major process investigated by scanning studies has to do with changes in the limbic system and in the neurotransmitters in this region of the brain. The limbic system is responsible for the processing of information to do with emotions, and many studies have drawn the conclusion that it is because of the changes in the limbic system that adolescents can be 'over-emotional' and easily affected by stress. It is also claimed in some research that changes in the limbic system account for the adolescent's increased need for novelty and sensation-seeking, and greater tendency for risk-taking (for summaries of these studies see Steinberg, 2007; Blakemore and Choudhury, 2007).

While recognising the importance of the research on the adolescent brain, it is important also to acknowledge some of the limitations inherent in this body of work. On the one hand there is general agreement about the ways in which the structure of the brain alters during adolescence. On the other hand the actual implications of these changes for adolescent behaviour and development are still open to wide-ranging debate among the scientific community. Few studies have been able to link changing images in the brain with changes in thought or emotion, so that many of the conclusions being drawn by researchers are really only matters of speculation at present. There is as yet a large gap between structure and function. Scanning studies allow us to see the structure of the brain, and how it changes, but they cannot at present tell us what the functions of those changes are.

Puberty

'I've always been one of the tallest, and then I grew, and then everyone caught up with me, and I was a bit like "Oh! I'm average". We all sort of went though it at the same time. But the thing was that most of the girls grew before all the boys, so all of the boys were at that little, small stage, and we were all quite a lot bigger for quite a while. And then they all suddenly went . . . and then suddenly they had grown up!'

(16-year-old girl)

'This summer holidays I went through a huge one. I've got stretch marks on my back because of it, growing so much in the summer. It does a lot on your personality, it makes you feel better about yourself being bigger, yeah, it makes you feel more confident.'

(14-year-old boy)

The word puberty derives from the Latin *pubertas*, meaning age of manhood, and among the general public it is usually thought to start with the onset of menstruation in girls and the emergence of pubic hair in boys. However, these two easily observable changes are each only a small part of the total picture, since puberty is in reality a complex process involving many bodily functions. It is common knowledge that puberty is associated with sexual maturation, but many other things are happening at the same time. In addition to rapid development of the reproductive system and of the secondary sexual characteristics of the individual, there are changes in the functioning of the heart, and thus of the cardiovascular system, in the lungs which in turn affect the respiratory system, in the size and strength of many of the muscles in the body, and so on. Puberty must therefore be seen as an event in the physical life of the body with wide-ranging implications, the most important of which will be considered in this chapter.

It is not the place here to explore the detailed endocrinology which underlies puberty. More detail can be found in Archibald *et al.* (2003) and Susman and Rogol (2004). For the moment we may note that a key concept helping to explain the arrival of puberty is the hormonal feedback loop. In essence a feedback loop develops long before adolescence, in fact before birth, and involves the pituitary gland (controlling hormone levels generally), the hypothalamus (that part of the brain that controls the pituitary gland) and the gonads (the testes in the male, and the ovaries in the female). This feedback loop works to control the level of hormones in the body, and puberty occurs when it does because several different signals instruct the brain to alter the level of hormones circulating in the body. It should be noted that these signals are complex, and originate from different sources.

Thus both genetic and environmental signals will be involved in prompting the hormonal feedback loop to trigger the first events associated with puberty.

One of the essential facts about this aspect of human development is that there are wide differences in the age of commencement of puberty, and these differences are both between individuals and also between communities. Thus, for example, puberty occurs later in less developed communities across the globe, as has been documented by Eveleth and Tanner (1977) and by Parent *et al.* (2003). In addition research has shown that, among African-American young woman early indicators of puberty such as breast development occur at significantly younger ages than they do in White Americans (Wu *et al.*, 2002). The primary explanation for variation in the age of puberty is likely to be genetic. Studies which compare identical twins with other siblings show that those who are genetically identical are far more similar in rates of pubertal development than those who are not genetically identical (Mustanski *et al.*, 2004). However, it is important to recognise that genetic factors are not the only ones to influence the start of puberty, and environmental factors do play a role too. The explanation for the international differences mentioned above is likely to be associated with variations in nutrition and health care, and other factors, such as body weight, also play a part. Young women who are very thin are likely to have delayed puberty, whilst those who are obese may start puberty earlier than their peers.

The growth spurt

Turning now to the actual events of puberty, one of the many changes involved here is known as the growth spurt. This term is usually taken to refer to the accelerated rate of increase in height and weight that occurs during early adolescence. Typical curves for individual rates of growth are illustrated in Figure 2.1. As noted above it is essential to bear in mind that there are large individual differences

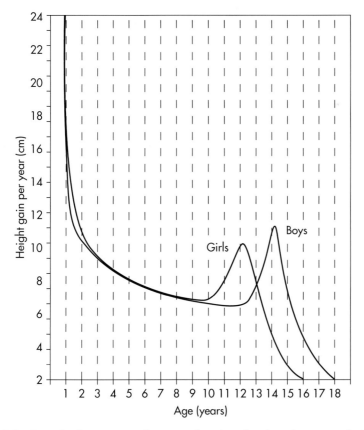

Figure 2.1 Typical velocity curves for supine length or height in boys or girls. These curves represent the velocity of the typical boy or girl at any given moment.
Source: Tanner *et al.* (1966).

27

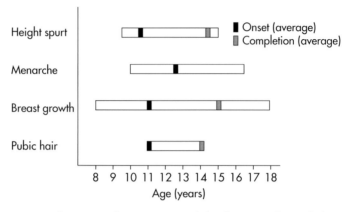

Figure 2.2 Normal range and average age of development of sexual characteristics in females.

Source: Tanner (1973).

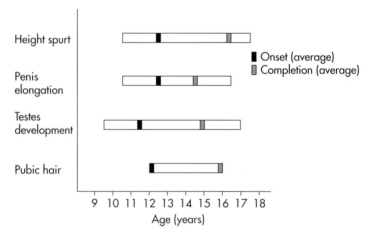

Figure 2.3 Normal range and average age of development of sexual characteristics in males.

Source: Tanner (1973).

in the age of onset and in the duration of the growth spurt, as is illustrated in Figures 2.2 and 2.3. Parents and adolescents themselves frequently fail to understand that such wide variation in timing is quite normal, and this lack of information may cause a great deal of unnecessary anxiety.

In boys the growth spurt may begin as early as 9 years of age, or as late as 15, while in girls the same process can begin at 7 or 8, or not until 13, 14 or even later. For the average boy, though, rapid growth is likely to begin at around 12, and to reach a peak somewhere in the 13th year. Comparable ages for girls are 10 for the onset of the growth spurt, and 11 for the peak age of increase in

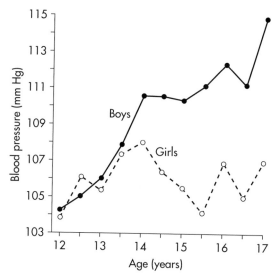

Figure 2.4 Differences in systolic blood pressure between boys and girls at puberty. Source: Montagna and Sadler (1974).

height and weight. Readers will note that girls, on average, are likely to commence puberty much earlier than boys. This fact has important implications for peer relationships at this age, a point we will return to in Chapter 9.

As already mentioned, other phenomena apart from changes in height and weight are also associated with the growth spurt. Thus the weight of the heart nearly doubles at this time, there is an accelerated growth of the lungs, and a decline in basal metabolism. Noticeable to children themselves, especially to boys, is a marked increase in physical strength and endurance. Gender differences are also reflected in less obvious internal changes, as Bancroft and Reinisch (1990) point out. For example, changes such as the increase in the number of red blood cells, and in systolic blood pressure, are far greater in boys than in girls. The extent of such differences, which seem likely to be evolutionary and to be associated with the male's greater capacity to undertake physical exertion, are illustrated in Figure 2.4.

Sexual maturation

Turning now to sexual maturation, there are a number of changes, both internal and external, associated with this element of puberty. In boys the sequence of events is relatively straightforward. Normally the first signs of puberty involve growth of the testes and scrotum, together with the appearance of pubic hair. Approximately a year later the growth spurt begins, and at this time there is also growth in the size of the penis. The appearance of other bodily hair, and especially facial hair, usually occurs quite late in the sequence, as does the deepening of the voice associated with the growth of the larynx. Lastly the internal sexual organs, such as the prostate gland, develop about a year after the growth of the penis, and lead to nocturnal ejaculations, or wet dreams.

For girls the sequence is not as straightforward, and there can be greater individual variation in the order in which the various changes occur. The following is therefore an approximation of what might happen for a typical girl. The first sign of puberty is usually early breast development, known as breast bud develop-ment, but in about a third of girls pubic hair may appear before any changes in the breasts are obvious. Breast development moves through a number of stages during puberty. Tanner (1962) identified five stages of breast development, taking in all about two to three years to complete. In addition there are internal changes taking place, such as the growth of the uterus, the vagina and other aspects of the reproductive system. The growth spurt usually occurs during the early or middle stages of puberty, whilst menstruation itself happens towards the end of the sequence, once a whole series of hormonal changes have taken place.

There has been much debate in the literature about how to measure puberty, and about when puberty can be said to commence. Whilst it is clearly easiest to date puberty in girls from the onset of menstruation, as we have seen this is far too simplistic a measure. However, there are no other obvious external markers, and carrying out a clinical examination of breast development, or assessing dental age is a skilled and expensive procedure. The situation with boys is even more difficult, as there is no externally obvious and agreed marker of pubertal status. Many different approaches have been used, as outlined in Coleman and Coleman (2002), but in reality there is no way of measuring pubertal status in a reliable fashion in boys without carrying out a clinical examination.

The secular trend

One of the fascinating debates relating to puberty and sexual maturation has to do with what is known as the secular trend. This term has been used to describe the biological fact that over the past century the physical growth of children and adolescents has accelerated, leading to faster and earlier maturation. This trend has been particularly noticeable in the growth rates of 2- to 5-year-olds, but it has also had many implications for adolescent development. Full adult height is achieved at an earlier age than was the case 50 years ago, final adult stature and weight have increased, and many investigators have reported that height and weight during adolescence are greater than they have ever been (Eveleth and Tanner, 1990).

In addition to changes in height and weight, the maturation of the reproduc-tive system is also affected by the secular trend. Tanner (1978) estimated that in average populations in Western Europe there has been a downward trend in the age of menarche of about four months per decade since 1850. This trend is illus-trated in Figure 2.5, from which it will be seen that broadly similar reductions in the age of menarche have taken place in a variety of countries. While there has been much debate about explanations for this trend, it is now generally agreed that better nutrition and health care are the primary reasons underlying the secular trend, although increasing body weight may also play a part.

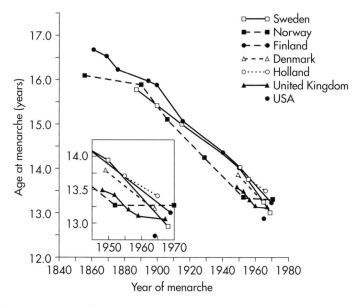

Figure 2.5 Secular trend in age at menarche, 1860–1970.
Source: Tanner (1978).

The question that arises is whether the trend illustrated by Tanner in 1978 has continued to operate in Western countries. There have been relatively few studies providing answers to this question, in spite of the obvious clinical and scientific relevance of such an enquiry, and those that are available refer primarily to young women growing up in North America. Herman-Giddens *et al.* (2004) reviewed several studies that were carried out from 1997 onwards in the USA, and these show that girls are continuing to mature earlier, although there are substantial ethnic differences, with African-American young women reflecting a much more marked trend towards earlier puberty. These authors note that while for White American girls the mean age of first menstruation is currently 12.6, for African-American girls it is 12.1. One publication describing the age of menarche in European countries in recent years is that by Parent *et al.* (2003). Here it is reported that there is a lower age in the southern countries such as Greece, Italy and Spain than in northern European countries. In the southern countries the mean age of menarche in the 1990s was between 12.0 and 12.6, whilst in countries such as Germany, the UK and the Scandinavian countries it was closer to 13 years of age. Herman-Giddens *et al.* (2004) point out that earlier puberty may not necessarily be a good thing. There is an association between being overweight and early puberty, and there are also some suggestions that the high level of pesticides in food may be affecting pubertal development. Anderson *et al.* (2003) analysed a number of large data sets in the USA since the 1960s, and were able to show that reducing age of menarche was associated with increased body weight, even when controlling for age and ethnic background.

Psychological effects of puberty

'I think it makes it more difficult for the people that don't mature faster, the people who are maturing at a later age. No-one's really, really horrible if they're smaller, but it can still make you feel worse if you're quite small and not maturing as fast as everyone else.'

(17-year-old boy)

'I know one of my friends started her period very young and didn't tell anyone for ages. Maybe it is like a source of embarrassment, I'm not sure. Not wanting to seem ... like wanting to hang on to childhood.'

(15-year-old girl)

The changes discussed above inevitably have an effect on the individual young person. The body alters radically in shape and size, and it is not surprising that many young adolescents experience a period of clumsiness and self-consciousness as they attempt to adapt to these changes. The body also alters in function, and new sometimes worrying physical experiences, such as the girl's first period, or the boy's first wet dream, have to be understood. Because these things are difficult to talk about, there is perhaps too little recognition of the anxieties that are common during this stage. Here is a girl of 16 talking about her first period.

'I remember my first fear, and hating it so much. I thought I really don't want to go through this, for so many years. And I hated that, I really did. I sat there and screamed, and I just did not want it. It wasn't that I hadn't been prepared for it, I mean, I knew it was going to happen and everything. But I hadn't really prepared for what I was going to feel, the sort of feeling that I've got to go through this every month, blah, blah, blah, blah. ... And my Mum just sort of said, yes, look on it as a gift rather than you know, sort of, like torture. But I mean to some extent you sort of think I hate going through this every month.'

(Coleman, 2001, p. 11)

The results of a study of Australian girls (Moore, 1995; Moore and Rosenthal, 2006) illustrate a remarkable degree of embarrassment, discomfort and concern about menstruation, indicating that the feelings expressed in the quote above are perhaps more widespread than is generally appreciated. Moore's research highlighted considerable ignorance about menstruation, despite the fact that the group of girls studied lived in a community where sex education at all levels was well integrated into the school curriculum. A similar study by Stein and Reiser (1994) looked at boys, and their attitudes to and knowledge of the first ejaculation. These authors too note that, in spite of good sex education, many boys felt unprepared for their first ejaculation, which on the whole had occurred earlier than expected. Those who felt they had been prepared had more positive attitudes, yet almost everyone reported that they did not tell anyone, and felt embarrassed and confused by the experience. What is clear from both these studies is that, even where sex education is in place in school, it is not dealing with these topics in a way that usefully informs and prepares young people. There are clearly important lessons to be learnt from these findings.

A further consideration is the effect that puberty has on identity. As many writers have pointed out (e.g. Kroger, 2004), the development of the individual's identity requires not only the notion of being separate and different from others, but also a sense of self-consistency. To have a stable identity one needs a firm knowledge of how one appears to the rest of the world, and a recognition that there is some continuity in how one looks to others. Needless to say, marked bodily changes are exactly the opposite of what is needed, therefore, for a firm sense of identity. Puberty thus represents a challenge in adaptation for most young people. It is unfortunate that many adults – even those in teaching and similar professions – retain only a vague awareness of the psychological impact of the physical changes associated with puberty.

Many writers have noted the sensitivity associated with the changing body in early adolescence (e.g. Alsaker and Flammer, 2006). In particular young people are likely to have idealised norms for physical attractiveness, and to feel inadequate if they do not match these unrealistic criteria. No doubt the advertising industry and the media play a significant role here in promoting images of beauty and success which depend on physical attributes that are unattainable for the majority of human beings. There is strong evidence to show that during early adolescence physical appearance is a more salient element of the self-concept for girls than it is for boys (see e.g. Harter, 1990). In addition it appears that girls are more dissatisfied with their bodies than are boys. In terms of specific attributes boys are more likely to be dissatisfied with their height, whilst girls are more likely to be dissatisfied with their weight (Stattin and Magnusson, 1990). Overall, however, at this stage girls dislike their bodies much more than boys do.

A large body of research on the development of the self-concept, to be discussed in more detail in Chapter 4, has indicated that, during the early years of adolescence, both boys and girls rely heavily on physical characteristics to describe themselves. As they progress through the adolescent years young people are able to make greater use of social and intellectual characteristics of personality to describe themselves, and as a result depend less on body image as a key element of their self-concept. It is worth noting therefore that, just at the time of most rapid change in terms of physical appearance, young people rely most heavily on their physical characteristics in relation to identity and self-esteem.

One further area that has received attention in the literature is the effect of puberty on family functioning (Ge et al., 2002; Susman et al., 2003). It has been suggested that the young person may experience increased moodiness at this time, thus putting a strain on relationships between parent and teenager, or that day-to-day hassles may become more frequent. Interestingly, although subjective reports from both parents and young people provide testimony to this situation, the research findings are mixed. Some studies, such as Papini and Sebby (1987) and Papini et al. (1989), have reported the onset of puberty as a time of increased tension and conflict within the family. However, other studies have questioned this, with some research (Paikoff et al., 1991) showing better relationships associated with the start of puberty, and others (Simmons and Blyth, 1987) showing no change at this time.

A possible explanation could be that the environment is as important here as the actual commencement of puberty. Thus Susman (1997) and Booth *et al.* (2003) have both reported that stressful life events, such as problems in the family, at school or with friends, are likely to play a bigger role in moodiness and depression than hormonal changes themselves. Furthermore the study by Booth *et al.* (2003) also shows that positive family relationships moderate the effects of puberty. Thus, where parents are aware of the psychological effects of this stage of development, and are accepting of behavioural change, then there is less likelihood of the young person being moody or irritable, and less effect on daily family life.

Early and late maturers

There has been a long-standing interest among social scientists in the effects on young people of being significantly earlier or later in pubertal development than their peers. As we have noted, individuals mature at very different rates. As an example, one girl of 13 may be small, with no breast development, and look much as she did during childhood. On the other hand another 13-year-old may look like a fully developed adult woman and appear to others as if she were 16 or 17. The question arises as to the nature of the consequences which flow from such marked physical differences .

By and large studies have shown that, for boys, early maturation carries with it social advantages, whilst later development can be more of a problem (Moore and Rosenthal, 2006). Early maturing boys feel more positive about themselves and about their bodies, and more satisfied with their development. Because they are stronger and have more advanced muscle development than others of the same age they will be better at sports, and this is a big advantage. Not surprisingly studies have shown that early maturing boys are likely to be more popular, and to do well in their school-work (Silbereisen and Kracke, 1997). By contrast late maturing boys are likely to be less popular, less successful in school achievements, less relaxed, and to have poorer relationships with both adults and peers.

For females the situation is more complex, since early maturation may have both costs and benefits. A number of writers have shown that girls who mature significantly earlier than their peers are less popular (among other girls), more likely to show signs of inner turbulence, and to be less satisfied with their bodies (Alsaker and Flammer, 2006; Moore and Rosenthal, 2006). Other studies have highlighted higher levels of eating disorders, increased depression and more contact with deviant peers. An important point about these findings has been made by Graber *et al.* (2006). They point out that one consequence of early maturation will be an increase in weight, so that girls in this situation are likely to feel less satisfied with their bodies, and therefore more prone to lower levels of self-esteem. In terms of their peer group relationships they may associate with older boys, especially if they are not particularly popular with other girls of their own age, and this may lead to early sexual activity and possibly to involvement in anti-social behaviour. Interestingly there has been much less research on late-maturing girls, but we may assume that they too suffer from being out of step with their peers, in the same way as boys do.

What explanations could there be for these findings? One explanation has been advanced by Simmons and Blyth (1987) among others. They call this the 'maturational deviance' hypothesis, by which they mean that those who are 'on-time' in relation to their developmental trajectory, and who fit in with the peer group in terms of what is happening to their bodies, are likely to adjust better than those who are 'off-time'. The two most deviant groups are early maturing girls and late maturing boys. Brooks-Gunn and Warren (1985) refer to this as 'goodness of fit'. They argue that there is a goodness of fit when the demands of particular social contexts mesh with the individual's physical and behavioural characteristics. These authors used this model to explain the results of their classic study of adolescent dancers.

Girls in dance and non-dance schools were compared for pubertal status. Because the dance student must maintain a relatively low body weight, it was expected that being a late maturer would be advantageous for the dancer. Results from Brooks-Gunn and Warren (1985) showed that more dance (55 per cent) than non-dance (29 per cent) girls were late maturers. In addition the on-time dancers (those who had already reached puberty) showed more personality and eating problems. Thus this study indicated that, for dancers who must maintain a low body weight, going through puberty at the normal time was a definite disadvantage. On the other hand those who in a normal population would be 'off-time' managed much better in the dance environment.

One key point about this study relates to the hormonal events which trigger the start of puberty. We noted in a previous section of the chapter that those with low body weight were likely to have delayed puberty, whilst those who are over-weight or obese mature earlier. No doubt many dance students were involved in serious dieting, which in turn may have acted to delay puberty. This study illustrates very well, therefore, how complex and multi-faceted are the variables that affect the onset of puberty, as noted by Alsaker and Flammer (2006).

For adults these events may seem like a long-distant memory, but for young people themselves they appear at the time to have profound implications for every-day life. Research shows that there are no long-term effects of early or late maturation, and thus young people can be reassured that the age at which they start puberty will have no consequences for their adjustment or sexuality as they become adults. However, adults themselves can help or hinder adjustment at this stage. The provision of good information, as well as acceptance and support from adults, can make a huge difference to an anxious teenager. There is an important role for adults here, especially in relation to those who are 'off-time' in their pubertal development.

Sleep in adolescence

All parents will be only too aware of the changing sleep patterns of teenagers, who like to stay awake into the night on school days and sleep until lunch time on weekends. Until recently it was assumed that this was just part of adolescent behaviour, reflecting general moodiness and contrary behaviour, and contributing to heightened levels of irritation among the adults in the family. Research has

shown, however, that this changing sleep pattern is caused by hormonal changes associated with the onset of puberty. One of the most important factors causing one to fall asleep is the secretion of a hormone called melatonin. Levels of melatonin change during the course of the day, partly triggered by the amount of light, but also by messages from the brain. As levels of melatonin rise we begin to feel sleepy, and as they fall we feel wakeful. During puberty increases in levels of melatonin occur later and later in the day, so that teenagers feel sleepy at later and later times. For those young people in the middle or at the end of puberty increases in melatonin occur about two hours later than in children and in adults (Carskadon and Acebo, 2002).

This is obviously an extremely important finding, and there are a number of implications. It would not matter if adolescents could just get up later in the morning. However, because of school this is not possible, although in one or two states of the USA starting times of the school day have been altered as a result of the research findings. A number of investigations of large samples of young people in the USA have supported the view that a majority of adolescents are getting less sleep than they need, and that those who get less sleep do less well academically, and have poorer levels of mental health (Wolfson and Carskadon, 1998; Fredriksen *et al.*, 2004). Roberts *et al.* (2009), for example, studied a large sample in the USA, and reported increased risk of poor academic performance and of depression in those with significantly reduced average hours of sleep. One study (Hansen *et al.*, 2005) compared sleep levels in the summer holidays with sleep levels during term time, showing that young people were getting around 9 hours sleep in the holidays, and an hour and a half less sleep in term time. In the study by Roberts *et al.* (2009) the authors reported that inadequate sleep was almost the norm for their sample, with over 40 per cent reporting less than 7 hours sleep during week nights.

Studies in Japan and in Taiwan have shown that this phenomenon is not limited to adolescents in North America, but would appear to be universal (Gau *et al.*, 2004; Ohida *et al.*, 2004). At present there are no reports of research which looks at this topic in Europe. From American studies, however, we have learnt that time of going to sleep may be determined not only by melatonin levels but by other factors as well. Because of the increase in the availability of television, the internet and other media that can be accessed in the bedroom teenagers have good reason to stay awake later (Van den Bulck, 2004). This would suggest that time of going to sleep may be determined to some extent by the environment as well as by biology. The most important conclusion that can be drawn from this body of research is that sleep patterns in young people during and after puberty are affected by hormonal changes. Young people are more likely to stay awake longer, and if they are getting up at a normal time then there is the possibility that they will be deprived of some degree of sleep, which could in turn affect their behaviour. Some adjustment in parental attitudes to adolescent sleep patterns is therefore required!

Implications for practice

1. Knowledge about brain development during adolescence has greatly increased as a result of new scanning technologies. Many of the behavioural changes during early and middle adolescence that have been observed for generations may have their basis in changes in the brain. It is helpful for adults to know that increases in thinking and reasoning skills are likely to be related to brain development. In addition the centres in the brain to do with the regulation of emotions also undergo rapid alteration, and this may have significant behavioural implications.
2. Puberty itself is poorly understood, not only by adolescents themselves, but also by adults in the family. It would greatly help if more information was available for parents and carers. Research has shown that young people who are properly prepared for the arrival of puberty adjust better than those who have had little preparation.
3. This point relates also to the need for more effective health education in junior school. While there may be debate over the rate of biological maturation, there is little doubt that those under the age of 11 are in need of appropriate knowledge of puberty and of the changes they will experience in the coming years.
4. A greater knowledge of the needs and potential difficulties of early and late maturers would be useful for parents, teachers and others who work with young people. As we have seen, both early and late maturers may be vulnerable in their social and emotional development. Support at the right time from a concerned adult will make a considerable difference to the young person's adjustment at this stage in their lives.
5. Increased awareness of the role of hormones in determining adolescent sleep patterns reflects an important advance in knowledge. Many young people are not getting as much sleep as they need, and their behaviour may be affected by this. Parents and other carers can be sensitive to this issue, and may be able to find ways of helping young people manage their levels of sleep more effectively.

Further reading

Archibald, A, Graber, J and Brooks-Gunn, J (2003) Pubertal processes and physiological growth in adolescence. In Adams, G and Berzonsky, M (Eds) *Blackwell handbook of adolescence*. Blackwell Publishing. New York.
An excellent review chapter by some of the leaders in the field.

Jackson, S and Goossens, L (Eds) (2006) *Handbook of adolescent development.* Psychology Press. Hove.
Contains a chapter on pubertal maturation.

Moore, S and Rosenthal, D (2006) *Sexuality in adolescence: current trends.* Routledge. London.
This is a really valuable book, with wide-ranging coverage including a strong emphasis on the biological background to sexual development. One of the chapters is entitled 'Changing hormones: changing bodies'. This is the second edition of a very popular book written by two Australian experts in the field.

Steinberg, L (2008) *Adolescence*, 8th edn. McGraw-Hill. New York.
Contains a good chapter on biological transitions.

Susman, E and Rogol, A (2004) Puberty and psychological development. In Lerner, R and Steinberg, L (Eds) *Handbook of adolescent development*, 2nd edn. Wiley. New York.
Again a fine review chapter, looking especially at the psychological concomitants of puberty.

Thinking and reasoning

'Things are probably less clear now, there's lots of shades of grey between right and wrong. Whereas before you knew that, what was, just right and wrong, and now you look at things in a more multi-faceted way. I guess it's less easy to tell, . . . no absolutes!'

(17-year-old girl)

'It's a lot harder to just categorise people or events, as say, just good or bad. Maybe I thought about it less when I was younger. The whole world seemed smaller I suppose.'

(16-year-old girl)

Cognitive development in adolescence is one of the areas of maturation which is least apparent to observers. There are no external or visible signs to show what is happening, as is the case with physical development, yet changes in this sphere are occurring all the time. Furthermore, alterations in intellectual function have implications for a wide range of behaviours and attitudes. As will be apparent from this chapter, changes in thinking, in reasoning and in information-processing determine not just school performance, but among other things they also affect moral thought, interpersonal problem-solving, political decisions and risk-taking. For many years this field was dominated by the work of Jean Piaget. Today, however, many writers believe that Piagetian theory is out of date, and that there are new approaches which better reflect the complexity of adolescent cognitive development. In this chapter Piaget's views will be briefly outlined, and his legacy explored, following which it will be possible to look at some modern thinkers. The chapter will also outline research on social cognition, decision-making, and on moral and political thought in adolescence.

The Piagetian approach

It was Piaget who first pointed out that a qualitative change in the nature of mental ability, rather than any simple increase in cognitive skill, is to be expected at or around puberty. He and others (e.g. Inhelder and Piaget, 1958) argued that at this point in development formal operational thought becomes possible. While a full description of Piaget's stages of cognitive growth is beyond the scope of this book, the crucial distinction is that which Piaget draws between what he called concrete and formal operations.

During the stage of concrete operations (approximately between the ages of 7 and 11) the child's thought may be termed 'relational'. Gradually he or she begins to master notions of classes, relations and quantities. Conservation and seriation become possible, and the development of these skills enables the child to formulate hypotheses and explanations about concrete events. These cognitive operations are seen by the child simply as mental tools, the products of which are similar to that which can be sensed through vision, hearing and touch. In other words the individual at this stage seems unable to differentiate between what is mentally constructed and what is perceptually given. When the child formulates a hypothesis it originates from the data, not from within the person. If new contradictory data are presented, he or she does not change the hypothesis, but rather prefers to alter the data or to rationalise these in one way or another.

With the appearance of formal operations a number of important capabilities become available to the young person. Perhaps the most important of these is the ability to construct 'contrary to fact' propositions. This change has been described as a shift in emphasis in adolescent thought from the 'real' to the 'possible'. It facilitates a hypothetico-deductive approach to problem-solving, and to the understanding of proposi-tional logic. It enables the individual to think about mental constructs as objects which can be manipulated, and to come to terms with notions of probability and belief.

The fundamental difference in approach between the young child and the adolescent was neatly demonstrated in a classic study by Elkind (1966). Two groups, children of 8 and 9, and adolescents of 13 and 14, were presented with a concept formation task, involving a choice between two pictures. Pictures were presented in pairs, with each pair including both a wheeled (e.g. a car) and a non-wheeled (e.g. a spaceship) object. Choosing a wheeled object made a light go on, whilst choosing a non-wheeled object did not. The problem was to determine what it was that made the light go on. Only half of the younger group were able to arrive at the correct solution, and those who did succeed took almost all of the allotted 72 trials to do so. On the other hand all of the older group solved the problem, and most did so in ten or fewer trials.

The tendency of adolescents to raise alternative hypotheses successively, to test each against the facts, and discard those that proved wrong was apparent in their spontaneous speech during the trials (e.g. 'maybe it's transportation . . . no, it must be something else, I'll try. . . .'). The younger group, however, appeared to become fixated on an initial hypothesis that was strongly suggested by the data (e.g. tool or non-tool, vehicle or non-vehicle). They then clung to this hypothesis even though they continued to fail on most trials.

Another, slightly different example of this situation is illustrated by the dolls-and-sticks problem (see Figure 3.1). Nine-year-olds can arrange these objects according to size with little difficulty. Furthermore they can match sticks to dolls according to height, no matter how the dolls and sticks are first presented. However, when the same problem is formulated in an abstract fashion, then this age group is unable to manage the task. Thus the problem 'If B is not as tall as C, and A is not as short as C, then who is the tallest?' cannot be tackled until formal operational thought has been developed.

Inhelder and Piaget (1958) developed a whole range of ingenious problems for the investigation of many different aspects of logical thinking, and some of these have been widely used by other researchers. One such test is the pendulum problem. Here the task involves discovering which factor or combination of factors

Figure 3.1 Piaget's dolls-and-sticks problem. Can the child establish a correspondence between the size of the dolls and the size of the sticks?
Source: Muuss (1996).

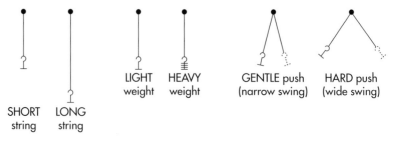

SHORT   LONG
string   string

LIGHT   HEAVY
weight   weight

GENTLE push   HARD push
(narrow swing)   (wide swing)

Figure 3.2 The Pendulum Problem. The task is to determine which factor or combination of factors determines the rate of swing of the pendulum.
Source: Shayer (1979).

determines the rate of the swing of the pendulum. The task is illustrated in Figure 3.2, and again depends for its solution on the ability of the individual to test alternative hypotheses successively. Many writers have attempted to set out what they consider to be the essential criteria for formal operational thought. One such example is Murray (1990), who argued that there are five elements that make up formal operations. These are:

1   *Duration*. Operational thought will continue over time, so that the same result will be obtained no matter how long has elapsed since the problem was first presented.
2   *Resistance to counter-suggestion*. Young people who are operational thinkers will not be influenced by persuasion or arguments which offer alternative explanations.

3   *Specific transfer.* The original problem-solving ability will remain unaffected, even where different materials or different situations are presented.
4   *Non-specific transfer.* Young people will show an understanding of the principles behind problem-solving, and will be able to apply learning obtained in one domain to any other domain.
5   *Necessity.* This notion refers to the idea of continuity in physical objects and materials. Thus, no matter in what form something is presented, of necessity it remains the same despite its appearance. Those who think in operational terms understand this principle.

Over recent years there have been many criticisms of Piagetian theory. Some of these criticisms will be outlined here. The first has to do with what is known as domain specificity (Byrnes, 2003; Lehalle, 2006). The argument here runs as follows. What young people learn will be a function of what they are exposed to, so that those who have more exposure to maths, for example, will have enhanced skills in this domain. Piaget's theory could be described as a domain-general theory, as he believed that formal operational thought would be applied across domains, no matter how much previous exposure the individual had had. As Byrnes (2003) points out, most contemporary cognitive theorists believe in domain specificity.

A second problem with Piaget's approach is that formal thought is more difficult to define than the earlier Piagetian stages, and this has raised questions over its applicability. It would also appear that not all young people are able to demonstrate formal thinking by middle adolescence, and indeed studies have shown that even some adults have not yet reached this stage of cognitive development (Shayer *et al.*, 1976; Shayer and Wylam, 1978). A third issue has to do with what Ward and Overton (1990) called a distinction between performance and competence. These authors pointed out that young people might be competent in logical thinking, but might not express that competence in performance if they were not interested in the task. They demonstrated this distinction by using two types of material – one set had to do with punishments for people breaking rules at school, while the other set of materials was to do with challenges for people facing retirement. Results were striking. At the age of 13 only about 20 per cent of the problems were solved correctly, regardless of the relevance of the material. However, at age 17 70 per cent demonstrated formal reasoning on problems to do with school, whilst only 30 per cent used formal reasoning on problems to do with retirement. Thus the relevance of the material makes a difference in the way young people use their developing cognitive skills.

The information-processing view of adolescent thinking

'I don't know, it's hard to explain, you sort of can think about things more, so if someone tells you something is right or wrong then you can sort of think about it yourself, and make a decision, rather than just listening to other people.'

(16-year-old boy)

In spite of the criticisms of Piaget current today, there is no doubt that he and his co-workers helped to map out some of the ways in which thinking changes during adolescence. However, others (e.g. Keating, 2004) have argued that this is only one part of the picture, and that it is also important to know what specific aspects of intellectual development contribute to the enhanced reasoning and problem-solving that differentiates adolescents from younger children. It is here that the information-processing approach comes into its own. Theorists making use of this perspective have been influenced by computer science, arguing that it is possible to look at human information-processing in much the same way as we analyse computer functions. Thus it is important to consider how the individual codes information, retrieves information, compares different bits of information, and makes decisions based on these comparisons. Studies of adolescent thinking which have been rooted in information-processing have concentrated on five areas which show improvement during this stage of development. These are:

- attention
- working memory
- processing speed
- organisation
- meta-cognition.

Each of these will be briefly discussed, considering attention first. Here advances can be seen in both selective attention, where the individual has to ignore irrelevant stimuli and concentrate on one thing only, and in divided attention, where it is necessary to pay attention to more than one thing at a time. Casteel (1993) carried out research that illustrated how adolescents improve over time in respect of these skills. As far as memory is concerned, this is another capability that shows improvement during the adolescent years. A distinction is usually drawn between working memory, i.e. that which is used to carry out a specific task, and long-term memory. Studies detailed in Keating (2004) show clearly how both aspects of memory improve with age.

In terms of speed of processing, again researchers have shown that, regardless of the task, older adolescents are able to process information faster than their younger peers (Hale, 1990; Kail, 1991). Improvements can also be seen in adolescents' organisational strategies (Siegler, 1988). Teenagers are more likely to plan tasks involving memory or learning, and they are more able to stand back and ask themselves which strategy might be most effective in any particular situation. Lastly young people, as they mature, are more able to think about their own thinking processes. The skill of reflection and the ability to take into account greater and greater amounts of information underlie an increasing competence in meta-cognition. However, it should be noted that being able to think about your own thinking can be both a blessing and a disadvantage, as will be shown when the topic of egocentricity is discussed below.

One interesting question has to do with whether these different aspects of information-processing relate to each other. Do they improve at the same rate across the age range? Do they enhance each other? And do they work together, or are they quite separate capabilities? In an important study by Demetriou *et al.* (2002) young people between the ages of 8 and 14 were studied over a long period of time. The researchers were able to show that, although all aspects of information-processing improved over time, the growth of each of the abilities was not affected by the state of the others at any one point in time. In other words it appears that the growth of these skills has to be explained by external agents, such as the learning environment, individual interests, and possibly encouragement from key adults, rather than the explanation lying in some internal developmental process. Demetriou *et al.* (2002) conclude that there is no single driver of cognitive change during this stage, but rather a multitude of both internal and external factors which underlie a complex developmental process.

Social cognition

'I have changed, like being able to manage my response in arguments and stuff like that. Letting something drop if someone says a remark which you understand is meant to be quite snide. Instead of sort of retaliating or react-ing to it, just sort of being able to think it doesn't matter, just leave it. And it does actually turn out fine anyway.'

(17-year-old girl)

The adolescent stage does not only involve changes in cognition to do with logic and reasoning of an academic nature. It is also a stage where there are marked changes in the way young people use their developing cognitive abilities to under-stand their social worlds. There are a number of arenas in which research has illustrated these changes, including moral and political judgements, perspective-taking, impression formation, and what has come to be known as adolescent egocentrism. This topic will be the first to be discussed here. It was David Elkind (1967) who originally drew attention to this notion, arguing that the attainment of formal reasoning powers frees the individual in many respects from childhood egocentrism, while yet paradoxically entangling the young person in a new version of the same thing. This is because the attainment of formal reasoning allows the individual to think not only about his or her own thought, but also about the thought of other people.

Elkind believed that it is the capacity to take account of other people's think-ing which is the basis for adolescent egocentrism. Essentially the individual finds it difficult to differentiate between what others are thinking and his or her own preoccupations. The assumption is made by the young person that if he or she is obsessed with a thought or problem, then others must also have that preoccupation.

45

The example often quoted is the adolescent's appearance. Young people are frequently concerned with the way they look to others, and they make the assumption that other people will be thinking about the same thing. Elkind linked this concept to another, that of the 'imaginary audience'. Because of egocentrism the adolescent is either, in actual or imagined social situations, anticipating the reactions of others. However, these reactions are based on the premise that others are as critical or admiring of them as they are of themselves. Thus the young person is continually constructing and reacting to an imaginary audience, which according to Elkind, explains a lot of adolescent behaviour. Thus such things as the self-consciousness of young people, the wish for privacy, the preoccupation with clothes, and the long hours spent in front of the mirror may all be related to the idea of an imaginary audience.

One other aspect of adolescent egocentrism, seen as an example of over-differentiation of feelings, is what Elkind has called the 'personal fable'. Possibly because the adolescent wishes to believe that he or she is of importance to so many people, individual concerns and feelings come to be seen as very special, even unique. A belief in the unique nature of the young person's misery and suffering is, of course, a familiar theme in literature. *The Diary of a Young Girl* by Anne Frank (1993 [first published in 1947]) and *Catcher in the Rye* (Salinger, 1994) are two celebrated examples, whilst two more recent, wonderful books illustrating the same theme are Lorrie Moore's *Who Will Run the Frog Hospital?* (1994) and Rose Tremain's *The Way I Found Her* (1997). It has been suggested by Elkind (1967) and others that it is the notion of uniqueness that underlies the construction of a personal fable in adolescence. In essence this is the individual's story about herself or himself, the myth that is created, which may well include fantasies of omnipotence and immortality. It is not a true story, but it serves a valuable purpose in buttressing the adolescent's fragile self-concept at a time of uncertainty and change.

A number of studies have explored the nature of egocentrism from an empirical point of view. Both Elkind and Bowen (1979) and Enright *et al.* (1980) have developed scales for the measurement of various aspects of egocentrism. In broad terms these investigations support the conclusion that egocentrism declines from early to late adolescence. However, findings are not clear-cut, and further research has been more critical. Some researchers have found it difficult to confirm the developmental trend (e.g. Riley *et al.*, 1984), while others have argued that certain aspects of egocentrism, such as the personal fable, may remain present throughout adolescence and even into adulthood (Quadrel *et al.*, 1993). Another approach to this topic has been to explore the link between egocentrism and self-consciousness. Thus a study by Rankin *et al.* (2004) showed that feelings of self-consciousness are more prevalent in girls than in boys, but that for both genders they increase during early adolescence, peak at around age 15, and then decline as social and cognitive competence develops. This suggests that egocentrism may be more a function of social and emotional factors rather than a reflection of a stage of cognitive maturation. Whatever the basis for egocentrism, however, it remains a useful concept explaining important aspects of behaviour in early adolescence.

Two further aspects of social cognition – impression formation and social perspective taking – will now be explored. Impression formation is a key element of the young person's development, indeed it is sometimes described as the basis for an implicit personality theory (Steinberg, 2008). It is generally agreed that there are four main elements of impression formation (Hill and Palmquist, 1978). The first of these is the gradual differentiation of impressions. Children are likely to describe other people, as well as themselves, in relatively concrete terms, concentrating on characteristics such as height, gender, hair colour and so on. Adolescents, by contrast, are more likely to see people in terms of their interests, attitudes and personality characteristics. A second element of impression formation is that during adolescence this aspect of thinking gradually becomes less egocentric. Adolescents begin to develop the ability to see that their impressions are their own, rather then being universal, and that therefore impressions are open to disagreement (Keating, 2004).

The next element of impression formation that develops during adolescence is that young people come to make greater use of inference. In contrast to children, adolescents begin to be able to interpret other people's feelings and behaviour, and to make inferences about aspects of other people's characteristics, even if those aspects are not manifest and clearly evident. Lastly young people's impressions of others slowly become more organised, so that attributes or characteristics become linked together in a coherent whole. Adolescents are also more able to associate particular types of behaviour with particular situations. Thus they can see that a friend may behave in one way when they are with their parents, but behave in a different way when they are with their friends. The ability to form impressions of others, and to be able to act upon those impressions, is clearly a key attribute for the development of new social relationships, as well as for the capacity to function appropriately in group situations.

Impression formation is of course closely linked with perspective taking, and it is here that the work of Selman (1980) has been extremely influential. For Selman social cognition involves role taking, perspective taking, empathy, moral reasoning, interpersonal problem-solving and self-knowledge. Selman's most important contribution is his proposal concerning a stage theory of social cognition. In broad terms he identifies four developmental levels of social perspective taking. These are:

Stage 1. The differential or subjective perspective taking stage (ages 5–9). Here children are beginning to realise that other people can have a social perspective different from their own.

Stage 2. Self-reflective thinking or reciprocal perspective taking (ages 7–12). At this stage the child realises not only that other people have their own perspective, but that they may actually be giving thought to the child's own perspective. Thus, the crucial cognitive advance here is the ability to take into account the perspective of another individual.

Stage 3. Third-person, or mutual perspective taking (ages 10–15). The perspective taking skills of early adolescence lead on to a capacity for a more complex type of social cognition. The young person moves beyond simply taking the other person's perspective (in a back and forth manner) and is able to see all parties from a more generalised, third-person perspective.

Stage 4. In-depth societal perspective taking (ages 15+). During this stage the individual may move to a still higher and more abstract level of interpersonal perspective taking, which involves coordinating the perspectives of society with those of the individual and the group.

These stages constitute the developmental structure of Selman's theory, and the assumption is that moves by the young person from one stage to another are accompanied by qualitatively different ways of perceiving the relationship between the self and others. Selman's own research demonstrates that there is an age-related progression with respect to social perspective taking (Selman *et al.*, 1986). It is important to note also that Selman sees these stages as having application in four different domains – the individual domain, the friendship domain, the peer group domain and the family domain. This domain-specific framework makes it possible to outline the progression of any one individual in these different areas, and to identify the interpersonal issues in which the stage structure will apply.

One of the great strengths of Selman's approach is its potential application to the world of social development. Selman himself was particularly interested in those young people with poor social skills, and he carried out some interesting interventions attempting to improve perspective taking and friendship regulation. This work has been described in Selman and Schultz (1990) and in Nakkula and Selman (1991). The way in which perspective taking underlies many aspects of human relationships is illustrated in work looking at information management by young people when in relationship with their parents. This will be referred to in greater detail in Chapter 5, but here it is of interest to note research by Marshall *et al.* (2005), in which they explore notions of deception and of lying. They quote one young person describing how he thinks about his behaviour towards his mother. He says: 'I don't need to lie to my Mom about what I am doing. Trust and honesty is important. But I don't need to tell her if I am going someplace where I think I will be safe but my Mom won't, then I just save her worrying.' A striking example of perspective taking in everyday life!

Moral thinking

'I think that when I was younger I was positive about everything, but now I'm positive about most things, but not as positive as I used to be. But then you think about things more deeply now, and you just think . . . Oh well!'

(14-year-old girl)

'I think quite differently about quite a lot of things now because you're sort of becoming your own person, so you're going to sort of develop your own opinions and stuff.'

(16-year-old girl)

Moral and political thinking are, of course, aspects of social cognition, but for understandable reasons both have been the focus of distinct and important research activity. Taking moral reasoning first, it is not difficult to see the relevance of this to adolescent development. As Eisenberg and Morris (2004) point out, young people's changing notions of justice, of morality and ethics, and of prosocial behaviour are all aspects of thinking and reasoning that are of great interest during the adolescent period. As with Elkind, Selman and others, once again it has been Piaget's concepts that have formed the springboard for later thinking about moral reasoning. Although there have been a number of different theories put forward to explain the develop-ment of concepts of morality in young people, there is little doubt that the 'cognitive-developmental' approach of Piaget and Kohlberg has been the starting point for most work in this area.

In his work on the moral judgement of the child Piaget (1932) proposed two major stages of moral thinking. The first, which he called 'moral realism', refers to a period in which young children make judgements on an objective basis. As an example, when asked which is worst, to break two cups or five cups, children are likely to base their reasoning on how much damage has been caused. In other words to break five cups must be a worse action than to break two cups, irrespective of the circumstances. The second stage, applying usually to these between the ages of 8 and 12, has been described as the morality of cooperation, or the morality of reciprocity. During this stage, Piaget believed, decisions concern-ing morality were usually made on a subjective basis, and often depended on an estimate of intention rather than consequences.

Kohlberg (1981, 1984) has elaborated Piaget's scheme into one which has six different stages. His method has been to present hypothetical situations containing moral dilemmas to young people of different ages, and to classify their responses according to a stage theory of moral development. Hypothetical situations which have been used include taking a decision about whether to hide your sister's wrongdoing from your mother, and whether it is better to cheat or to let someone down. Perhaps the best-known dilemma is one which has come to be known as the Heinz dilemma. It goes as follows:

> In Europe a woman was very near to death from a very bad disease, a rare form of cancer. There was one drug that doctors thought might save her. It was a form of radium that a druggist in the same town had recently discovered. The drug was expensive to make, but the druggist was charging ten times what the drug had cost him to make. He paid $200 for the radium, and charged $2,000 for a small dose of the drug. The sick woman's husband, Heinz, went to every-one he knew to borrow the money, but he could only get together $1,000, which is half of what it cost. He told the druggist that his wife was dying, and asked him to sell it cheaper, or let him pay later. But the druggist said: 'No, I discovered the drug, and I'm going to make money from it'. So Heinz got desperate, and broke into the man's store to steal the drug for his wife.

> Question: Should the man have done that?
>
> (Kohlberg, 1981)

Based on responses to questions like this, Kohlberg has described the following stages of moral development.

Pre-conventional

Stage 1   Punishment–obedience orientation. Behaviours that are punished are perceived as bad.

Stage 2   Instrumental hedonism. Here the individual conforms in order to obtain rewards, have favours returned etc.

Conventional

Stage 3 Orientation to personal relationships. Good behaviour is that which pleases or helps others and is approved by them.

Stage 4 Maintenance of social order. Good behaviour consists of doing one's duty, having respect for authority, and maintaining the social order for its own sake.

Post-conventional

Stage 5 Social contract and/or conscience orientation. At the beginning of this stage moral behaviour tends to be thought of in terms of general rights and standards agreed upon by society as a whole, but at later moments there is an increasing orientation towards internal decisions of conscience.

Stage 6 The universal ethical principle. At this stage there is an attempt to formulate and be guided by abstract ethical principles, for example the Golden Rule, or Kant's Categorical Imperative.

Broadly speaking research has supported Kohlberg's notion of a progression through various stages of moral reasoning during adolescence. Colby *et al.* (1983) demonstrated a similar progression, and Kohlberg and colleagues were able to show that even in different cultures there was evidence of a stage process. In a classic study (Kohlberg and Gilligan, 1971) the authors compared three very different cultures: the USA, Taiwan and Mexico. Results showed an almost identical sequence of stages, with variation being shown in the rate of development and the fact that later post-conventional stages of reasoning were very rarely seen apart from in the USA. In a more nuanced study Walker *et al.* (2001) explored the actual process of the move from one stage to another. They showed that young people experienced periods of consolidation and of transition. Thus in a period of consolidation there is stability in the type of reasoning employed, whilst in a period of transition there will be some fluidity of reasoning, with young people possibly using more than one type of reasoning. Once another period of consolidation is reached it will be at a higher level of reasoning than that achieved earlier.

In spite of this support Kohlberg's writings have raised contentious issues, and there has been extensive critical discussion over the validity and meaning of this stage theory of moral reasoning (see Eisenberg and Morris, 2004, for review). In particular the methodological problems associated with the testing and scoring of moral dilemmas have worried some critics. One proposal has been to suggest alternative forms of assessment which can be scored more objectively. Rest (1973), for example, developed a multiple-choice format, known as the Defining Issues Test, which has been widely used by researchers. Another criticism has concerned the meaning of hypothetical moral dilemmas. Some writers have argued that it would be better to use real-life situations, and using this method Walker *et al.* (1995) found little difference in moral reasoning between those aged 16–19 and those aged 21–25. These authors argued that changes in moral reasoning when applied to real-life situations appear to be more gradual than changes relating to hypothetical situations.

There is also the question of whether moral reasoning has any relation to actual behaviour. Do individuals whose moral reasoning is at an advanced level demonstrate that thinking in their behaviour? Interestingly the research does in fact support this contention. Eisenberg and Morris (2004) review studies which indicate that, although young people do not always act in an entirely consistent manner, on average, those who reason at higher stages act in more moral ways.

The most sustained criticism of the cognitive-developmental approach to moral reasoning has come from one of Kohlberg's former colleagues, Carol Gilligan. In essence her argument has been that the framework used in scoring Kohlberg's dilemmas has depended on a justice orientation, based on the assumption that moral reasoning has to do with notions of justice, fairness and equity. Gilligan suggested that there could be an equally valid orientation, namely the care orientation. This can be defined as being to do with not turning away from some-one in need rather than treating others unfairly. Gilligan's care orientation is similar to the concept of prosocial reasoning developed by Eisenberg and others (Eisenberg et al., 1991, 1995). Of course the most interesting aspect of this has to do with gender. Gilligan argued that women were more likely to view moral dilemmas from a care perspective, whilst men might be more likely to make judge-ments according to a justice framework. Not surprisingly this has created some interesting debates, especially as Gilligan suggested that the very traits that have defined 'goodness' for women, i.e. their care and sensitivity to others and the responsibility they take for others, are not traits especially valued by men!

Thinking back to the Heinz dilemma quoted earlier, one can see that using a justice orientation ('the theft of someone else's property is wrong') would lead to a very different assessment of higher order morality than the use of a care orientation ('looking after the sick is paramount'). Gilligan herself proposed some new dilemmas, including the following:

> A high school girl's parents are away for the weekend, and she's alone in the house. Unexpectedly, on a Friday evening, her boyfriend comes over. They spend the evening in the house, and after a while they start necking and petting.

> Questions: Is this right or wrong? What if they went on to have sex? Suppose the girl is less willing than the boy? Do you think issues about sex have anything to do with morality?

> (Gilligan et al., 1990)

Of course dilemmas like this involve situations that are much closer to real life, and as we have noted the progression through stages of moral reasoning is slower under such conditions in contrast to reasoning about hypothetical moral issues. In terms of gender it is interesting to note that, whilst Gilligan's arguments have received a lot of attention, in fact the research findings are not so clear-cut. As Steinberg (2008) points out, studies have noted that males and females approach moral dilemmas from both a justice and a caring perspective, depending on the problem. Where researchers have tried to identify gender differences they have largely been unsuccessful (e.g. Pratt et al., 2004). In spite of the popularity and intuitive appeal of Gilligan's arguments, it would appear that morality is not as gender-based as might be imagined.

Another interesting question that has been raised by investigators is whether interventions can accelerate or enhance the level of cognitive thought or moral reasoning. Work by Michael Shayer in the UK has received some prominence, especially in the educational setting. He and his colleagues have argued that when appropriate classroom activities are put in place cognitive development can be enhanced (Shayer and Adey, 2002). The role of parents has also been a focus of enquiry, with the work of Walker and colleagues (Walker and Hennig, 1999; Walker et al., 2000) being particularly useful here. These researchers have been able to show that whether moral reasoning can be accelerated by parental intervention or not depends very much on the style of intervention. Thus where parents use criticism or direct challenge there is no influence on the young person's level of moral thinking, but where a more inductive, encouraging style (what is known as a Socratic style of dialogue) is used, then indeed the adolescent's level of moral reasoning can be facilitated and in some cases advanced.

Political thought

'Being able to understand why people do things. Yes, I think that's definitely true. You go through different experiences, and you can sort of imagine more extreme versions of them, like having political views and things like that. You can imagine what it would be like if you weren't allowed to think the way you wanted to . . . I'm sure I do think differently, and you have more context to understand the "baddies", as you would have imagined them when you were younger.'

(17-year-old girl)

In this chapter on thinking and reasoning the final topic to be explored is that to do with political thinking. In view of what has been covered already it is not surprising to find that thinking and reasoning to do with political issues shows a similar developmental process as that for other aspects of social cognition (Torney-Purta, 1990; Flanagan, 2004). The classic study in the field of political reasoning is that of Adelson and colleagues (Adelson and O'Neill, 1966; Adelson et al., 1969), and their work remains pre-eminent in this field. Adelson and O'Neill (1966) approached the issue of the growth of political thinking by posing for young people of different ages the following problem:

Imagine that a thousand men and women, dissatisfied with the way things are going in their own country, decide to purchase and move to an island in the Pacific; once there they must devise laws and modes of government.

These authors then explored the adolescent's approach to a variety of relevant topics. They asked questions about how a government would be formed, what its purposes would be, whether there would be a need for laws and political parties, how you would protect minorities, and so on. The investigators proposed different laws, and explored typical problems of public policy. The major results may be discussed under two headings: change in modes of thinking, and a decline in authoritarianism with age.

As far as the first issue is concerned, there was a marked shift in thinking from the concrete to the abstract, a finding which ties in with all that has been already discussed in this chapter. For example, when asked: 'What is the purpose of laws?' one 12-year-old replied: 'If we had no laws people would go round killing each other'. By contrast a 16-year-old replied: 'To ensure safety, and to enforce the government'. Another commented: 'They are basically guide-lines for people. I mean, like this is right and this is wrong, to help them understand' (Adelson, 1971).

The second major shift observed was a decline in authoritarian solutions to political questions. The typical young adolescent of 12 or 13 years of age appeared unable to appreciate that problems can have more than one solution, and that individual behaviour or political acts are not necessarily absolutely right or wrong, good or bad. The concept of moral relativism was not yet available for the making of political judgements. When confronted with law-breaking or even mild forms of misbehaviour the younger adolescent's solution was, characteristically to:

> simply raise the ante: more police, stiffer fines, longer prison sentences, and if need be, executions. To a large and varied set of questions on crime and punishment they consistently proposed one form of solution: punish, and if that does not suffice, then punish harder. . . . At this age the child will not normally concede that wrongdoing may be a symptom of something deeper, or that it may be inhibited by indirect means. The idea of reform and rehabilitation through humane methods is mentioned only by a small minority at the outset of adolescence.
>
> (Adelson, 1971, p. 1023)

By contrast the 14- or 15 year-old is much more aware of the different sides of any argument, and is usually able to take a relativistic point of view. Thinking begins to be more tentative, more critical and more pragmatic.

> Confronting a proposal for a law, or for a change in social policy, he scrutinises it to determine whether there is more to it than meets the eye. Whose interests are served, and whose are damaged? He now understands that law and policy must accommodate competing interests and values, that ends must be balanced against means, and that the short term good must be appraised against latent or long term or indirect outcomes.
>
> (Adelson, 1971, p. 1026)

While Adelson and his colleagues did not propose a stage theory relating to growth in political thought, it will be apparent from what has been outlined above that the move from concrete to abstract, and from absolute to relativistic reasoning is consistent with all that has been said about developments in social cognition. Of particular interest is Adelson's finding that in late adolescence a broadly consistent and coherent set of beliefs, akin to an ideology, begins to be expressed that was not apparent at earlier stages. This ideology is 'more or less organised in reference to a more encompassing . . . set of political principles' (Adelson, 1972, p. 121). These principles may concern a wide range of topics, and could include things like civil liberties, freedom of speech and so on.

In more recent times research has concentrated on some of the possible background factors that might influence political thinking (Flanagan, 2004; Lehalle, 2006). For example studies have compared young people from different social backgrounds, showing that poverty and disadvantage clearly affect both knowledge of and attitudes to the political process (Flanagan and Tucker, 1999). In Europe there have been a number of studies looking at the impact of German re-unification, and a concern with the factors that might encourage the growth of right-wing ideologies. Broadly speaking research shows that there are fewer differences between countries and political contexts than there are between generations and family types.

Noack *et al.* (1995) concluded that comparisons between adolescents and their parents in attitudes to social change yielded greater differences than comparisons between families from former East and West Germany. In both countries young people were more optimistic than their parents about the results of re-unification. Similarly Rippl and Boehnke (1995) found few differences in authoritarianism between the USA and the two countries of Germany. As they said: 'The central results of this study are as follows: that an authoritarian character seems to exist in all three countries included in the present study. There is no evidence that state socialism produced distinctly more authoritarian personalities than Western democracies do' (Rippl and Boehnke, 1995, p. 66). Lastly Noack *et al.* (1995) reported that adolescents are more likely to develop right-wing, authoritarian attitudes if they have right-wing parents and live in communities that promote or support right-wing policies. Thus it is apparent that, where political reasoning is concerned, it is possible to see both developmental change and influence from the context in which the young person is growing up.

Implications for practice

1. First, the very notion of a major shift in the early adolescent years towards more abstract thought is something that needs to be taken into account by any adult who comes into contact with this age group. A growing capacity for logical and scientific reasoning will affect the young person's skills in communication, decision-making and negotiation.

2. In addition there is a broader concern about the school curriculum, and its impact on the type of thinking exhibited by adolescents today. Does the curriculum encourage formal operational thinking, or does it inhibit its development? For some writers (e.g. Keating, 2004) there is a real anxiety about the way current educational practice inhibits what is called 'critical habits of mind' in young people. For writers like this schools are places in which too much emphasis is placed on examination performance instead of fostering imaginative and creative thought.

3. In terms of concepts of egocentrism and other aspects of social cognition examples have been given of ways that these can be applied in everyday interactions with young people. It has been noted how Selman, Elkind and others have used their theories to develop new approaches to interventions,

and more is said about this in Chapter 10. To take egocentrism as an example, it will be apparent that an understanding of the way young adolescents think about themselves might be helpful to parents as well as to professionals. Young people can appear to those who live and work with them to be intensely self-centred. An awareness of the fact that egocentrism is a normal feature of the cognitive development of adolescents could assist adults to put this behaviour in perspective.

4. An understanding of moral thinking has implications for practice. Kohlberg himself developed a training course which attempted to accelerate adolescent moral development, although there have been some doubts as to the success of such a venture. However, subsequently there have been a number of attempts to use Kohlberg's framework in programmes with young people. Some of these have been in the broad field of values education, while others have continued the search for a means of enhancing or hastening moral thought.

5. Another field for the application of the work of Kohlberg and others has been to develop it in the context of anti-social behaviour. Here the belief is that those whose behaviour appears to exhibit some deficit in moral reasoning can be helped by training in this area. While there has been work of this kind in North America as well as in Britain, the notion that offending behaviour can be modified by cognitive skills training has not been universally accepted. Nonetheless this remains a fruitful field for further work.

6. To conclude, it will be clear that there are many ways in which an understanding of adolescent thinking and reasoning may have applications in practice. All too often professionals become preoccupied with the outward behaviour of young people, ignoring some of the less obvious aspects of development. Changes in thinking and reasoning are good examples of this. It is important to take account of some of the limitations in the thinking skills of the younger adolescent. It is also necessary to recognise how these skills develop with time, allowing older adolescents to manifest a range of new capabilities.

Further reading

Keating, D (2004) Cognitive and brain development. In Lerner, R and Steinberg, L (Eds) *Handbook of adolescent psychology*, 2nd edn. Wiley. New York.
An excellent review, with a strong neuroscience perspective, by one of the USA's recognised experts in the field.

Lehalle, H (2006) Cognitive development in adolescence: thinking freed from concrete restraints. In Jackson, S and Goossens, L (Eds) *Handbook of adolescent development*. Psychology Press. Hove.
A good chapter with a strong European slant.

The self and identity

Introduction

'I'm not really worried about what I look like, because I know it's going to change, because it does change most of the time, because I change nearly every week. I notice it. People say I look like my older brother, and if I don't turn out like him it will be bad on my confidence I guess, because I want to be like my older brother. But then if I want to be like him, then it's not really me, so I've got to deal with who I am, and I've got to make sure I like what I look like. I guess I've got more figuring out to do. It's really weird, it's weird actually.'

(14-year-old boy)

Adolescence is usually thought to be a time of both change and consolidation in respect of the self-concept. There are a number of reasons for this. First, the major physical changes that have been documented in Chapter 2 inevitably carry with them an alteration in bodily self-concept and thus in a highly significant element of the overall concept of self. Second, intellectual growth during this stage makes possible a more complex and sophisticated self-concept. Third, some development of the sense of self seems likely as a result of changes in social relationships, in particular increasing autonomy, changes in family interactions and the growing influence of peers. Lastly, as pointed out by Alsaker and Kroger (2006), this is also a time of transition in relation to the social environments experienced by young people. There will be a move from junior to secondary school, and in middle and late adolescence many will experience some aspects of the workplace. In such situations they will be expected to interact with adults in more mature ways, leading to alterations in the perception of self.

The ways in which young people understand and perceive themselves, their own agency and personality, have a powerful effect on their subsequent reactions to various life events. The essential dilemma for an individual young person who wishes to be fully integrated into society is that between 'playing appropriate roles' and 'selfhood'. On the one hand it is important to play the right roles in a range of social settings, and to follow the prescribed rules for these situations. On the other hand it is equally important to maintain elements of individuality or selfhood. Adolescence is a time when an individual struggles to determine the exact nature of his or her self, and to consolidate a series of choices into a coherent whole which makes up the essence of the person, clearly separate from the parents and from other formative influences. Without this process towards individuality the young person can experience depersonalisation.

The relative freedom for the adolescent to escape from behaviour which is regulated by rules set up by adults can be achieved through taking on different roles, and through the selection of alternative social contexts in which to develop outside the home. In the process of socialisation the various adults (parents, teachers and other mentors) which whom the young person interacts are important as role models and social agents, but so too are the functions of selfhood, perceived competence and coherent identity. The young person is engaged in a process in which making sense of the social world, and finding a comfortable place in it, is the key to psychological maturation.

In this chapter the evidence available relating to the self-concept and to identity development will be briefly reviewed, with a particular focus on four major themes:

- factors associated with self-concept development;
- self-esteem in adolescence;
- theoretical approaches to identity development;
- a review of research on ethnic identity.

Before commencing a discussion of these topics, a word needs to be said about terminology. Unfortunately in this area a number of terms tend to be used inter-changeably by writers and researchers, so that, for example, 'self-concept', 'self-worth' and 'self-esteem' may all be used to refer to the same notion, while there is also often confusion between 'identity' and the 'self' or the 'self-concept'. For the present the term 'self-concept' will be used to refer to the overall idea of a sense of self, which includes body image, self-esteem and various other dimensions of the self. The term 'self-esteem' will be used as far as possible to refer to the individual's self-evaluation or sense of self-worth. Finally the term 'identity' will be used when discussing the work of Erik Erikson and those who have built on his original ideas, including writers such as Marcia, Waterman, Cote, Phinney, Bosma and Kroger.

Factors associated with self-concept development

'I don't really think like that massively. I don't really have a problem with who I am. It's not that you can do much about it. I think it's pretty much set, you know. You see people trying to fit in and be whatever, you know, to make sure people like them, but it's just fraud, and you know that from a mile they stick out.'

(16-year-old boy)

'You start to question yourself. You're just thinking "Well, I am growing up and making my own choices". And, like, you're not too sure about the person you are, or you're becoming, and it gets a little bit worrying. I mean you could turn into anyone! . . . I'm changing still, I think. I think I'm getting there, and working it out, 'cause I did sort of know who I was before, and then I changed again, and now with all my other friends who I prefer being with, and I think, yeah, I'm still trying to work it out.'

(16-year-old girl)

There are many different ways of conceptualising the self-concept. Indeed this is a topic with a long history in psychology and related disciplines, and a wide range of theoretical positions can be identified within the literature. For the purposes of this chapter discussion will remain primarily within the field of psychology, focussing on research and theory relating to the adolescent life stage. The most common way of delineating the self-concept has been to describe a number of dimensions which may be said to constitute the totality of the self. One good example may be found in the work of Offer and colleagues. Offer is well known for the development of the Offer Self-image Questionnaire (Offer, 1969; Offer *et al.*, 1992). In this questionnaire the adolescent self-image is broken down into five global areas of psychosocial functioning. These are:

- the psychological self (including impulse control, emotional health and body image;
- the sexual self;
- the social self (including social functioning and vocational attitudes);
- the familial self (including family functioning);
- the coping self (including self-reliance, self-confidence and mental health).

An alternative multi-dimensional view may be found in the work of Harter (for a description see Alsaker and Kroger, 2006; Steinberg, 2008). Harter developed a self-perception profile, based upon a factor-analytic procedure, and as a result of this procedure she identified eight specific dimensions of the self-concept: scholastic competence, job competence, athletic competence, physical appearance, social acceptance, close friendship, romantic appeal and conduct.

An even more complex model has been developed by Shavelson, who supports a hierarchical view of the self-concept in adolescence. This model is illustrated in Figure 4.1. Shavelson *et al.* (1976) and Marsh *et al.* (1988) believe that at the top of the model is a fairly stable general self-concept, which is based on two main dimensions – the academic and the non-academic self-concept. Within the non-academic self-concept a distinction is made between social, emotional and physical self-concepts, each of which is built on other more detailed facets of the self. These are placed lower in the hierarchy, since it is believed they are less stable and more situation-specific in nature.

It is important to note that these are not the only examples in the literature of approaches to the adolescent self-concept, but they do give an idea of the way social scientists have viewed this topic. Such approaches are also helpful when the manner in which the self-concept changes and develops during adolescence is considered. First it can be said that a greater degree of differentiation occurs. On the one hand aspects of the self-concept are more likely to be linked to specific situations. Thus a child will describe himself or herself simply as sad, lazy, sporty or friendly. A teenager is more likely to say that he or she is friendly in such and such a situation, or sad under certain circumstances. On the other hand an adolescent is also more likely than a younger child to be able to include a notion of who is doing the describing. Thus a teenager might say: 'My parents see me as quiet and shy, but my friends know that I can be quite the opposite.' This ability to see the self from different points of view is a key feature of the changing world view

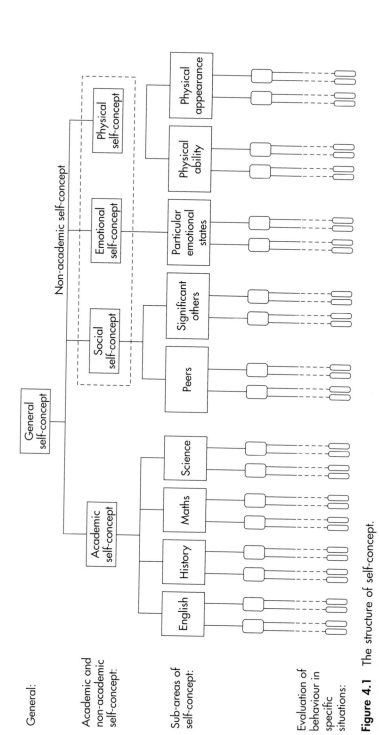

General:

Academic and
non-academic
self-concept:

Sub-areas of
self-concept:

Evaluation of
behaviour in
specific
situations:

Figure 4.1 The structure of self-concept.

Source: Shavelson *et al.* (1976).

of the young person in the early years of adolescence, and is dependent on the cognitive development outlined in the previous chapter.

In addition to greater differentiation, better organisation and integration of different aspects of the self also develops (Dusek and McIntyre, 2003; Alsaker and Kroger, 2006). When asked to describe themselves children may simply list attributes in no specific order or relationship to each other. As they get older young people show evidence of a greater need to organise traits so that they become linked together and form a coherent whole. Interestingly, this increased awareness of the importance of having a coherent view of the self may create some problems for those in the middle years of adolescence, since with this awareness also comes a recognition that within one's personality there will be conflicting attributes. In an important study Harter and Monsour (1992) asked young people to characterise their personalities by placing various traits on a series of concentric circles, from most important in the centre to least important on the outside. It was apparent from this study that most young people saw themselves as having conflicting attributes, and being different sorts of people in different situations. Presumably the resolution or acceptance of these conflicts is part of the developmental process that contributes to the move towards maturity. In this respect it is of interest to bear in mind the view of Harter (1988) and others, who believe that the self-concept is most usefully understood as a theory one constructs about oneself. The gradually increasing differentiation and organisation which occurs during adolescence is evidence of precisely this construction that Harter talks about.

Harter and others have also been interested in two other aspects of the global self-concept. One is the preoccupation with the self which is characteristic of this stage, and the other is the question of how much the self-concept fluctuates during this period. In terms of the first of these, there is little doubt that adolescence brings with it a marked increase in introspection. This has been well described by Erikson (1968) and Rosenberg (1979). This shift towards an often painful awareness of the self and how one appears to others is likely to result from a variety of factors. Increased cognitive ability plays its part, together with the physical growth associated with puberty. A changing body will almost certainly lead to a sense that the self is altering, and this in turn can cause intense self-consciousness as the young person becomes increasingly aware of other people and of how he or she appears to them. The idea of adolescent egocentrism has already been mentioned, as has the link between new cognitive skills and enhanced awareness of the perceptions of others. Egocentrism and introspection are closely linked, for as the adolescent begins a new phase of attempting to understand the emerging self, so for a while this aspect of the inner world becomes a major preoccupation.

Turning now to the issue of stability in the self-concept, it is the case that more empirical research has been carried out on the stability of self-esteem than on the global self-concept. This research will be considered in the next section of the chapter. Nonetheless it is certainly the case that some aspects of the self will change more than others. Indeed Shavelson's model, described above, specifically implies that the higher in the hierarchy the element of the self, the more stable it will be. In addition to this there will also be a growing awareness on the part of the young person that some aspects of the self will be subject to day-to-day fluctuation. Such awareness, however, will not necessarily prevent anxiety about the lack of stability. As Harter notes, a young person may well ask: 'I really do not understand how I can switch so fast. I mean, how can I be cheerful one minute, anxious the next, and then be sarcastic?' (1990, p. 363). Of course this is a question that parents too may well be asking, as they struggle to cope with a teenager who appears to be many different people all rolled into one.

Self-esteem

'You do see people changing at this age. I'm not saying I'm special or any-thing, but I can see people I know changing, or not changing while I am, you know. Like I have friends who have always been really good at school, like top of the class, try hard types, and they always do well in tests and exams, blah! blah! blah! But when you get down to it I don't think they're actually that amazingly bright. I think that they've done well because they can learn by rote, like learning facts, repeating facts, and there's not a lot behind it. So yeah, I'd like to think I'm a bit different to that. And I've noticed it. I've changed my way of thinking so I notice that way of thinking in other people who haven't changed. It's made me grow away from people, because I don't know if they're going to change ever. It makes me feel like I've changed and grown but they haven't got there yet.'

(17-year-old girl)

Self-esteem has received more attention than most other aspects of the self, since it is seen as a barometer of coping and adaptation. Since the early days of research in this field it has been apparent that low self-esteem was likely to be associated with adjustment difficulties, and that those with high esteem were likely to be doing well in many different domains. To take one example, the classic study of Rosenberg (1965) illustrates this general conclusion. He was able to show that low self-esteem, characteristic of approximately 20–30 per cent of the sample he studied, was linked to a range of variables. The research focussed on older adolescents, the sample including roughly 5,000 17- and 18-year-olds in randomly selected schools in New York. Self-esteem was measured with a ten-item self-report scale (i.e. the degree to which the respondents agreed or disagreed with statements such as 'I feel I am a person of worth, at least on an equal level with others').

Low self-esteem was shown to be related to depression, anxiety and poor school performance. Both high and low self-esteem adolescents were similar in wishing for success on leaving school, but the low self-esteem group were more likely to feel that they would never attain such success. In addition they were more likely to prefer a job which they knew was beyond their grasp, and to feel they did not have the resources necessary for success. The young people who were high in self-esteem were significantly more likely than those with low self-esteem to consider the following as personal assets: self-confidence, being hard-working, having leadership potential, and being able to make a good impression. Low self-esteem adolescents were characterised by a sense of incompetence in social relationships, social isolation and the belief that people neither understood nor respected them. Finally, the belief that their parents took an interest in them was significantly more apparent in those with high self-esteem.

It may appear to readers that this is a study from the past. However, the results have stood up over time, and have served as the foundation for later studies. Since the appearance of Rosenberg's study in 1965 a large body of research on self-esteem in adolescents has developed. Most of it has come to acknowledge that it is not only the global self-concept which is multi-dimensional, but that self-esteem itself is also likely to be multi-dimensional. Thus a young man may have high self-esteem when it comes to performance in the gym, but a low sense of self-worth when he has do deal with school work, or manage a tricky social situation. Work in this area has become more sophisticated since Rosenberg's day, but nonetheless researchers have continued to look at similar issues, such as the correlates of high self-esteem. Thus, for example, Dusek and McIntyre (2003) review studies that explore the relation between academic achievement and self-esteem. As these and many other authors point out, the problem is to try to identify which variable influences which. Is it high self-esteem which leads to better school performance, or is it the other way round?

As Dusek and McIntyre state: 'Although several longitudinal studies have been conducted to clarify issues of causation and direction of effect, the results have been far from crystal clear. In fact it seems that the more research that is done, the more murky the waters' (2003, p. 300). In an attempt to come to some conclusions on these issues, recent research has used structural equation modelling and other complex statistical techniques. Commentators such as Hoge *et al.* (1995) take the view that, while influences between the variables are weaker than earlier correlational studies implied, nonetheless performance in school has somewhat more influence on self-esteem than the other way around. A final point here is that the Shavelson model mentioned earlier continues to be influential, since the highest correlations are found between achievement in specific subject areas and self-esteem directly related to those domains.

Apart from work of this nature, two areas of self-esteem research have attracted interest in the recent past. The first has to do with understanding the attributes which contribute most to self-esteem, and the second relates to the longitudinal course of self-esteem stability during adolescence. There have, in addition, been studies of self-esteem in different ethnic groups, an issue which will be considered in a subsequent section of the chapter. For the moment consideration will be given to the attributes which contribute to self-esteem. On this subject there appears to be consensus among researchers – most agree that in early adolescence it is satisfaction with one's physical appearance that contributes most to self-esteem. Harter (1990, p. 367) quotes one adolescent who says: 'What's really important to me is how I look. If I like the way I look, then I really like the kind of person I am.' Among young people, especially in the earlier stages of adolescence, body image satisfaction correlates most highly with global self-esteem, followed by social acceptance by peers. Academic achievement and sporting success also contribute, although to a lesser degree. As many authors have shown, there is a marked gender difference in respect of the salience of body image, with this being a more important factor for girls than for boys (see for example Cole *et al.*, 2001).

A number of classic studies in the literature have reported lower levels of self-esteem among girls in early adolescence (e.g. Simmons and Rosenberg, 1975; Simmons and Blyth, 1987). It seems probable that these findings can be explained by the high level of importance attributed to body image satisfaction in global self-esteem, and the fact that girls are particularly sensitive to, and dissatisfied with, their body image during the pubertal years.

Another important contributor to self-esteem is the opinion of important others, but which others make most difference in adolescence? The work of Harter (1989, 1990) has been important here. Her research shows that there is a developmental shift, with parents becoming less important as a function of age. Thus, for children, the perceptions of parents play a larger part than any other variable in determining self-esteem, a finding supported in the research of Cole *et al.* (2001). However, with the onset of adolescence peers become increasingly salient. Interestingly classmates appear to be of more importance than close friends in influencing self-esteem. As Harter says:

> Acknowledgement from peers in the public domain seems more critical than the personal regard of close friends, since close friends, by definition provide support, and their positive feedback may not be perceived as necessarily self-enhancing. . . . Thus it would appear that the adolescent must turn to somewhat more objective sources of support – to the social mirror, as it were, in order to validate the self.
>
> (1990, p. 368)

In spite of this important conclusion there is no evidence that parents cease to be influential in respect of adolescent self-esteem. Parents continue to have an impact, but not to the over-arching degree that is apparent during childhood. As noted earlier, Rosenberg in 1965 reported that those whose parents showed an interest in their academic performance had higher self-esteem; indeed research which will be reviewed in Chapter 5 shows that self-esteem is one of the variables most obviously influenced by parenting styles in adolescence. Parents and peers both play a part in this important arena, but the balance of influence between the two shifts during the adolescent years in line with the increasing significance of social relationships outside the home.

The second theme which is noteworthy in this context is the stability or otherwise of self-esteem during this stage. Early studies reported contradictory results, yet with hindsight this is not surprising. On the one hand many different measures of self-esteem were used, and on the other researchers did not distinguish between different groups of young people. More recent research has shown that varying groups of young people show different trajectories of self-esteem during the adolescent period. The first people to note this possibility were Hirsch and Dubois (1991), who identified four very different paths taken by groups of adolescents in respect of self-esteem development. The sample they looked at were between the ages of 12 and 14, and their findings indicated that approximately one-third of the group could be classified as being consistently high in self-esteem, and a further 15 per cent consistently low in self-esteem during this period. However, roughly half the sample showed marked change during the two-year period. Twenty per cent showed a steep decline, while nearly one-third showed a small but significant increase in self-esteem during the course of the study. This is clearly of considerable importance in contributing to a clearer understanding of self-esteem in adolescence, and underlines the point that within the adolescent age group there are wide individual differences in all domains.

Since the publication of the Hirsch and Dubois (1991) study, others have looked more closely at this issue. In the European context Alsaker and Olweus (1992) showed stability of self-esteem over short periods of time (e.g. one year) but greater change over longer periods (e.g. three years). Block and Robins (1993) found that boys are likely to be over-represented in the group whose self-esteem increases, whilst girls may be over-represented in the group showing a decline in self-esteem. Alsaker and Olweus (2002) looked at the question of victimisation, and were able to show that a particular stressful experience, such as being bullied in school, could contribute to changes in self-esteem. Not surprisingly those who were bullied showed a decrease in self-esteem, and the higher the levels of bullying, the more self-esteem was affected. Zimmerman *et al.* (1997) looked at a wider age range than that studied by Hirsh and Dubois (1991). They included young people between the ages of 12 and 16 and, remarkably, were able to replicate in broad fashion the four trajectories first described by Hirsch and Dubois. Their results are illustrated in Figure 4.2.

Zimmerman and colleagues (1997) note that the groups with consistently high self-esteem and those with rising self-esteem were more likely to resist peer pressure, and less likely to misuse alcohol and to become involved in deviant behaviour. Of even greater importance is their conclusion that the most striking effects of self-esteem change may be found by comparing the groups which show declining and improving self-esteem. These two groups often start at much the same point, at age 12, but gradually diverge in respect of scores on every dependent variable studied. As these authors point out, these results have highly significant implications for intervention programmes, and indicate that one programme design cannot be expected to fit all young people. As they say: 'One strategy might reach youth with steadily decreasing self-esteem, while a different approach might be more effective for youth with rising self-esteem' (p. 137). Finally they note that the use of a single model to describe adolescent development may inhibit the discovery of meaningful differences between individual young people. As in so many areas discussed in this book, a more nuanced approach to adolescence is now being recognised as essential. Key studies, such as that carried out by Zimmerman and colleagues, illustrate just how important it is to avoid generalisation, and to take a more finely grained approach to the understanding of young people's development.

Theoretical approaches to identity development

'At school they put a lot of pressure on about, sort of, what are you going to do. Then it sort of makes you think who you want to be, and what you want to do, and all of this. Everyone wants to be successful, but then you're just like, you stop and think, well, "what if I'm not?" "What if I'm one of those

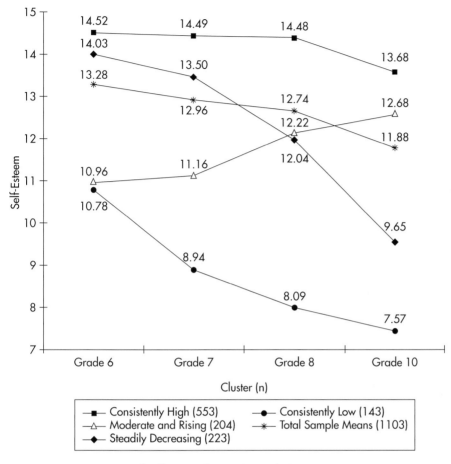

Figure 4.2 Trajectories of self-esteem for total sample (*N* = 1103).

Source: Zimmerman *et al.* (1997).

people who just can't do what they want to do?" Especially if you're like me and if you have no clue!'

(16-year-old girl)

'I've always had some vague idea – maybe it changes, I don't know – but as you grow older I've always had some vague idea about who you are and what you are going to be. Since I can remember I've always been sporty, and that's just kind of gone with me. And it's just developed, and I've found sports which I'm better at, and it just progresses from there. I've never really had a time when I've been "What am I good at?" or something like that. . . . Something to do with sport, that's what I hope to be doing, because that's what I enjoy doing, and I'd like to do something that I enjoy doing.'

(16-year-old girl)

A key figure in any discussion of identity development is Erik Erikson (1968). For those who wish to read of his work in detail an excellent review may be found in Kroger (2004). Erikson viewed life as a series of stages, each having a particular developmental task of a psychological nature associated with it. In infancy, for example, the task is to establish a sense of basic trust, and to combat mistrust. The maternal relationship is here considered to be critical in creating a foundation upon which the infant may build later trusting relationships. As far as adolescence is concerned, the task involves the establishment of a coherent identity, and the defeat of a sense of identity diffusion. Erikson believed that the search for identity becomes especially acute at this stage as a result of a number of factors. Thus Erikson laid stress on the phenomenon of rapid biological and social change during adolescence, and pointed especially to the importance for the individual of having to take major decisions at this time in almost all areas of life. In many of his writings Erikson either stated or implied that some form of crisis is necessary for the young person to resolve the identity issues and to defeat identity diffusion.

According to Erikson identity diffusion has four major components. First, there is the challenge of intimacy. Here the individual may fear commitment or involvement in close interpersonal relationships because of the possible loss of his or her own identity. This fear can lead to stereotyped, formalised relationships, or to isolation. Another possibility is that the young person may, as Erikson puts it, 'in repeated hectic attempts and dismal failures, seek intimacy with the most improbable partners' (1968, p. 167). Second, there is the possibility of a diffusion of time perspective. Here the adolescent finds it impossible to plan for the future or to retain any sense of time. This problem is thought to be associated with anxieties about change and about becoming adult, and often 'consists of a decided disbelief in the possibility that time may bring change, and yet also a violent fear that it might' (1968, p. 169).

Next there is a diffusion of industry, in which the young person finds it difficult to harness his or her resources in a realistic manner in work or study. Both of these activities represent commitment, and as a defence against this the individual may find it impossible to concentrate, or may frenetically engage in one single task to the exclusion of all others. A young person who opts out of taking exams at the last minute, or who drops out of a course just at the point when it is getting interesting, are good examples of the adolescent struggle with a diffusion of industry. Finally Erikson outlines the concept of negative identity. By this is meant the young person's selection of an identity exactly the opposite to that preferred by parents or other important adults.

> The loss of a sense of identity is often expressed in a scornful and snobbish hostility towards the role offered as proper and desirable in one's family or immediate community. Any aspect of the required role, or all of it – be it masculinity or femininity, nationality or class membership – can become the main focus of the young person's acid disdain.
>
> (Erikson, 1968, p. 172)

These four elements constitute the main features of identity diffusion, although clearly not all will be present in any one individual who experiences an identity crisis. In addition to such concepts one other notion needs to be mentioned as an important feature of Erikson's theory, that of psychosocial moratorium. This means a period during which decisions are left in abeyance. It is argued that society allows, even encourages, a time of life when the young person may delay major identity choices and experiment with roles in order to discover the sort of person he or she wishes to be. While such a stage may lead to disorientation or disturbance, it has, according to Erikson, a healthy function: 'Much of this apparent confusion may be considered social play – the true genetic successor to childhood play' (1968, p. 164).

The real problem with Erikson's theory is the fact that he is never specific about the extent of the adolescent identity crisis. His use of terms such as 'normative crisis' and 'the psychopathology of everyday adolescence' implies that all young people may be expected to deal with such crises, yet nowhere does he acknowledge the broad range of adolescent experience. He prefers instead to deal in the qualitative aspects of identity development, and while there is a wealth of clinical insight evident in his thinking, it has been left to others to translate his ideas into a form that can be tested empirically.

The work of Marcia (1966, 1993), also outlined in Kroger (2004), is seminal in this respect. Marcia has used Erikson's conceptual dimensions of crisis and commitment to define four identity statuses. The four stages, or identity statuses, as they are called, are as follows:

1   *Identify diffusion*. Here the individual has not yet experienced an identity crisis, nor has he or she made any commitment to a vocation or set of beliefs. There is also no indication that he or she is actively trying to make a commitment.
2   *Identity foreclosure*. In this status the individual has not experienced a crisis, but nevertheless is committed in his or her goals and beliefs, largely as a result of choices made by others.
3   *Moratorium*. An individual in this category has not yet resolved the struggle over identity, but is actively searching among alternatives in an attempt to arrive at a choice of identity.
4   *Identity achievement*. At this stage the individual is considered to have experienced a crisis, but to have resolved this on his or her own terms, and now is firmly committed to an occupation, an ideology and to a choice of social roles.

The identity achievement, moratorium, foreclosure and diffusion statuses characterise those attempting to resolve or avoid the identity work of adolescence. Identity achievement and foreclosure individuals share a commitment to adult roles; however, the former have synthesised important childhood identification figures into an original and personal configuration, whereas the latter have bypassed such development work by adopting identities created for them by others. By contrast, moratorium and diffusion young people share a lack of commitment. However, for the moratorium group that lack is instrumental in acting as a stimulus towards identity synthesis, while for those in diffusion it represents an inability to make a commitment to some form of adult identity.

In Marcia's view these four identity statuses may be seen as a developmental sequence, but not necessarily in the sense that one is the prerequisite of the other. Only moratorium appears to be essential for identity achievement, since the searching and exploring which characterises it must precede a resolution of the identity challenge. In Marcia's (1966) original research, he found that as students moved through the four years of college the proportion of those in the identity diffusion category declined, while the number of identity achievement subjects steadily increased.

Marcia's conceptualisation of identity development has spawned a huge amount of research activity. Two key questions were addressed by researchers who followed Marcia. First, and most obviously, it was important to discover whether Erikson's theory of identity development was supported by the methodology proposed by Marcia. Broadly speaking this proved to be the case. For example, identity achievers appear to be psychologically healthier than other individuals on a variety of measures. They score highest on achievement motivation, moral reasoning, career maturity and social skills with peers. Individuals in the moratorium group score highest on measures of anxiety, and show the highest levels of conflict with authority. Those in the foreclosure category have been shown to be the most authoritarian, to have the highest need for social approval and the lowest level of autonomy. Finally those in a state of identity diffusion are found to have the highest levels of psychological and interpersonal problems. They are also the most socially withdrawn and have the poorest social skills with peers. Reviews and summaries of this research may be found in Kroger (2004), Nurmi (2004), and Alsaker and Kroger (2006).

The second important question addressed by those who wished to test Marcia's hypothesis has been to do with the developmental sequence of the four identity statuses. It has been shown by a number of researchers that identity achievement is unlikely to occur much before the age of 18. Those who have looked at young people in the middle adolescent years find little differentiation between groups. It appears that, although self-examination may take place during this period, the actual formation of an adult identity does not occur until late adolescence at the earliest. Indeed, it may be that, with the increased delay in achieving adulthood seen currently in Western societies, identity achievement does not occur until much later. Studies by Pulkinnen and Koko (2000) in Finland and by Luyckx and Goossens (2006) in Belgium support this notion.

There has also been considerable interest in whether individuals shift from one identity status to another over time. How stable are the statuses, and is it to be expected that there will be more variation among some individuals than among others? A study by Adams and Fitch (1982) showed that over 60 per cent of students who were classified as being in the identity diffusion category had moved to a different status within a period of one year. The research of Waterman and his colleagues illustrates a similar conclusion. In one study (Waterman and Goldman, 1976) approximately 90 per cent who were in the moratorium category had shifted to another group by the end of the study. It is clear, therefore, that the challenge of identity is not necessarily resolved at any one point in time, but continues to re-emerge again and again as the individual moves through late adolescence and early adulthood.

As Kroger (2004) makes clear, the vitality of the research endeavour which originated with the work of Erikson and Marcia is still very much in evidence. Studies in the recent past have incorporated longitudinal designs (e.g. Fadjukoff *et al.*, 2005), and there has been an increasing focus on identity development in context (e.g. Phinney and Goossens, 1996), looking at how identity development varies according to the circumstances, the situation and the location that young people find themselves in. A number of writers have asked how young people go about resolving the identity question. Berzonsky (2004), for example, differentiates between young people who actively seek information and approach the task with an open mind, as opposed to those who attempt to conform to family and social expectations. This latter group often may also show a tendency to 'get identity questions over as quickly as possible', leading to an unsatisfactory resolution which only impacts on the individual in later life. Others in Berzonsky's framework procrastinate and avoid decisions for as long as possible. Not surprisingly those in the first group, described as being in 'informational mode', are most likely to be identity achievers. Another approach has been outlined by Cote (2000), who is interested in the concept of agency. In his research Cote shows that a strong sense of personal agency is predictive of identity achievement across ethnic and social class groupings. As Cote and his colleagues note, those who feel in control of their lives, and who are able to take decisions for themselves are most likely to be able to resolve the identity challenge (Schwartz *et al.*, 2005).

Finally it should be noted that the identity status model has not been without its critics. Some writers have questioned whether Marcia's concept of identity status actually does justice to Erikson's original theoretical concept of identity (e.g. van Hoof, 1999). A second focus has been on whether adequate validity has been established for the four identity statuses, and it should be noted that there are a variety of measures being used in research to identify these statuses (Alsaker and Kroger, 2006). Not unnaturally the use of different measures can lead to uncertainty about the conclusions of such a wide variety of studies, and more rigour in the field would be of help here. Lastly there are a number of writers who have questioned whether identity status change follows a developmental sequence, or whether the change is random (e.g. Meeus *et al.*, 1999). Underlying this concern is a question about what factors lie behind the move from one status to another. Are these environmental, psychological or biological, or a combination of all of these? It may be that future research will look more closely at this question. It is certainly the case that one key variable that has featured prominently in recent research is that of ethnicity and its effects on identity development, and it is this topic which forms the next section of the chapter.

A review of research on ethnic identity

While this topic has been of interest for decades, it is only recently that there has been a marked and increased focus on identity and ethnicity. It will be noted that much of the thinking in this area has come from North America, although European research has also been making a mark, and will be reviewed here later in the section. In terms of a historical perspective, theories which are of an essentially linear nature can be mentioned first. So, for example, early work by Phinney (Phinney, 1992, 1993; Phinney and Rosenthal, 1992) presented a model which envisaged three stages in the development of ethnic identity. First, young people who had not explored or thought about their ethnic identity were described as 'unexamined'. Young people in the next stage were known as 'searchers'. For these young people some incident or event, such as witnessing or experiencing racial harassment, marked a turning point in their view of themselves, and led to a process of enquiry concerning the roots of their identity.

Young people in the third group described by Phinney were those who had managed to come to a resolution of their identity, accepting a position vis-à-vis both their own culture and the majority culture. These adolescents were known as the 'achieved' group. Such a schema is similar to that of Marcia and others in that there are a number of identity statuses, and an implication that individuals may move from one to another in a developmental process. Considerable research has been carried out using Phinney's model (e.g. Martinez and Dukes, 1997) but at the same time others (e.g. Berry, 1990) have been arguing that acculturation may be a more complex and multi-dimensional concept, so that a three-stage model will hardly do justice to the process whereby an individual comes to terms with his or her ethnic identity. It has been suggested that the position of those from minority ethnic groups may best be described in terms of two independent dimensions: the retention of one's cultural traditions, and the establishment and maintenance of relationships with the larger society. Phinney herself accepts this argument, as is made clear in Phinney and Devich-Navarro (1997). It is possible to envisage a model in which there are four positions for any one individual if the two dimensions – retention of cultural traditions and relationships with the wider society – are dichotomised as high and low. These positions are:

1   *Integration.* Such individuals would be high on retention of cultural traditions but would also develop and maintain relationships with the mainstream culture.
2   *Assimilation.* Here young people would have a high maintenance of relationships with the majority culture, while having a low level of maintenance of cultural traditions.
3   *Separation.* Those in this group would have high cultural retention, and low identification with the mainstream culture.
4   *Marginalisation.* Individuals in this group would be low on both dimensions.

As Phinney and Devich-Navarro (1997) note, this model is more useful than a linear one, but it still requires further elaboration to accommodate the variation in ethnic and mainstream involvement among minority groups. This has led these two authors to propose an even more elaborate model, which is illustrated in Figure 4.3. As will be apparent, there are three panels in the figure. The top panel represents the pattern of assimilation and fusion with the mainstream culture, where the individual rejects their own culture entirely, or manages to fuse the two cultures so that they become one. In the second panel more complex bicultural possibilities are envisaged. Here the two cultures are perceived as overlapping, with the individual occupying the middle ground in blended biculturalism, and

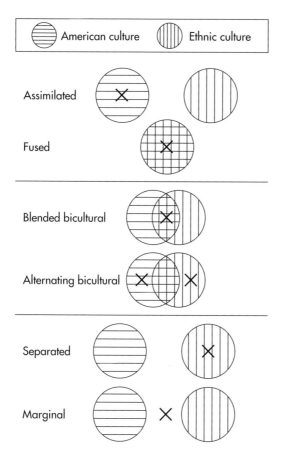

Figure 4.3 Identification patterns based on the individual's perception of American and ethnic cultures (represented by circles) as separated, combined, or overlapping, and his or her position relative to each culture (represented by 'X').

Source: Phinney and Devich-Navarro (1997).

moving from one culture to another in alternating biculturalism. The third panel represents those for whom the two cultures cannot be reconciled. An individual can either identify solely with their own culture and reject the mainstream culture, or be forced to find a position outside both cultures.

In the study by Phinney and Devich-Navarro (1997), which included African-American and Mexican-American young people, a number of interesting examples of biculturalism are reported. Some who fitted into the category of blended biculturalism appeared reluctant to choose between the two cultures, describing themselves as equally American and ethnic. Thus an African-American young woman described herself as like 'half and half . . . to me it is the same thing', and a Mexican-American young man said he was 'both cultures, I am both'. Another young person said 'I am more American I guess, but that does not mean I am not very Black'.

As far as those fitting the category of alternating biculturalism are concerned, most described themselves as more ethnic than American. Thus an African-American student responded by saying 'I am mostly Black, I am both, but I am more Black'. A Mexican-American young man said 'I am American and Hispanic, but I consider myself more Hispanic'. The authors of the study compared the two groups in terms of their bicultural identity, and revealed interesting differences between the two ethnic groups. Essentially they showed that African-American young people are more likely to be in the blended bicultural or separated groups, whereas Mexican-American adolescents were significantly more likely to be in the alternating bicultural group.

Comparisons between different cultures in the European context are relatively rare, although the work of Verkuyten (1993, 1995) is an exception. In the 1995 study young people from four cultures living in Holland were compared for self-esteem and ethnic identity. The groups were from mainstream Dutch culture, from Turkey, Surinam and Morocco. Results showed that there were no differences in global self-esteem between the four groups, but that ethnic identity was of more salience for those from minority cultures. Similar findings were reported by Martinez and Dukes (1997) in their comparison of four cultural groups in the USA. It should be added that within the European context Sabatier (2008) recently investigated second-generation immigrants and their identity development in France, whilst Wissink et al. (2008) looked at different cultural groups in the Netherlands, comparing ethnic identity and self-esteem among Dutch, Turkish-Dutch, and Moroccan-Dutch young people. A special issue of the *Journal of Adolescence* edited by Beyers and Cok (2008) gives a valuable overview of current work on the relationship between identity development and contextual factors, looking at the topic within the framework of developmental contextualism which was reviewed in Chapter 1.

A number of studies have looked at family influences on ethnic identity, and the evidence is consistent in showing that family environment shapes development in minority cultures just as it does in those from mainstream cultures (for review see Collins and Laursen, 2004). The attitudes of parents to their own culture will have a profound impact on children and young people, and will inevitably affect the process of ethnic identity formation. The term racial socialisation has been used to describe this process. In a study by Marshall (1995) parents from minority cultures were asked which aspects of race they saw as important to discuss with their children. Responses included racial pride, racial barriers, equality and the physical attributes of the particular culture. Interestingly research shows that, whilst racial socialisation may speed up the process of ethnic identity development, it does not necessarily lead to a stronger sense of ethnic identity (Phinney and Chavira, 1995).

One important issue is the possibility of conflict between parents and young people over the degree of identification that is expected in relation to mainstream and minority cultures. Thus in Asian cultures in Britain parents are frequently characterised as expecting a greater degree of commitment to ethnic values, whether they are to do with religious beliefs, attitudes to family life or anti-social behaviour (Webster, 2009). Phinney and Rosenthal (1992) quote a Mexican-American young woman describing this problem: 'My parents are sort of old-fashioned, so they tell me that I have to do things. . . . Like I am a girl, so I am always sent to the kitchen to cook. But I am more American than them, and I don't believe in that girl thing. We end up in an argument, and it does not get solved' (p. 153). In the context of conflict over ethnic identity, some studies have looked at the mental health of young people from minority backgrounds. Thus for, example, Birman *et al.* (2002) and Liebkind *et al.* (2004) have explored the impact of immigration on adjustment, and shown that having a strong ethnic identity is associated with positive adjustment in a new country.

A number of writers have also looked specifically at gender issues in relation to race. Thus Shorter-Gooden and Washington (1996) have explored the difficulties for young women in North America of what they call 'weaving an identity'. Results showed that, for the women studied here – a sample of late adolescent, educated African-American young women – ethnic identity was of much greater salience than gender identity. This is not to say that gender was not of importance, but it was clear that for most race was the defining feature of their identity. A study carried out in Britain by Mirzah (1992) explored the same theme, underlining the talents of young Black women, and the barriers they face as they seek to obtain an education equal to that obtained by their White peers. As the author puts it:

> Young Black women bear all the hallmarks of a fundamentally inegalitarian society. They do well at school, do well in society, are good efficient workers, and yet as a group they consistently fail to secure the economic status and occupational prestige they deserve. This study asked why it is that Black women suffer these injustices, and attempted to reveal the processes of inequality that, despite the ideology of a meritocracy, persist in this society.
>
> (1992, p. 189)

In the UK context both Back (1997) and Frosh *et al.* (2002) have explored gender, but from the perspective of boys and young men. Both authors explore the difficulties faced by males from minority backgrounds. They point out that young Black men are, on the one hand, admired for their athleticism or musical ability, but on the other, feared for their potential for violence and trouble-making. In such a context the formation of masculine identity is problematic, and creates enormous difficulties for young men from particular minority backgrounds. Something similar has happened recently in relation to terrorism and Asian young men, but there is, at the time of writing, no research on this phenomenon.

Finally it is important to turn to a different aspect of ethnic identity, that experienced by young people of mixed race. At least individuals from one minority culture have a recognisable background to which they belong. For those from mixed backgrounds the situation is considerably more difficult, and yet there is little research on this aspect of ethnic identity. One exception is the work of Tizard and Phoenix (2002), who explored the identity of young people in Britain who had mixed parentage. They found that, while roughly 60 per cent of the sample had a positive ethnic identity, 20 per cent had what the authors described as a 'problematic' identity, and a further 20 per cent were mixed in their attitudes to their race. Examples of a positive identity are as follows (2002, pp. 58–60):

> 'I'm lucky. I'm proud of my colour. (What makes you proud?) I'm an individual class. I don't know the word, like we are only a few, sort of thing.'

'It's a lot more interesting. If people ask me what nationality I am, I can spend half an hour telling them.'

Examples of a problematic identity are:

'When I started to mix with boys I just felt different, because in my class I am the only coloured person. I felt actually at a disadvantage because everyone is like weighing up what they look like, and I'm different.'

'Recently I wanted to be White. I haven't come across a lot of racial hatred and stuff, but it still hurts, you know. I know that if I was White, I wouldn't be at all worried about my colour.'

The adolescents in the study were given eleven topics which might contribute to their overall sense of identity, and were asked to rank these according to how important they were for their sense of identity. Interestingly one-third of the sample put their colour at or near the top of the list, while 39 per cent did not mention it at all. This finding reflects the general impression given by the research that, while some see their mixed race as a central feature of themselves, others hardly think about it. Those with a positive identity tended to be most likely to attend multi-racial schools, while those with a problematic identity were most likely to be affiliated to adults from the mainstream White culture. There seems little doubt that the context in which young people grow up has a major impact on the way ethnic identity is shaped. This section will conclude with the words of two young people who make this point.

'I suppose it is on my mind most of the time. (Why is that?) I worry that people will discriminate against me, because of my colour, and being aware that I am the only coloured person in my class.'

'In the country, or in cities where there are not a lot of Black people, if you go there, it's nudge, wink, over there's a Black person, as if they'd never seen one before, but when you come back to London , it's like nobody cares whether you are Black or White.'

(Tizard and Phoenix, 2002, p. 62)

Implications for practice

1. It is clear from the research reviewed here that the self-concept develops rapidly during the adolescent period. This development is linked to concomitant physical, cognitive and emotional growth. In particular, the self-concept becomes more differentiated, while at the same time the young person shows an increasing ability to perceive themselves from the point of view of others. For any adult working with teenagers it is essential to take into account these changes, and to recognise the impact they may have on interpersonal relationships.

2. In terms of self-esteem, there is general agreement that this variable has a powerful influence on adjustment across a wide range of domains. Educational achievement, social relationships, mental health, the ability to deal with stress – all these are affected by self-esteem. Much thought has gone towards establishing the factors which determine the individual's level of self-esteem, and in this chapter the changing balance between parents and peers in terms of influence has been noted. Research has been highlighted which shows differences in self-esteem trajectories during the adolescent period, and the importance of shaping interventions that are appropriate to the individual's own developmental pathway has also been noted.

3. It is important for practitioners to recognise that the classic 'adolescent identity crisis' as originally described by Erikson does not appear to be true of the majority of young people. Research indicates that, although identity development is central during this stage, it does not necessarily take the form of a crisis. Rather, an individual is likely to pass through various stages, with considerable fluctuation at different times in respect of the salience or difficulty of the identity question. In view of the fact that so many young people do not attain full adult maturity and independence until well into their twenties, it is probable that a final resolution of issues to do with identity will not necessarily be achieved during the teenage years.

4. One of the striking changes in the literature in recent years has been to do with an increased focus on ethnic identity, coupled with a realisation that identity is as much to do with the context in which the young person grows up as it is to do with personality factors. It has become clear that those working with young people from minority backgrounds need to be aware of this dimension of adolescent development. Of course there are wide individual differences, and culture, context and social background will all have their effect on identity development. Nonetheless practitioners have much to learn from the research described in this chapter, and it is to be hoped that these findings will become increasingly available to those in the field.

Further reading

Alsaker, F and Kroger, J (2006) Self-concept, self-esteem and identity. In Jackson, S and Goossens, L (Eds) *Handbook of adolescent development*. Psychology Press. Hove.
A comprehensive review with a strong European slant.

Erikson, E (1968) *Identity, youth and crisis*. Norton. New York.
One of the great classics in the field. Easy to read, and full of challenging ideas.

Kroger, J (2004) *Identity in adolescence: the balance between self and other*, 3rd edn. Routledge. London.
One of the best books on adolescent identity, now in its third edition, and a mainstay of the '*Adolescence and society*' series. Kroger summarises four of the main theoretical approaches to identity. A very popular book.

The family

'I think parents are something that you can come back to and rely on, because we're supposed to be out there learning about life, but you need something to fall back on if it goes wrong. I know that me and my Mum scream like we're going to kill each other, but she's always there. I know she's never going to abandon me if I'm in trouble and stuff.'

(15-year-old girl)

'Probably being just a safe environment where you feel like you can step back from everything else that goes on around you and be, like, a warm loving generalness! My parents were always very open with me, and talked about everything that went on in school and with my friends, but in a very non-judgemental way. I think non-judgemental is good, because you get judged from every angle all the time, and it's quite good to have a place where you can talk and not be, I don't know, not be judged.'

(16-year-old girl)

Adolescence brings with it a major change in the way that parents and young people interact with each other. Such change is gradual, and contrary to popular belief, does not lead to the complete breakdown of relationships. As we shall see, research and discussion about these matters in the recent past have emphasised continuity as much as change, and there has been a greater emphasis on the positive role that parents can play during this period of life. Since the 1960s research on family relationships has indicated that conflict is a less dominant theme than was once assumed. Many adolescents get on well with their parents most of the time, and when there is conflict it tends to be over day-to-day domestic issues rather than over the big questions to do with such things as values or career choices. As has been noted in Chapter 1, the transition to adulthood experienced by young people has, over the past 30 years or so, altered beyond recognition. This has had significant implications for the family, with young people remaining at home for much longer periods, and in many cases, returning home after college or university.

In setting the scene for a consideration of adolescents and the family there are some important points to be made. In the first place much has been learnt from research carried out in the last decade of the twentieth century and the first decade of the twenty-first century. This research has brought to the fore a much more nuanced view of family change. Whereas in the past research questions tended to focus on concerns such as how much conflict is there between parents and teenagers, or at what point does a young person gain autonomy, the perspective has shifted and there is a recognition that these questions are too simplistic. Research is now asking more refined questions, such as what types of autonomy are there, and in what areas are adolescents autonomous, and at what ages.

A second key consideration is that the very definition of the family is undergoing radical change. In terms of family arrangements it is important to note the increase in families headed by a lone parent (see Figure 5.1). For some couples marriage is being postponed, or not taking place at all. Marriage and child-bearing are also occurring at a later age, and there are smaller families than in previous generations. There are more family types that have to be recognised, so that we

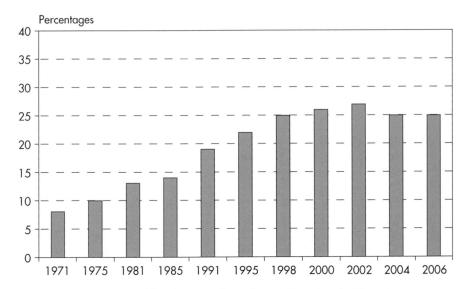

Figure 5.1 Proportion of families with dependent children headed by a lone parent in Britain, 1971–2006.

Data from: General Household Survey, 2006. ONS.

Source: Coleman and Brooks (2009).

can no longer think about nuclear families and single parent families, but have to include step-families, as well as what are known as blended families where children from two different couples live together in a new arrangement. Then in addition more mothers are now going to work. In the review by the Nuffield Foundation (2009) it is estimated that, of mothers with children over the age of 11, around 80 per cent are now in the labour market, at least on a part-time basis. This change has major implications for child care and for the way families with teenagers function on a day-to-day basis (Millar, 2008).

As was noted above, another facet of the changing family is that young people remain in the parental home for longer today than was the case in previous generations. This is true across Europe (Lila *et al.*, 2006) as well as in North America (Steinberg, 2008). A review of changing patterns of leaving home can be found in Mulder (2009). The fact that the ability to set up home independently is being postponed in Western societies is related to the phenomenon of emerging adulthood discussed in Chapter 1. This pattern of delayed independence has significant implications for the achievement of full autonomy, as well as for various aspects of family life. Among other things parents are likely to remain financially responsible for their older adolescents for longer, space in the home for the young adult will be needed, and parents will stay involved with the lives of their sons and daughters for a longer period than was the case in previous generations.

The next point to mention is that there has in recent years been an increased acknowledgement of what is known as directionality. In other words writers and researchers are recognising that influences between parents and adolescents go both ways, and that it is insufficient to look only at the impact of parents on their adolescent sons and daughters. Young people have an influence on their parents, and their behaviour affects the way parents respond and the parenting style they adopt. This notion is congruent with the ideas outlined in Chapter 1, to do with the focal model and with the idea of young people as constructors of their own development, and fits with concepts of agency and individuality. As will be suggested in the section on family environments in this chapter, it has been the work on monitoring and supervision that has made the point about two-way influences particularly strongly.

A word about gender is important. In discussions about parenting it is all too often the case that little distinction is made between mothers and fathers. Yet the two parents are likely to play very different roles, and to be perceived differently by young people themselves. Research by Noller and Callan (1991) illustrated this point neatly by showing how adolescents share much more with mothers, but also how they discuss different things with the two parents. Mothers are more likely to receive information about personal and family issues, whilst money, politics and careers are more likely to be discussed with fathers. There has been far too little research on the role of fathers with teenagers, one exception being the book by Shulman and Seiffge-Krenke (1997). These authors make the point that most commentary about fathers has implicit in it what they call 'the deficit model'. Because the mother is seen as being the more involved parent, they argue, the father is seen as in some way failing as a parent. Yet we know that fathers play a different yet critical role in the parenting task, and more recognition and understanding of this is necessary. Two studies by Flouri and colleagues (Flouri and Buchanan, 2003; Flouri, 2006) point in particular to the importance of fathers in the context of the adolescent's mental health.

Thoughts about parents lead on naturally to a recognition that, with all the focus on the development of the adolescent, it is easy to lose sight of the fact that the adults in the family will themselves be experiencing life changes at this time. They may have their own parents to care for, or they may be facing challenges in relation to employment and family finances. What can be called 'mid-life' for parents will bring with it many new concerns and worries, possibly to do with declining physical health, possibly to do with the changing nature of marriage or partnership. Many studies report mothers and fathers finding the adolescent period the hardest stage of parenting, with a resultant impact on relationships and on parental mental health. In Fortner et al. (2004) it was reported that parents of adolescents were spending more time at work to escape the pressures at home, and Steinberg and Silverberg (1987) documented higher levels of mental ill-health among parents of adolescents than among parents of younger children. Keeping in mind the life stage of parents as well as that of adolescents links well with a lifespan approach to human development.

This chapter will examine the way in which independence is negotiated in a context in which young people appear to mature earlier, and yet remain dependent on their families for longer. It will look in more detail at the question of conflict and the 'generation gap'. It will be important to keep in mind the fact that the whole concept of the family has changed, and is continuing to change. There are fewer conventional nuclear families, and a much wider range of family types. The nature of the labour market has altered, so that fewer mothers now remain at home involved in full-time child care. In addition to this the role of parent is dispersed to more adults, with grandparents, step-parents and non-residential parents all potentially playing a part in family life. The chapter will look at autonomy, at questions to do with race and ethnicity, and at the impact of divorce. The chapter will conclude by considering some of the challenges involved in the parenting of young people, and will look at recent research on interventions designed to enhance the parenting of teenagers.

The development of autonomy

'I mean once you get out of your first school, you go on to secondary school, they lose the importance they had. So that's a big thing, because you can't have your parents coming in to talk to the teachers all the time, and they can't be as much help as they were. They're still important, and when you are a teenager you're probably going to need more guidance than when you were younger, but they lose some importance. It's for different things basically. . . . They should sort of be there for everyday stuff. They can get you to places, and help you do things that you want to do outside of school, but with really important things, like school and friendships and stuff it's a lot more difficult for them to be involved.'

(17-year-old boy)

It could be argued that the development of independence, or autonomy, is one of the key tasks for the adolescent. To be free from parental restraint, and to achieve control over one's life, is the goal of every young person. Yet progress towards this goal is never straightforward. To some extent the way in which autonomy is achieved will depend on the circumstances of the family, on ethnic background, and on the cultural, social and economic opportunities available in the environment. Gender too will play a part, since independence for women is understood differently from independence for men. It may be stating the obvious, but autonomy will not mean the same for an Asian young woman growing up in an inner-city environment as it will for a White young man from an isolated rural community. In addition the personality of the young person will be important, as will the parents' own situation and their attitudes to their son or daughter.

In terms of our understanding of this feature of adolescent development, there have been some significant shifts over the past decades. In early writings about adolescence it was assumed that emotional disengagement from parents was a fundamental element of the move towards independence, and that unless separation and detachment occurred, it was not possible to become a mature adult. This view was very much influenced by psychoanalytic theory. More recently, however, empirical research has cast a different light on the matter. In the first place, from the 1960s onwards, investigators were reporting more positive relationships between parents and teenagers than had been expected. The work of Douvan and Adelson (1966) in the USA, and of Fogelman (1976) in the UK are good examples of these landmark studies.

As a result of this empirical work commentators came to believe that it was possible to develop autonomy without the separation and disengagement that had been envisaged in early writings. Youniss and Smollar (1985), for example, talked of interdependence, a stage during which both parent and adolescent work together to redefine their relationship. In this situation close ties are maintained, without the young person's growing individuality being threatened. One of the most frequently quoted papers of this period is that of Grotevant and Cooper (1986), in which they put forward the notion of connectedness. In this view the young person can move towards a state of individuation while remaining connected to the family. It is of interest to note that ideas about connectedness were at first seen to be especially true of young women, as a result of close relationships between mothers and daughters, but in more recent writing this concept is seen to apply to males just as much as to females. Excellent summaries of this approach can be found in Grotevant and Cooper (1998) and in Lila *et al.* (2006).

A theoretical perspective which encompasses both autonomy and the continuation of close relationships with parents can be seen to have some inherent contradictions in it. As a result of this, a new wave of empirical studies originated in the 1980s which attempted to measure autonomy, and to distinguish various elements of a complex phenomenon. The best-known of the instruments used in these studies was the Emotional Autonomy Scale (the EAS) first proposed by Steinberg and Silverberg (1986). This scale measures four aspects of emotional autonomy:

1 'de-idealisation', i.e. the extent to which the young person sees the parent as fallible and human;
2 'non-dependency', i.e. the absence of childish dependencies on the parents;
3 'individuation', i.e. the perceived lack of parental knowledge and understanding about the young person and their life;
4 'parents as people', i.e. the realisation that parents are ordinary people who have separate lives, existing in a world not known to the young person.

Results from early studies using the EAS showed a steady increase with age in all aspects of autonomy, but they also showed that high scores on various elements of the EAS scale were linked to less positive behavioural outcomes. Thus young people with high scores on the EAS experience greater degrees of parental rejection (Ryan and Lynch, 1989) and report higher degrees of conflict in the family (Goossens, 2006c). Research also shows that those who are more separated, as measured by the EAS, are also more likely to have emotional problems, especially internalising problems such as depression and anxiety (Beyers and Goossens, 1999). These were unexpected findings, and they have led some authors to question whether the EAS is measuring adaptive autonomy, or whether it is tapping into something more dysfunctional. This debate has continued in the literature, and is well summarised in Goossens (2006c).

One sensible conclusion is that there may be two different trajectories for young people. On the one hand there are those who start adolescence already at a high level of separation, and change relatively little during adolescent development. These young people are likely to have a poorer level of adjustment. On the other hand there will be another cohort who start at a low level of separation, and whose degree of separation increases from puberty onwards. This group may be considered to be better adjusted than the first group. Further research is needed to explore this hypothesis, but it would appear to have some face validity.

Another approach to this topic has been to distinguish between different types of autonomy, with the most common classification being between emotional, behavioural and value autonomy. Behavioural autonomy refers to 'active, overt manifestations of independent functioning, including the regulation of one's behaviour and decision-making' (Sessa and Steinberg, 1991, p. 42). Emotional autonomy is more to do with the internal representations of parents, so that it could be said that this type of autonomy involves 'the de-idealisation of the parental figures, leading to a more mature conception of parents as individuals who have a life of their own, thus . . . adolescents are no longer at the behest of unconscious feelings, often of an ambivalent nature, towards their parents, as children tend to be' (Goossens, 2006c, p. 136). Finally values autonomy refers to the development of one's own system of values and morals.

These ideas have been developed further by Smetana and colleagues, who have developed the social domain theory of parental authority (Smetana, 2002). This theory states that parents and adolescents will hold different opinions on who has the final say regarding different aspects of family life. Thus we might imagine that an adolescent believes that she has the final say about which friends she chooses, or whether her bedroom remains tidy. However, she might agree that her parents should have a say when it comes to school work and decisions about career choices. On the other hand her parents may take a very different view, holding the belief that they should have some say over her choice of friends, or the state of her bedroom.

This work has been extended by Collins (1990), who has looked at what he calls 'violations' of parental and teenage expectations. In his view, if the parents believe they should have a say in the state of this girl's bedroom, they are violating her expectations of her autonomy, leading inevitably to conflict. Collins is also interested in broader concepts of adolescence. He gives, as an example, a teenager who believes that, with increasing age, there will come greater freedom and less parental direction. On the other hand the parents may believe that it is precisely at this adolescent stage that they need to exercise greater control, to protect their son or daughter from the temptations and risks that are present in our society. The result of such divergent beliefs about adolescence will not be hard to guess.

Before leaving this topic, we should make some mention of two other studies in which approaches to the topic of autonomy are rather different. First, the work of Kracke and Noack (1998), carried out in Germany, distinguishes between three stages of adolescence. This enables the authors to show that it is in the middle stage of adolescence that the most intense negotiations take place regarding autonomy. As they say, it is at this stage that young people are most in need of establishing their right to freedom, while at the same time it is the stage for parents when they least wish to lose control. Kracke and Noack also note that changes in family members' behaviour indicate a much more verbal type of negotiation at this stage. However, in spite of the intensification of negotiation over autonomy, their results still showed relatively low levels of conflict at all three stages of adolescence. More recent work on autonomy in Germany (Haase *et al.*, 2008) indicates that political change, coming about as a result of re-unification, can have significant influences on the autonomy timetable. Those growing up in East Germany after re-unification were much more likely to adhere to a 'Western' timetable.

It is also important to mention the work of Larson and colleagues in this context, and in particular their methodological approach. In Larson *et al.* (1996), for example, a study is described which looks at the topic of autonomy from the perspective of young people's daily interactions with their families. The authors use a method known as the Experience Sampling Method (ESM), in which teenagers receive texts at random moments during the day. Following the text, the young people are asked to complete a report indicating what they are doing, and the emotions associated with this activity. Incidentally mobile phones were not available when this method was first devised, so in the 1990s pagers rather than mobile phones were used.

Using such a method has enabled Larson and others to track daily activities, and to gain an invaluable picture of the lives of adolescents. In the Larson *et al.* (1996) study it emerged that, while the overall time spent with the family decreased throughout the teenage years, time spent with mothers and fathers on a one-to-one basis hardly changed at all between the ages of 10 and 18. Their results, which are illustrated in Figure 5.2, underline the fact that close relationships with parents continue to serve an essential function. Autonomy may be important, but so is connectedness.

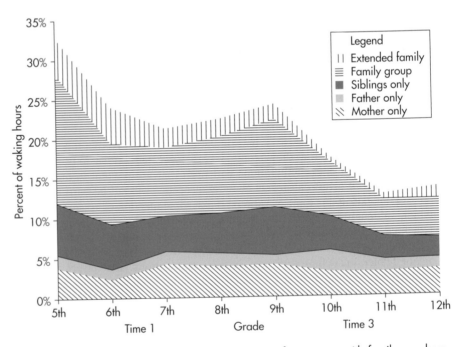

Figure 5.2 Age differences in adolescents' amount of time spent with family members.
Source: Larson *et al.* (1996).

Conflict and the generation gap

'My parents might give me ideas about what I want to do, but I'm still going to do what I want to do.'

(14-year-old girl)

'If they say something like "You can't do that" or something, then I argue back saying "Yes, I can". And they'd say "That's wrong" and I'd be like "It's right" and stuff like that, arguing and arguing. I think that's just growing up, quite a few people, I think, do that as well.'

(16-year-old girl)

One of the areas that has been the subject of more research than most is that concerned with parent–adolescent conflict. In popular terms this is known as 'the generation gap'. What is especially interesting about this topic is that there appears to be a clear divergence of opinion between researchers and the general public. It is commonly believed by parents and other adults that the adolescent years bring with them conflict and disagreement in the home, as well as widely divergent views on such things as sex, drugs and morality. Researchers, on the other hand, report that for the majority there are broadly positive relationships between parents and teenagers, with little evidence of a generation gap in attitudes to careers, education, values and morality.

Fogelman's (1976) research has already been mentioned. This involved a study of 11,000 young people and their parents in the UK, and results showed that most parents reported good relationships with their teenagers, while the young people themselves endorsed this view. Teenagers indicated that they respected their parents' opinions, and sought their advice on the important issues that they faced. To give one example, 86 per cent of adolescents told of getting on well with their mother, whilst 80 per cent reported positive relationships with their father. A similar proportion said they rarely disagreed with their parents regarding their choice of friends or on health issues.

A series of recent research studies have supported these findings. In the North American context a review by Collins and Laursen (2004) may be noted, and as far as the European situation is concerned a good outline is to be found in Honess *et al.* (1997) and Jackson *et al.* (1998). It may reasonably be asked: what is the explanation for these findings? However, it is perhaps not so surprising. After all, values and attitudes are primarily influenced by social and economic background, and of course parents and teenagers will share rather than differ in their backgrounds. It is reasonable to expect that our central beliefs will be influenced more by background than by age. Indeed Steinberg (2008) makes the point that there is greater diversity in values and beliefs between adolescents than there is between the two generations. There are, of course, exceptions to this rule, but in general this would seem to make sense.

The next question then arises, if parents and young people are relatively close in their values and opinions, what is it that they disagree about? Numerous studies have looked at this question, and the answer is that the disagreements occur in relation to subjects such as styles of dress, choice of music and

TV programmes, and patterns of leisure activity. These issues are ones which are more likely to be influenced by friends and the immediate social environment, rather than the wider family and the community. Studies, such as that by Montemayor (1983), show that issues such as these have been the focus of family conflict for as long as the topic has been investigated, with time of coming home at night, choice of clothing, and tidy bedrooms being some of the most common flash points. Findings also show that these issues are of international relevance, as shown in the study by Yau and Smetana (2003) of teenagers in China and Hong Kong. Results of this study showed that exactly the same topics were relevant in these countries as in Europe and North America.

It is important to note that disagreements can occur between parents and young people over these domestic issues without relationships completely breaking down. In interesting work by Smetana and others (Smetana, 1988; Smetana and Asquith, 1994) it is argued that one of the reasons for disagreements is because the generations define the problem differently. Thus, parents are more likely to believe that behaviour is a matter of convention, i.e. the choice of clothes is dictated by what would be expected by others, or what is normal in these circumstances. Young people, on the other hand, see something like choice of clothes as a matter of personal freedom. If they can choose what they want with no reference to convention, then that is a reflection of their autonomy and maturity.

Smetana and others believe that parents and teenagers are more likely to clash over the definition of an issue rather than over the specific details. In other words it is more a matter of 'who has the authority' than 'who is right'. If young people and their parents define daily issues differently, then it may be that the resolution of conflicts will prove difficult. However, it is at this point that the idea of communication between the generations becomes critical. In a number of studies it has been shown that the better the communication between parents and teenagers, the more likely it will be that conflicts will be resolved (Coleman et al., 2004).

As we have already noted, it is important to remember that young people do not rebel against their parents on all issues. If the young person believes that parental authority is legitimate in a particular arena, then there is less likely to be conflict. Reference was made in the previous section to Smetana's theory known as the social domain theory of parental authority. A good illustration of this can be found in a study by Smetana and Daddis (2002). They showed that adolescents will accept their parents' rules when they believe the issue is a moral one, or when it involves safety, but they are less likely to accept parental legitimacy when they believe the issue is a personal one (such as clothing or leisure). It would appear therefore that it is not all issues that are at stake, but rather for certain issues (personal ones in particular) the question is who has the authority, and by whom the issue should be decided. One important conclusion here is that young people who believe their parents are trying to regulate what for them are personal issues will be likely to describe their parents as overly controlling, and to show poorer levels of adjustment (Hasebe et al., 2004; Smetana et al., 2004).

To conclude this section, it can be seen that there is little evidence to support the notion of a generation gap over the big issues to do with morality and fundamental beliefs. There is, however, clear support for the idea that during adolescence there will be a series of areas to do with personal choice where parents and young people will disagree. Such disagreements need not necessarily lead to the breakdown of relationships. However, it is also essential to recognise that in some families there will be high levels of conflict, either as a result of battles over autonomy, or because of a complex variety of relationship problems within the home. Some of the factors that underlie chronic conflict, such as divorce and family separation, or styles of parenting, will be examined in later sections of this chapter. Lastly we are still faced with the problem of finding an explanation for the public's belief in the generation gap. Some might say that the notion is fed by the media, while others believe that too much attention is paid to the small number of young people who are troubled or in serious difficulty. Possibly a negative stereotype of adolescence serves an important function for a society which sees teenagers as challengers of the status quo. Whatever the truth of these notions, we should not lose sight of the research findings. For the great majority of families there will be disagreements, but these will not lead to catastrophe or disaster. There are many things that parents can do to minimise the degree of conflict, and some of these strategies will be discussed at the end of the chapter.

Family environment and adolescent development

'Having some trust is definitely important. Letting go a little bit, as well as being there and caring what you're doing. You see a lot of people who do go off the rails, and you think "Don't their parents care that they're 13 and out till 2 o'clock in the morning, and they don't know where they are?" But I think caring, and being interested, but not having to know everything all the time.'

(17-year-old girl)

'I have a friend whose Mum is, like, you know, really cool! Like she lets her smoke weed in the house, and she's really nice, and you can talk to her, but I wouldn't want her as a Mum. Because it's all a bit random, like she's too much of a mate, and there's no security, rules and stuff. And I think my friend feels like that too sometimes.'

(15-year-old girl)

In thinking about family environments and their effects on young people it is important to look first at the role of parents, and in particular at their parenting styles. For any consideration of this topic it is essential to acknowledge the work of Diana Baumrind and Eleanor Maccoby. Indeed it can be argued that their writing has had a profound effect on our understanding of parenting behaviour, and there are few studies of parenting that have not been influenced by the work of these two eminent psychologists. In the early 1970s Baumrind (1971) first put forward her view that there are two dimensions of parenting behaviour which need to be distinguished: parental responsiveness and parental demandingness. Baumrind believed that parents vary on both these dimensions, and also that the dimensions are more or less independent of each other. This made it possible to look at various combinations of the characteristics of parenting behaviour, and numerous studies have indicated how significant this classification is for an understanding of family functioning.

According to the scheme developed by Maccoby and Martin (1983), parental behaviour can be classified as:

- authoritarian
- authoritative
- indulgent
- indifferent.

Authoritarian parents place a high value on obedience and conformity. They are more likely to punish for misbehaviour, and tend not to encourage autonomy. Authoritative parents are warm but firm. They set standards, and hold to boundaries, but are more likely than other parents to give explanations and to reason with the young person than to be punitive. Indulgent (or permissive) parents behave in a benign, accepting, but essentially passive manner. They are unlikely to set standards, or to have high expectations for their children and do not see punishment as important. Finally, indifferent parents are often also called neglectful. This group of parents takes little interest in the lives of their children, and is likely to spend the minimum amount of time on child care activities.

As has been indicated, there have been numerous studies of parenting which have made use of this classification, and the results are consistent. They show that, in almost all cases, children and young people brought up in families where parents use an authoritative parenting style do better on a range of outcome measures. These include having higher self-esteem, being more advanced on such skills as perspective-taking, and having a greater likelihood of avoiding problem behaviours such as drug-taking, early sexual activity, and anti-social behaviour. These results are summarised, for example, in Lila *et al.* (2006) and Steinberg (2008). Young people who are brought up by indulgent parents are often less mature, more irresponsible and more likely to conform to peer group pressure. Those who grow up with neglectful or indifferent parents are those who are most at risk, as might be expected. They are more likely than others to be impulsive and to get involved in high risk behaviours.

The finding that authoritative parenting leads to such positive outcomes has, not surprisingly, led many to question what it is about this style of parenting that makes such a difference. Steinberg (2008) is one of the writers to have put forward perhaps the most convincing explanation of these results, and he notes that there are three key components of authoritative parenting. The first element in this style of parenting is warmth, in that parents love and nurture their children. The next component is structure, an especially important aspect of parenting for teenagers. This means that children and young people have clear boundaries, an understanding of the rules, and an understanding of what is expected of them by their parents. Lastly authoritative parents give autonomy support, in that they accept and encourage the young person's individuality, and the young person's gradual moves towards taking greater control over his or her own life. All these things are critical in providing a family environment in which independence is facilitated while parents also set limits, provide support and acceptance, and endorse achievement.

It may be thought that this description of parenting is too good to be true! Studies have shown that, while this may be the ideal, few parents manage to hold to this style of parenting all the time. Indeed some studies have shown that parenting style may vary depending on the circumstances and indeed on the behaviour of the child or young person (Mounts, 2002, 2004). It is all very well to imagine a benign style of parenting with a happy, responsive and well-balanced teenager. However, when faced with stress, tension and constant arguments even the most effective parents could be forgiven for slipping into authoritarian or even indifferent parenting styles. This leads on to the question of directionality. Whilst for many years there has been an awareness of the fact that influence between parents and children goes both ways, in other words, that influence is bi-directional, it has proved difficult to incorporate that insight into research designs, a point well made by Schaffer (2006). All too often researchers in the social sciences slip back into assuming that influences go one way, i.e. certain types of parental behaviour lead to certain types of outcomes in children and young people.

Research in the field of monitoring and supervision has helped to make this point most forcibly. Work by the team of Margaret Kerr and Hakan Stattin has shown how the behaviour of parents is directly affected by the behaviour of the teenager. Many early studies had appeared to demonstrate that low levels of parental monitoring and supervision resulted in a variety of adjustment problems in young people, including poor school performance and various types of offending behaviour (e.g. Patterson and Stouthamer-Loeber, 1984; Fletcher *et al.*, 1995). However, Stattin and Kerr (Stattin and Kerr, 2000; Kerr and Stattin, 2000) argued that these findings were open to question. Based on their own empirical work, they suggest that, rather than parental monitoring, it is the young person's disclosure or non-disclosure which makes parental monitoring possible. Thus the key variable which explains problem behaviour may be linked to poor communication between parent and young person, as opposed to the parent's actual behaviour or parenting style. This makes sense, since clearly parents can only monitor and supervise if they have a teenager who is willing to share with them what he or she is doing.

Such research underlines the importance of the notion of directionality when trying to understand the impact of parenting on young people's development. Teenagers who are constantly challenging their parents, or who are distant and uncommunicative, will induce particular behaviours in their parents. Thus Laird *et al.* (2003) showed that, when parents had little knowledge of their adolescents' whereabouts, there was a greater likelihood of the young people being involved in anti-social behaviour. In other words we can envisage a cycle of effect and counter-effect. Difficult behaviour leads to either harsh or lax parenting, which in turn leads to greater distance between parent and adolescent, which in turn leads to further difficulty in family relationships. On the other hand mature or competent behaviour on the part of the young person could encourage authoritative parenting, which in turn has positive effects on the young person's development.

One interesting notion that has been introduced into the discussion about parents and young people is that of information management. Implicit in this is the concept of reciprocal relationships between the generations, but it goes further in pointing out that young people take an active role in managing the flow of information between themselves and their parents. A paper by Marshall *et al.*

(2005) was the first to point this out, showing that adolescents make use of a sophisticated set of categories into which they place different types of information. Thus a young person might decide not to disclose something because they believe it is none of the parents' business, or alternatively they might take the view that they will not tell the parent because the information might be hurtful. The classification developed by Marshall *et al.* (2005) is set out in Table 5.1.

Table 5.1 Definitions and frequencies of adolescents' strategies for conveying information about their whereabouts and activities.

Theme	Definition	Examples	Frequency
Jurisdiction	Decision to inform parent is founded upon whether activities are under the jurisdiction of the adolescent (i.e. nearby, shorter period of time) or parent (i.e. far away, longer period of time)	'When you're within town and visiting friends or going to the library or to a store' 'When it's night, when they don't know who I'm going with, when I go somewhere I've never been before'	67
Social support	Decision to inform parent is associated with support such as protection from safety or assistance with daily tasks. Social support may be from the parent to the adolescent or vice versa	'...when my mother needed me to babysit my sister I would give the number where I was' 'When there is a potential for danger. For example, if I'm going hiking in the woods they should know exactly where I am in case I get hurt or something'	37
Ask me no questions, tell you no lies	Information is conveyed only if the parent asks; not conveyed if parent doesn't ask	'only if they wanted to know' 'if they are going to check [on where I am]'	6
Sort of tell	Parent is provided with partial information as to the adolescent's whereabouts and activities	'When they won't let me go, we don't explain exactly where I'm going' 'For example, if I'm out with friends they don't need to know where. At least they know I'm out and will be back later'	38
Tell or else	Adolescent conveys whereabouts and activities to avoid consequences of parent not being informed	'If I don't tell them I get into big trouble' 'The consequences [of not telling] are too high'	5

Source: Marshall *et al.* (2005).

Further studies on information management have appeared in Keijsers and Laird (2010). Two examples may be given here. Daddis and Randolph (2010) looked at information management in the context of romantic relationships, and showed that trust between parent and teenager made a difference to disclosure, but so did the young person's estimate of the impact of disclosure. If he or she believed that sharing information with the parent would positively impact on others they would be more likely to disclose. These findings reinforce the notion of active management by the young person depending on awareness and assessment of the consequences of disclosure. In another study Tilton-Weaver *et al.* (2010) used a longitudinal design, and they were able to show that the parent's response to disclosure at Time 1 influenced the young person's management of information at Time 2. In other words whether the parent responded positively or negatively in the first place had an impact on the future disclosure patterns of the young person. Findings such as these provide graphic support for the idea that adolescents are actively shaping their environment; that they are constructing their own development. This idea is one to which we will return in the final chapter.

In thinking about the impact of the family environment on adolescent development, one further topic is worth mentioning, and that is changes over time in parenting behaviour. In an important review, the Nuffield Foundation (2009) has summarised what is known about this subject in the UK, based on evidence to be found in some of the major longitudinal studies of family life. Some of these findings are counter-intuitive, since most people believe that family life has deteriorated, and that parents are less involved with their sons and daughters than in previous generations (Layard and Dunn, 2008). The results of the Nuffield review are of great interest, in that they show quite the opposite. In the first place parents' expectations of good behaviour appear to have increased between 1986 and 2006. The proportion of young people reporting that their parents expected them to do their homework increased from 90 per cent to 95 per cent, and the proportion reporting that their parents expected them to be polite increased from 75 per cent to 87 per cent.

Secondly there is an increase in the time parents and young people like to spend together. Young people's own reports of the amount of quality time they opt to spend with their mothers increased over 30 years from 23 per cent to 30 per cent. Lastly the level of monitoring seems to have increased. The proportion of parents who routinely asked their teenagers who they were spending time with rose, between 1986 and 2006, from 67 per cent to 77 per cent, whilst the number of adolescents who actually said they told their parents who they were with increased from 78 per cent to 86 per cent (Collishaw *et al.*, 2007). The documentation of these changes in family life provides an interesting background to the broader range of

social changes that we have already noted. Increased awareness of risk may be leading to higher levels of parental anxiety. However, the belief that parents and adolescents are growing further apart does not seem to be the case. Finally, and it can only be speculation, but it may be that these findings reflect an increased awareness of parenting in the UK, together with a growing recognition that parents and parenting behaviour really do matter.

Culture and ethnicity

As the world becomes more multi-cultural it becomes increasingly important to recognise that there are cultural differences between families in the way they approach the rearing of children, and especially in the way they manage the adolescent stage of development. Nonetheless there is far less research evidence on this than there is on many other aspects of parenting. It is also true that the majority of research originates from North America, with European textbooks paying very little attention to this topic. In this section we will review a selection of studies that have investigated the role of ethnicity in this area.

One comparison that is often drawn between families with different cultural backgrounds has to do with differences in time spent in the family setting, and variations in the emotional closeness of parents and adolescents in different cultures. Thus Cooper (1994) showed greater expectations of family closeness in Chinese, Mexican and Vietnamese families in the USA than in White American families. In a study by Facio and Batistuta (1998), a comparison was drawn between the family relationships described in Hendry et al. (1993) in a Scottish sample and those found in a small city in Argentina. The comparison was illuminating. In Argentina nearly 80 per cent of young people in the 15–16-year age range reported having meals with their parents, while only 35 per cent of the Scottish sample did so. A general picture emerges of warm and positive relationships with both parents in Argentina, similar to studies of family life in countries such as Spain and Italy, where parents and young people are close, and where young adults remain in the family home well into their twenties, or even into their thirties.

Japanese culture provides an important comparison point, since as Gjerde and Shimizu (1995) point out, the role of the father differs significantly from that to which we are accustomed in the West. In Japan the mother is the central parental figure, with the father being 'absent' for most of the time. In addition any open expression of discord in the family is discouraged, so that conflict is difficult to manage. As Gjerde and others have made clear, little thought has yet been given to the ways in which Japanese cultural values impact on adolescent development. However, in the Gjerde and Shimizu (1995) study they were able to show something of the complexity of family relationships.

They examined parental agreement or disagreement on how the adolescent should be socialised, and linked this to mother–teenager cohesion and the adjustment of the young person. In brief, results showed that close relationships between teenager and mother (high cohesion) was adaptive so long as the parents were in agreement on matters to do with adolescent socialisation. However, where mother and father disagreed, then mother–teenager cohesion was related to poor adjustment. As the authors note, these results illustrate the fact that the father's role is highly significant, even if he is away from the home and participates relatively rarely in family life.

Young people are likely to have a very different experience of family life growing up in Israel. There has been considerable interest in adolescent development in this country, since, for those brought up on a Kibbutz, peers and non-family members have historically been more influential than parents. However, during the last decades of the twentieth century there was a clear move away from this form of upbringing and a shift towards what Kaffman (1993) calls 'the familistic revolution'. Partly as a result of the difficulties experienced by the Kibbutz-reared young people in the 1960s and 1970s, the family has grown in importance in Israel, to the point now that relationships with parents are as central as they are in other European countries. The changes in family functioning are documented in Mazor (1993), providing a fascinating account of a shift in values concerning the role of the parent in family life. In particular it is argued that, as a result of fears concerning a pervasive drug culture, and also the involvement of a number of young Israelis in cults and other destructive group experiences, Israeli society began to believe that it needed to place much more emphasis on the family, and reduce the power and influence of the peer group.

Because of the multi-ethnic nature of society in the USA there have, not unnaturally, been a wide range of studies on parenting practices in this country. One major focus has been on the variation in parenting styles across ethnic groups. One key finding is that there is less evidence of authoritative parenting (as defined in the previous section) in African-American, Asian-American and Hispanic-American families than there is in White American families (Dornbusch et al., 1987; Smetana and Chuang, 2001; Yau and Smetana, 1996). This finding no doubt reflects differences in values and beliefs across different cultures. However, young people in ethnic minority families whose parents do use this style of parenting appear to benefit as much as those in European cultures. Two further findings are of importance here. First, authoritarian parenting (where there is a greater emphasis on demandingness and control) is more common in ethnic minority communities. Second, young people from White backgrounds are more adversely affected by authoritarian parenting than are minority young people (Lamborn et al., 1996; Ruiz et al., 2002). One possible explanation for this finding may be that higher levels of parental control are more adaptive in communities where violence and risk are prevalent. On the other hand it may be that, as Chao (2001) has suggested, these dimensions of parenting style have less meaning in non-European cultures.

In this context it may be helpful to draw a distinction between 'individualistic' and 'collectivist' cultures. This is a distinction well known to commentators on culture and values (e.g. Hofstede, 1983), but it has particular relevance for any consideration of family life for adolescents. Essentially, in a collectivist culture it is believed that the young person's behaviour and aspirations should centre around the reputation and success of the family and the community, rather than around the wishes of the individual. In an individualistic culture the opposite value system obtains. Here it is expected that the young person will seek to identify his or her own personal goals, and will be encouraged to find ways of reaching these goals without undue regard to the needs and wishes of the family. This distinction can be helpful in understanding differences in adolescent experiences, as for example in Gilani's (1999) research, which showed that Asian young women in the UK were, in the main, obedient to their mothers' wishes and experienced low levels of mother–daughter conflict. However, White British young women experienced much higher levels of conflict with their mothers, while at the same time reporting satisfaction with their own autonomy and right to make their own decisions.

Webster (2009) makes the point that, in the British context, there is a complex situation with many different cultural groups whose value systems vary according to their particular backgrounds and experiences of immigration. It is sometimes suggested (e.g. Smith, 2005) that first-generation immigrants assimilate relatively easily, becoming overly conformist and law-abiding in relation to the host culture. Their children, however, may take the opposite position. In this situation young people find assimilation hard to cope with, and end up rejecting mainstream values. One explanation for this is that such young people resent the prejudice and disadvantage they experience, and, in a vicious circle, become marginalised and excluded, and thereby attracted to high risk and anti-social peer group cultures. However, as Mason (2003) points out, this does not apply to all immigrant groups. Some ethnic groups, such as some Asians, arrive in the host country with significant social capital, thus protecting their young people from many of the risk factors which affect other groups. In conclusion we can reflect that these considerations will be highly significant for family life, and therefore for the types of parenting experienced by young people from different ethnic backgrounds.

Divorce and the changing nature of families

'My Mum and Dad have split up, so my Mum lives at the top of the town, and my Dad lives down here, so I can always go. . . . Like I've done in the past, have an argument with my Mum and come and stay at my Dad's. I've got all my friends around the place as well, and some of them – their parents are the same as well, so sometimes I go and stay at a friend's house, or they come and stay at mine, and we can just talk about it.'

(14-year-old girl)

It was noted at the beginning of this chapter that the very notion of family has undergone substantial alteration over the last few decades. In most commentary today writers distinguish between four family types – couple families, single parent families, step-families and blended families (e.g. Halpern-Meekin and Tach, 2008). While it was the case that for a long time research tended to focus on divorce as the topic for investigation, it is now recognised that there are many other factors to take into account. Indeed some single parent families exist, not as a result of divorce, but as a result of parental choice. It is also recognised that divorce is only one event, and that the process, including the family circumstances both before and after divorce, may be more important as determinants of the child or young person's adjustment than the divorce itself. Other factors too play their part, such as the role of the wider family, the impact of economic hardship which may occur as a result of relationship breakdown, and the differences between ethnic groups in their response to family change. Arguably one of the most significant changes has been the emergence of parenting roles carried out by non-biological partners, and the necessity to understand how these impact on family life. In past decades there was concern over the role of the non-residential father. Today, however, it is as much the place of step-parents, step-grandparents and even non-married partners that offers challenges both to biological parents and to children and young people in their development.

A primary consideration in this context relates to a comparison of the advantages and disadvantages for children and young people growing up in intact married couple families and those growing up in other family types. Much is made in cross-country comparisons and in political debate about the importance of marriage for children's well-being (Layard and Dunn, 2008), and it is of importance therefore to examine this issue. In Britain in 2006 25 per cent of families with dependent children up to the age of 16 were headed by a lone parent. This has profound social implications, not all of which are necessarily apparent today. Work by Scott (2004, 2007) and others suggests that there are undoubtedly disadvantages for those living in reconstituted families, but that these disadvantages are as much about economic disadvantage as they are about stress in relationships. The evidence is clear that parents who bring up children on their own are significantly more likely to be living in poverty, and that this in turn has an impact on a wide variety of aspects of family life including housing, health, opportunities for further education and the transition to adulthood.

In order to understand the impact of family change and reorganisation it is essential to recognise that divorce or breakdown is a process rather than an event. Research is unequivocal in indicating that events taking place before the breakdown, as well as what happens subsequently, play a larger role than the event itself. Thus Kelly (2000) reports that a high level of family conflict prior to breakdown is a significant factor in determining the adjustment of young people post divorce. Collishaw et al. (2004) also showed that chronic parental conflict was related to disorder among adolescents in subsequent years. Equally significant are the findings to be found in Jenkins et al. (2005), who compared intact and step-families with children between 4 and 17. They showed that marital conflict about children increased children's problem behaviour, but that children's problem behaviour predicted marital conflict, especially in step-families. However, siblings differed in their exposure to conflict, and thus the long-term impact is not the same for all children and young people. Variation in impact is greater in step-families than in intact families.

Research also shows that what happens after family breakdown is closely related to young people's adjustment to divorce. The phrase 'caught in the middle' was first used in the work of Buchanan et al. (1996). Following research carried out in California, these writers identified the damaging effect on young people of continuing conflict between parents over access and other arrangements. More recent research (e.g. Dunn et al., 2005) into family conflict reflects the complexity of family relationships today. This research recognised that conflict could occur between different members of reconstituted families, including mother and former partner, mother and step-father, and father and new partner. Such complexity makes research extremely difficult of course, but in this study the investigators were able to show that some types of conflict – that between mother and non-resident father for example – were more likely to lead to poor adjustment than other types of conflict. This research also led the investigators to conclude that, as others have found, it was the young person's involvement in their parents' conflict that was significant rather than the frequency of such conflict. Finally Dunn *et al.* (2005) make the point that where young people experience conflict in more than one family environment, e.g. at home and in a step-family, the impact is likely to be particularly detrimental in terms of mental health problems.

Looking at the other side of the coin, there is some evidence that parental divorce and family reorganisation can be a protective factor against further psychological harm (Scott, 2007). Firstly it may be that, following a change in family circumstances, young people are relieved of having to witness chronic conflict or even violence. As this young woman makes clear, being so close to hatred and anger between one's parents is very difficult to manage.

> 'The worst thing has been the hate between the two of them. Knowing how much they hated each other, and being in the middle of that. They were really so horrible to each other all the time, and all they'd do was slag each other off to me. And I hated it, I really did. I felt really in the middle and like I couldn't do anything about it. I think at first I felt like part of it was my fault, and I should have stopped it, but I mean, I just couldn't. But I always carry it around, that I should have been able to stop it.'
>
> (16-year-old girl, quoted in Coleman, 1990)

Another potentially positive experience that may stem from family reorganisation is the opportunity to take on new roles within the family. For some young people growing up with a single parent or in a reconstituted family may allow more rapid movement towards the assumption of maturity and of adult roles. Adolescents may be given the opportunity to take on more responsibility and to play a greater role in decision-making within the family in a way that was not possible when both parents were living together. Finally the possibility for adolescents of making new relationships with different adults should not be ignored. As one parent finds a new partner this brings with it an opportunity for a young person to form a different type of relationship with someone who comes from outside the family. So much research and discussion focusses on the negative aspects of the introduction of a step-parent into a family, but there are undoubtedly many examples of positive and supportive relationships which can develop between young people and previously unknown adults.

One final protective factor not yet mentioned has to do with the role of friends. Research (e.g. O'Connor *et al.*, 2001; Dunn and Deater-Deckard, 2001) illustrates how important friends can be in situations of family change. In studies that look at young people's communication patterns, and the role of confidants at times of family difficulty, the findings are clear. Friends play a key role, and for those who lose friends because of moving home and changing school, things are more difficult than for those who remain in the same environment. Thus it can be concluded that it is not the family breakdown itself that is the damaging factor, but rather it is the circumstances that surround such an event. Serious conflict between parents both before and after separation is one of the key risk variables determining the outcome for young people, whilst being removed from violence or hatred between parents, and being able to keep the same group of friends can help to mitigate some of the most damaging effects of family breakdown.

Parenting teenagers

'Listening. Listening is what's important. Because if you don't really have anyone to listen . . . I think . . . You get these kids that, like, hide in their rooms, don't you? And I think that's mainly because their elders don't really listen to them.'

(14-year-old boy)

'You ask for something, like with parents, if you want something quite simple, but they say no and stuff. If you want to do something, and they say no. Sometimes they go straight in and say no, but then sometimes they listen and say "No, because I don't want you going and doing this because of so and so . . ." I can see why they say it, but then sometimes I think, like, "I'm not going to go and do anything stupid or anything."'

(15-year-old girl)

The topic of parenting has received greatly increased attention over the past decade. Books and journals dedicated to parenting have appeared in many countries, and there has been an upsurge in the number of parenting programmes available for parents of teenagers. In Britain much of this has been driven by the government's concern over anti-social behaviour, and an associated attempt to provide greater support to parents whose sons and daughters might be getting into trouble. Quite apart from this, however, there has been a growing focus on this topic apparent since the 1990s, with researchers becoming interested in how best to translate their findings into practical advice for parents (see Roker and Coleman, 2007; Kerr *et al.*, 2008).

One important difference between parents of teenagers and parents of younger children has to do with uncertainty about the parenting role. For parents of young children there is relatively little difficulty in defining roles and responsibilities. Yet this is not the case for parents of teenagers, particularly in the context of changing families and the arrival of step-parents, non-residential parents and so on. Part of this has to do with the changing nature of power and authority in the family. Today parents of teenagers are not clear what is expected of them in relation to monitoring and supervision, or in setting boundaries and limits for a 14-year-old, or in regulating homework or the amount of screen time (computer and television use) that is allowable. In addition there are issues such as confidentiality in relation to medical treatment, and the appropriate age for a young person to start having sex. Most parents feel at a loss over such matters, which leads to lowered self-confidence, heightened anxiety, and less effective parenting (Coleman and Roker, 2001).

In fact there is much in the literature that can be used to guide and assist parents of teenagers. Questions to do with parenting style have already been mentioned in this chapter, as has the topic of monitoring and supervision. To take one example of a review of research findings, Grolnick *et al.* (2008) highlight the importance of reciprocity in parent–adolescent relationships, arguing that for parents to understand the two-way nature of relationships is a key to better parenting. They also identify three areas that need attention – the type of control used, the importance of involvement, and the provision of structure. As far as control is concerned, they draw a distinction between behavioural and psychological control, and go on to argue that both these types of control can be positive or negative depending on other factors. As they note, control can be helpful if it aims to create rules that are perceived as fair and reasonable, and if it does not involve too much intrusion into the life of an adolescent. Control is also very much age dependent, so that what might be appropriate for a 13-year-old will not be appropriate for a 16-year-old. Parental involvement also has an important part to play. Parental involvement refers to the extent that parents are interested in, knowledgeable about, and active in various elements of their teenagers' lives. However, the opposite side of the coin is over-involvement, or intrusiveness, which can be counter-productive and lead to continual tension between parent and young person.

The question of structure is an important one for any parent, and Grolnick *et al.* (2008) have set out a very helpful classification of six dimensions of structure that may underlie effective parenting for this age group. These are:

- clear and consistent communication of expectations
- opportunities for young people to meet or exceed expectations
- predictability in parental behaviour
- feedback of information to young people
- the provision of explanations and rationales for any rules or expectations
- parental authority must be coupled with the taking of leadership roles in the home.

It is these ideas that underlie many of the parenting programmes that have been developed over the past decade or so. Barrett (2003) and Roker and Coleman (2007) provide useful reviews of some of the most widely used programmes. Today there are simply too many programmes to document here, but significant dimensions to bear in mind are such things as the length of the programme, whether it is a general parenting programme or designed for problematic behaviour, whether it has been properly evaluated for outcomes, and whether there is an adequate training programme for practitioners to use before offering it to parents. Much has been learnt over the recent past about the challenges and difficulties of running parenting programmes for parents of teenagers, and some of these will be briefly reviewed here.

The first question has to do with how best to get information to parents. Most parenting programmes are based on the notion of group work. The programme aims to get a number of parents together who then meet eight or ten times as a group to explore various dimensions of parenting. However, as Roker and Foster (2007) showed, not all parents want to attend a group. Some prefer to talk on a one-to-one basis to an expert, whilst others may prefer to have information that they can take home and read in privacy. Other parents may want to use the internet to obtain information about parenting, but as Roker (2007) illustrated in her study of the use of websites, this too has its challenges. The conclusion from this work is that different media suit different parents, and if the intention is to provide information to parents in the most effective manner, then a menu of opportunities should be offered.

A second issue has to do with parenting in circumstances of poverty or disadvantage, and the problems that this creates for those running parenting programmes. Ghate and Hazell's (2002) book entitled *Parenting in poor environments* highlighted the obstacles that face parents in such circumstances. Many have to take part-time jobs during unsocial hours, making it extremely difficult to attend a parenting group in the evening. Others cannot arrange child care for younger children, or have no access to suitable transport to the parenting group venue.

A third and fascinating question has to do with how to involve young people in parenting programmes. If the intention of a programme is to facilitate more effective parenting, then clearly some thought needs to be given to the reactions of the young people in the family. Yet this is a question that is far from resolved.

Few writers on the topic of parenting programmes pay sufficient attention to this, but without doing so a key feature of the potential efficacy of any programme is being missed. One of the few evaluations of different ways to involve young people was described by Hoskin and Lindfield (2007). These authors evaluated five different models, all of which involved young people in different ways. In one the organisers ran parallel groups for parents and young people, in another family therapy was offered, in a third a family skills training programme was available, and so on. Results showed that it was not so much the model that made the difference, but the very fact that young people were part of a programme created both advantages as well as additional challenges. The challenges arose because having young people involved demanded extra resources and at times distracted from the needs of the parents. On the other hand everyone welcomed the fact that adolescents were playing a part in the programmes, recognising that this was a challenge that should not be avoided. In years to come this will be a feature of parenting interventions that will have to be addressed.

Implications for practice

1. The first point to make is that recent studies of the development of autonomy indicate that young people do not separate entirely from their parents during the adolescent stage. By and large it is true to say that a continuing connectedness with parents, for both young men and young women, is helpful for a transition to adulthood.

2. In spite of a general public belief that adolescence is characterised by high levels of conflict in the home, research does not support this conclusion. While there are many issues about which parents and young people disagree, in general relationships appear to be more positive than negative. In the majority of families there is no evidence of substantial inter-generational conflict. Many factors will have an impact on whether there is conflict, and if so, what the level of conflict is. In particular good communication between parent and teenager will have the effect of reducing conflict. As might be expected, conflict is highest when parents themselves have poor relationships, where the family is experiencing stress or difficulty, or where there is a long-standing risk factor such as the parent having chronic ill-health or experiencing unemployment.

3. Research on parenting styles has shown consistently that authoritative parenting has the most beneficial effect on adolescent development, since this includes warmth, structure and support for autonomy. By contrast authoritarian, indifferent or indulgent parenting styles have effects which, while differing to some extent, all encourage less adaptive adolescent development.

4. In recent years there has been a recognition that relationships between parents and teenagers are bi-directional. In other words both influence each other, and in addition to looking at what parents do, it is essential to understand how the young person's behaviour influences parental behaviour. Studies of adolescent information management have made this point forcefully, and these investigations underline the view that young people are active agents in their own development.

5. Studies have begun to address the issue of race and ethnicity where families are concerned. While more research in this area would be welcome, it can be concluded that ethnicity plays a key role in the way parents behave towards their teenagers. For practitioners therefore it is essential to recognise that there will be variation between cultures, and that what is expected in one setting will not necessarily be expected in another. Where cultural background is associated with disadvantage or overt racism, parents may respond to these circumstances with strategies which they see as adaptive or protective of their teenage children. Such strategies may differ from those seen as adaptive in the majority culture, where there is less likelihood of prejudice or harassment.

6. Relatively little attention has been directed to the role of the father in relation to adolescent development, but what research there is underlines the importance of this role for teenagers. The necessity of avoiding a 'deficit' model of fathering has been stressed, and it is clear that more effort is needed to support fathers during the stage when their children become teenagers.

7. Research findings on the impact of divorce have emphasised the complexity of the experience for children and young people. Today a young person may have relationships with a number of adults all of whom may play some form of a parental role. The impact of this complexity needs to be kept in

mind. Research shows that conflict between parents, especially between the biological parents, has damaging consequences for young people, whether that conflict predates the divorce or separation, or occurs after it. It is clear that the economic effects of divorce are almost as significant as the psychological consequences, with relative poverty having a major influence on adolescent outcomes. The most significant practical conclusion from research findings is that divorce is part of a process, and that adjustment will be influenced by a range of factors rather than by the divorce itself.

8. The parenting of adolescents has received greatly increased attention in recent years. There are many parenting programmes, and there has been a change of culture so that it is now much more acceptable for parents to seek advice and help. Practitioners need to bear in mind that different programmes are suitable for different groups of parents, and that the circumstances of individual parents (e.g. child care arrangements) need to be taken into account when planning a parenting intervention.

Further reading

Ghate, D and Hazell, N (2002) *Parenting in poor environments: stress, support and coping.* Jessica Kingsley. London.
A book that has already become a classic. Describes ground-breaking research which has wide-ranging implications for the parenting of teenagers.

Kerr, M, Stattin, H and Engels, R (Eds) (2008) *What can parents do? New insights into the role of parents in adolescent problem behaviour.* John Wiley. Chichester.
This book is one in a series called '*Hot topics in developmental psychology*', and it describes new research looking at the way parents and adolescents mutually influence each other, with a particular focus on troubled young people.

Lila, M, Van Aken, M, Musitu, G and Buelga, S (2006) Families and adolescents. In Jackson, S and Goossens, L (Eds) *Handbook of adolescent development.* Psychology Press. Hove.
A good review of European research on young people in the context of the family.

Roker, D and Coleman, J (Eds) (2007) *Working with parents of young people: research, policy and practice.* Jessica Kingsley. London.
A review of a variety of innovative interventions with parents of teenagers. The chapters summarise the research and outline the implications for policy and practice.

Health

'I used to think that smoking was completely horrible, but now I think, well I wouldn't do it, but I understand that people get addicted to it. I think it's best to do it in the teenage years than when you're older because you'll get less addicted I think.'

(14-year-old girl)

Understanding adolescent health is no easy matter. There are a variety of contentious questions which are associated with this topic, and this chapter will address the most important of these. One obvious example relates to the very definition of health, and it will become apparent that adult and adolescent perspectives on this differ in important ways. Then there is the issue of health and risk. Do young people need to take risks in order to learn about themselves, or is it necessary for the adult world to do all it can to limit what is seen as risky behaviour? Many adults are pessimistic about adolescent health, and numerous publications can be cited (e.g. Nathanson, 2003) in which those in the medical professions catalogue the apparent downward spiral in the use of drugs and alcohol, and in the engagement in unsafe sexual behaviour. Others write about the fact that, comparing all age groups in the population, it is only among adolescents that no material progress has been made over the last decades in health improvements (Viner and Barker, 2005). It can be seen, therefore, that this is a topic which arouses considerable debate, and about which there are very many contrasting views. In this chapter there will be an introductory discussion, followed by sections on physical exercise, smoking, alcohol and substance misuse, nutrition and eating, mental health, and health promotion.

Introduction

'I do get moody, I think everyone does at some point. I remember getting very upset about it, and thinking "is this it?" kind of thing. Am I just going to be like this, day after day, live my life like this? And my Mum talked to me, she told me like, that everything was transient, and every mood that I had was going to go away eventually, and so you could be right down, but, you know, eventually it will go and you'll be back up. It's all a bit like – "I'm growing up!" And it never seemed like such a big thing then, it wasn't like such a big thing anymore. But yes, there was a point before I realised that, and I just felt, like, I'm going to be miserable forever, and my life is always going to be in this system, going to school, or work, or whatever, and it's never going to end.'

(15-year-old girl)

It is essential to recognise that adolescent health is a developmental phenomenon. In this book there have already been discussions about brain development and about the importance of puberty in the overall development of the young person, and issues to do with health have to be seen in this context. Thus health concerns for a young person aged 12 or 13 are bound to be associated with the major physical changes that are occurring in the body at that time. Worries over moods, body image, anxieties about the size of breasts or penis, and concern about the timing of puberty are likely to be paramount. As the young person grows up, however, these concerns will alter, so that in middle adolescence there may be more focus on health as it relates to social relationships. How does the young person look to friends? What about acne and skin care, having greasy hair, being overweight and so on? Health at this age will be very much to do with popularity and acceptance among friends, and the beginning of romantic relationships. Then at a later stage there are likely to be concerns about behaviour that is expected by the peer group, such as smoking, using illegal substances and so on. It has often been argued that decisions about health behaviour by adolescents represent a trade-off between knowing what is good for you, and dealing with pressure from friends and the wider peer group (Coleman *et al.*, 2007).

Health for young people has more to do with the here and now, rather than with an abstract notion of health, or with a concern about preventing future ill-health. Young people are less interested in the relation between smoking and long-term morbidity rates of lung cancer, and more interested in how to deal with peer pressure, or how smoking might link to dieting and appetite for food. Adolescents tend to adopt a subjective definition of health, and they prefer to learn skills which help them cope with conflicts relating to health decisions rather than being given basic information about health. Information about drugs is a good example. Whilst they may be quite knowledgeable themselves about different types of illegal substances they lack the social skills to manage the social pressures and to apply what they know in their daily lives.

Young people are also very aware of the contradictions apparent in many health messages that come to them from adults. Thus it is hard to accept that drinking alcohol is damaging to health when you can see an adult culture around you that places drinking at the centre of much social activity. Similarly it is illogical to teach young people about health and nutrition in school settings where the food on offer in the canteen is anything but healthy. There is no doubt that adults manifest a paradoxical attitude to young people's health, and this has the effect of magnifying the differences between teachers or parents and adolescents.

Differences between the generations are also apparent when the concept of risk is considered. Health behaviours relating to such things as drinking, smoking, poor diet, unsafe sex and the use of illegal substances are frequently described as 'risky' or as 'health risk behaviours'. However, what is considered by the adult world to be risky is not necessarily seen in the same light by young people. Michaud and colleagues (2006) have been in the forefront of a European movement to distinguish between risk that is manifestly linked to the development of problem behaviour, such as drug addiction, and risk that could be considered to be normative, such as drinking alcohol at a party or smoking cannabis, which is better described as experimental rather than risky. This is a complex argument, but there is considerable force behind it. Michaud argues that very often risk behaviours occur because of situations that bring about new and unexpected challenges to an inexperienced adolescent, rather than because of characteristics inherent in the individual (Michaud, 2006; Michaud *et al.*, 2006).

As Michaud and others write, the use of the term risk may be associated with a negative stereotype of adolescence, and can be used to describe things about young people that adults either fear or mistrust. As a result many behaviours, such as having sex, doing physically dangerous sports, getting drunk, trying drugs and so on are classified as 'bad' or 'damaging', whilst they ought to be considered as 'experimental or exploratory'. This distinction between different concepts of risk (which will be discussed further in Chapter 11) has implications for many aspects of adolescent health. It has links to health promotion, because one's view of risk determines the approach to be taken, and it has links to the provision of services, because the perception of health risk will affect the priority given to the needs of young people. Both these topics will be considered in more detail later in the chapter.

Physical exercise and sport

'I play quite a lot of tennis with my friends and stuff. In the earlier years I did football, but as you get older you don't really have as much free time, you get a lot more work, and I just didn't really want to do it. And then I got more into tennis, and they don't really do that at school.'

(16-year-old boy)

Young people's involvement in sport and exercise is considered to be an important indicator of good health. In recent times an increased focus on two separate measures of poor health, namely obesity and coronary heart disease, has prompted adult concern over the question of exercise and sport in adolescence. It is not entirely clear that there are direct links between these two things, so that for example it may be that rising rates of obesity are more to do with wider lifestyle issues such as diet and nutrition, rather than low levels of exercise. Nonetheless all agree that exercise is a protective factor against a range of

health risks, and that it is important to ensure that young people have opportunities to engage in sport and other physical activities during the school years (Kremer *et al.*, 1997; Cale and Harris, 2005).

In many European countries there has been concern over whether there is a historical trend towards lower levels of exercise in the population as a whole, and in the adolescent age group in particular. The pervasive influence of television and of the computer are often blamed for this, and many governments have put in place policies attempting to reverse such a trend. In fact surveys over time do not support the contention that there has been any major decrease in exercise levels among young people. If anything it would

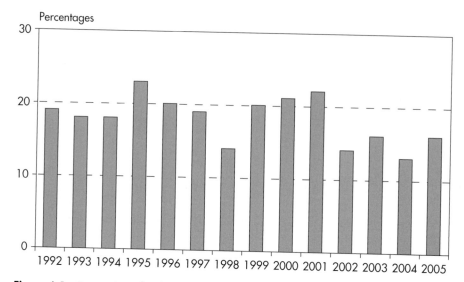

Figure 6.1 Proportion of girls aged 14–15 years who did not participate in any active sports on a weekly basis, 1992–2005.

Data from: Balding (2006).

Source: Coleman and Schofield (2007).

appear that the trend is going the other way, as can be seen from Figure 6.1, showing a reduction over time in young women not engaging in some physical activity at least once a week.

Much the same trend can be seen in Figure 6.2, illustrating that between 2004 and 2007 in the UK there was a slight increase in school pupils participating in at least 2 hours of high quality physical exercise during the school week. However, this chart also shows another important trend, the reduction in sporting involvement with age. Whilst over 90 per cent are engaging in high quality sporting activity in early adolescence, by age 15 this drops to around 60 per cent. The changing levels of involvement as young people get older is a topic for further discussion below.

In terms of participation one other finding is of importance, and that is the gender difference in engagement with sports and physical activity during this stage. Whilst for most boys there remains a high level of engagement during the school years, this is not the case for girls. As can be seen from Figure 6.3, the engagement of girls clearly diminishes as they move towards middle adolescence. This is a finding that has important implications for the health of women in our society, and is a topic that is poorly researched or understood. Clearly sport plays a very different role for males and females in the adolescent years, with sport having a central role in male social activity and a very limited role in female social activity. Thus contextual and attitudinal factors will be playing their part in determining both levels of involvement and loss of interest in sport.

In an extensive review of the place of sport and exercise in adolescent health Lowry *et al.* (2007) explore some of the reasons why young people might opt out

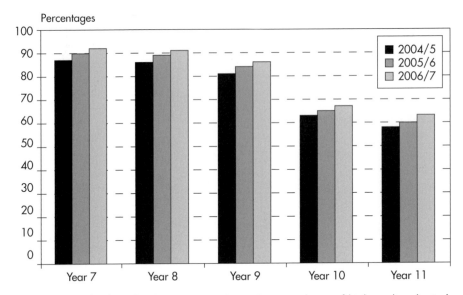

Percentages

Figure 6.2 School pupils who participated in at least two hours of high quality physical education in a typical week (including out of hours provision) in England 2004–2007.

Data from: Craig and Mindell (2008).

Source: Coleman and Brooks (2009).

of participation. These authors suggest the following are what they call 'drop-out motives':

- Limited improvement. A lack of progress or any noticeable improvement in skills related to sport.
- Conflict of interest. Other activities being more interesting or rewarding.
- Pressure from others. A feeling of being under pressure from a coach, parents or other adults.
- Lack of time. Increasing demands from school work or other activities could conflict with time for sport.
- Boredom. A low level of interest in the activity.

Two other factors could be added to this list, both of which are of particular relevance to young women. The first is the social context of sport, and the resulting peer pressure that militates against girls being involved in sporting activity. The second has to do with the physical nature of sport, the unpleasant feeling of getting sweaty, the need to change into sports clothes and therefore go to the changing rooms, and the very 'male' nature of sport. All these things may play a role in determining involvement.

Thinking about drop-out motives prompts some reflection on the opposite side of the coin, and on the benefits that participation in sport might offer young people. Based on the work of Lowry *et al.* (2007) the following motives might be suggested:

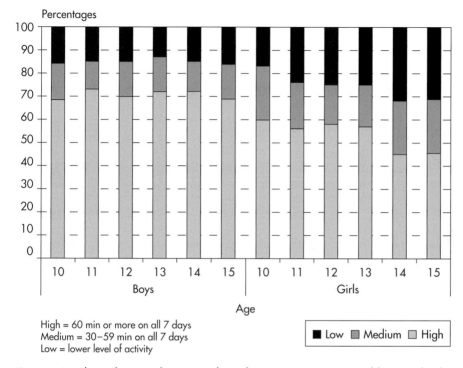

High = 60 min or more on all 7 days
Medium = 30–59 min on all 7 days
Low = lower level of activity

■ Low ▨ Medium ▢ High

Figure 6.3 Physical activity by age and gender among 10–15-year-olds in England in 2006.

Data from: Craig and Mindell (2008).

Source: Coleman and Brooks (2009).

- Skill. To gain feelings of accomplishment or ability.
- Social. To gain a sense of belonging to a social group, and having shared experiences.
- Fitness. To improve body image, strength or stamina.
- Competition. To perform well in one domain, and to achieve success.
- Enjoyment. Sport or physical activity might be fun or give pleasure.

Many writers have linked well-being with engagement in sport, as well as suggesting that those with emotional health problems might benefit from participation in sport or other physical activity (Heaven, 1996; Cale and Harris, 2005). This could be because of an increased level of endorphins in the blood, or because of what is known as 'the time out hypothesis' (Alfermann and Stoll, 2000), which suggests that distraction and involvement in alternative activities can help to lift a depressed mood or divert attention from anxiety or stress. It is also the case that work with young people who are disadvantaged or 'at risk' has often involved sport and outdoor adventure as a mechanism to enhance self-esteem, develop skills and enhance peer relationships (Jeffs and Smith, 1990). Outdoor adventure pursuits such as hill-walking, mountaineering and canoeing have all been used in this way, and have a long tradition within youth work as a means of encouraging psychosocial development amongst those who are most vulnerable (Cotterell, 2007).

Smoking, drinking and the use of illegal drugs

'What am I proud of? Well, a bit of a weird one, but everyone gets to the stage where everyone goes through the smoking thing, and it's like this big "hoo hah". I was just, like, OK, whatever. If everyone else is trying it, try it. And I realised it was kind of crap, and I didn't get much out of it. So I was, like, can't be arsed. I was quite proud that I didn't get swept up in that 'cause they all looked a bit stupid.'

(16-year-old girl)

When adults think about health in relation to young people the topics of drink and drugs come most readily to mind. A significant proportion of health education for adolescents tends to focus on these subjects, and when parents are asked what worries them most about the behaviour of teenagers these are the things that are most often mentioned. If adolescence is perceived as a stage of 'health risk' (Heaven, 1996) then it is most likely that drinking and the use of illegal substances will be in the forefront of behaviours that are associated with this idea. As has already been noted, this is far too simplistic a view, and for many young people drinking alcohol or smoking cannabis are behaviours associated with social situations and are far closer to notions of experiment or enjoyment than to a notion of risk, a point neatly illustrated in a study by Rodham *et al.* (2006) which looked at adolescents' understanding of risk and risky behaviour. However, there is no doubt that both alcohol and drug use can cause risks to health. This may be because the young person is engaging in these behaviours when alone, when considerations of safety are ignored, or when the use of these substances is chronic and long term or involves multiple substances. Thus it is important to recognise that smoking, drinking and illegal drug use can occur in different circumstances and have different meanings depending on the situation and on the individual young person.

Looking first at smoking, in line with the general social trend towards a reduction in this behaviour, it can be seen from Figures 6.4 and 6.5 that young people are following the direction of adults in this respect. However, it is worth noting that the downward trend is more marked in the older age group, with adolescents in the 11 to 15 age group showing less of a reduction. Nonetheless there was a sharp drop in the younger age group in 2007, and it is to be hoped that this will continue (Warren *et al.*, 2006). Perhaps the most important feature of these data is the gender gap among young adolescents. Girls are smoking more than boys in this age group, and whilst it is encouraging to see that this difference is hardly apparent in the 16 to 19 age group, it is a notable feature of smoking behaviour in the early stages of uptake. Numerous studies have attempted to identify the reasons for the gender difference, including Lloyd and Lucas (1998), who carried out one of the largest studies in the UK. They argued that social factors, especially concerns about weight and diet, were the primary reasons for

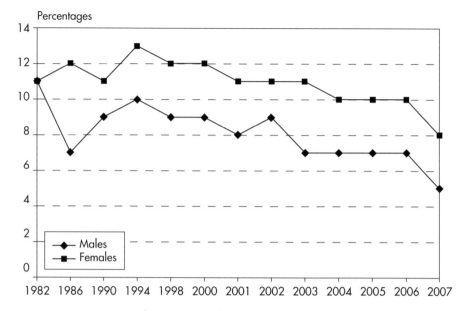

Figure 6.4 Proportion of 11–15-year-olds who were regular smokers, by gender, 1982–2007.

Data from: Drug Use, Smoking and Drinking among Young People in England in 2007. The NHS Information Centre, 2008.

Source: Coleman and Brooks (2009).

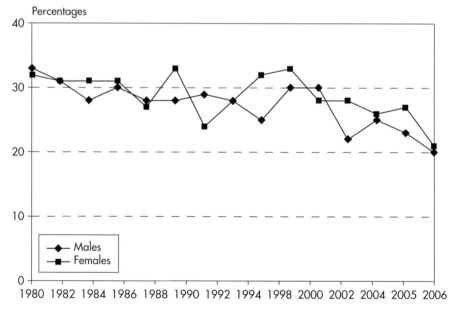

Figure 6.5 Proportion of 16–19-year-olds smoking in Britain, by gender, 1980–2006.

Data from: Statistics on Smoking, England, 2008. The NHS Information Centre.

Source: Coleman and Brooks (2009).

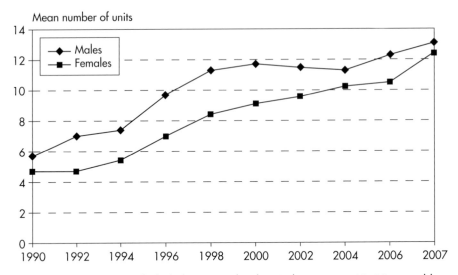

Figure 6.6 Mean units of alcohol consumed in last 7 days among 11–15-year-olds, by gender, in England 1990–2007.

Data from: Drug Use, Smoking and Drinking among Young People in England in 2007. The NHS Information Centre, 2008.

Source: Coleman and Brooks (2009).

this finding. In terms of reasons for smoking more generally, it is agreed that having parents and siblings in the family who are smokers is one key factor, whilst other factors such as low self-esteem, high levels of anxiety, the wish to relieve boredom, peer influences, and a means of fitting in socially all contribute to smoking behaviour (Tilleczek and Hine, 2006; Michaud *et al.*, 2006).

Alcohol use is widespread amongst young people, and such behaviour cannot be understood without a recognition of the place of alcohol in the social life of the adult population. It is clear that drinking is seen as a badge or indicator of being grown up, and it is hard to expect young people to abstain from alcohol when they see their parents and their communities using alcohol so widely. Most young people only drink on rare occasions, and so once again it is important to distinguish problematic behaviour from behaviour that is appropriate to the social situation. Drinking is likely to serve similar functions for young people as it is for adults (West, 2009). These functions include the fact that drinking can be pleasurable, that

it is a 'social' activity which is a marker of someone's involvement with the peer group, and that it is a helpful way to reduce anxiety in social situations. Studies of drinking behaviour illustrate two trends that have raised adult concerns about alcohol consumption in young people. The first trend is an increase in drinking levels among younger teenagers. This trend is illustrated in Figure 6.6, where it can be seen that over a decade and a half alcohol consumption in the UK among the 11 to 15 age group has nearly doubled. This is clearly a disturbing phenomenon, and may be to do with increased ease of access to alcohol through supermarkets and corner shops. The second piece of evidence that has concerned policy makers is the position of the UK countries in the league table of drinking behaviour. Figure 6.7 illustrates this finding, and shows that England and Wales in particular come close to the top of the table in respect of experiences of drunkenness in early adolescence. These two facts about alcohol consumption emphasise the importance of effective health education, a topic which will be considered later in the chapter.

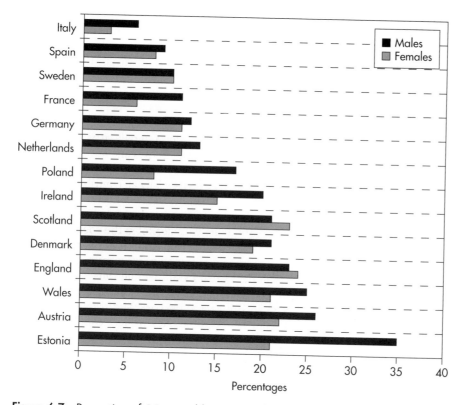

Figure 6.7   Proportion of 15-year-olds reporting first drunkenness at age 13 or younger in selected countries in 2006.

Data from: Currie *et al.* (2008).

Source: Coleman and Brooks (2009).

The topic that arouses the greatest anxiety among adults is undoubtedly young people's use of illegal drugs. There is continuing debate over the classification of different substances, especially with regard to the regulations concerning cannabis. It is essential to recognise that drugs do not all have the same effect, and that adolescents themselves are very much aware of the differences between cannabis and other substances such as cocaine and heroin. Again there has been wide-ranging research looking at the reasons for the use of illegal substances among young people, as well as the long-term consequences of drug use in adolescence (e.g. Engels and van den Einjden, 2007). The reasons given by young people for their use of cannabis are much the same as those given for drinking and smoking tobacco. Cannabis use is enjoyable, it is pleasurable and relaxing, and above all else it is a sociable activity. There is currently contradictory evidence about the effects of cannabis use, with some arguing that regular cannabis use can lead to psychosis and to other mental health problems (Hall, 2006), whilst other studies do not indicate any long-term damaging consequences. One explanation for the different findings may be that the long-term effects vary depending on the frequency of use, the underlying personality of the young person, and the type of cannabis being used, as demonstrated by Moore and colleagues (2007) in a systematic review of the evidence. Research in relation to heroin or cocaine use is less controversial, with studies showing clearly that the use of these substances leads very easily to drug dependence, and thus to serious health risk. In terms of the frequency of the use of these different substances, surveys show that between 25 per cent and 35 per cent of 15-year-olds across Europe have used cannabis at least once in the past year (Currie *et al.*, 2008). As far as heroin and cocaine are concerned the numbers are very much lower, with no more than 5 per cent involved in such activity (NHS Information Centre, 2008).

Nutrition, dieting and eating behaviour

'My friends, like, they all care a lot about what they look like, and now I sort of care more about it because I've been with them, and you feel a bit pressured, like, you want to be like them. I still try to eat exactly the same things. I don't want to be as slim as them and everything, I just want to be myself, but. . . . My sister used to call me loads of stuff, fat and things, so that sort of made me want to change and things. My Mum's been saying stuff too, and that's made me want to sort of lose weight and stuff, 'cause my sister always used to annoy me, but like, now, 'cause I've lost weight she can't really say anything.'

(14-year-old girl)

Behaviour associated with food and food intake is important for adolescents for a number of reasons. In the first place puberty brings with it major changes in bodily characteristics, including weight and the shape of the body. For all the reasons already mentioned such changes have both psychological and physical implications, and therefore food intake becomes significant as it has the potential to influence these characteristics. Those who wish to be thinner may diet, whilst others who wish that they were heavier may overeat. Much has been made of the role of the media here, with many believing that images of the 'perfect body' put pressure on girls to be slim and on boys to be muscle bound. Food intake is also important because of the secular trend in children and young people towards being heavier, with the associated fear among adults of increasing rates of obesity in the young. One of the reasons for the emphasis on sport and exercise in adolescents is linked to anxiety about increasing levels of obesity. A third factor in eating behaviour has to do with the foods that are popular among young people. Studies show that adolescents are more likely than adults to eat crisps, sweets and chocolates, and other fatty foods. This has resulted in a drive to improve nutrition in families and schools, which is part of a much larger social movement towards greater awareness among the adult population of the characteristics of different foods. In this section of the chapter there will be a discussion of food and eating habits, dieting and body image, obesity and eating disorders.

The quality of food that we eat is important to all of us, but for the reasons outlined above food comes to have particular salience for young people during the adolescent years. One of the factors rarely discussed is that food choice in young people has strong elements of 'adolescent identity' associated with it. Young people may choose certain foods, such as pizza or hamburgers for example, as they represent foods that are different from those chosen by adults. It is also the case that cultural and social factors play a big role in food choice, so that fruit and vegetables are more likely to be eaten in families where parents have higher levels of education (Currie *et al.*, 2000). Research shows that snack foods, such as crisps, are chosen more frequently by adolescents than by adults, as are fizzy drinks and sweets (Michaud *et al.*, 2006). Such food choices have implications for health, and may well be linked to increased weight or obesity. Studies carried out by the Health Behaviour in School Aged Children project (Currie *et al.*, 2000, 2008) indicate that adolescent food choice across European countries is changing, with the eating of both chocolate and crisps increasing over time. Such a trend poses a major challenge for health promotion.

One feature of food-related behaviour that is common among a proportion of adolescents, particularly girls, is dieting, or the restriction of food intake. As can be seen from Figure 6.8, the number of 15-year-old girls who engage in weight control ranges from 17 per cent in France to nearly 35 per cent in Italy. This is related to a sense of dissatisfaction with the shape of the body, and research by Balding in the UK indicates that 55 per cent of girls between the ages of 13 and 15 would like to lose weight. This compares with only 20 per cent of boys who believe they are too heavy (Balding, 2006). The most likely reason for this finding has to do with self-perceptions of body image (Heaven, 1996). Girls are very much influenced by what they believe to be the expected or most highly valued body shape, an image that is purveyed by films, television and the print media. Faulkner (2007) calls this a 'culture of thinness'. It is not surprising, therefore, that a significant proportion believe that they are too heavy or not the right shape, and at a developmental stage of heightened sensitivity to popularity and social acceptance this leads to attempts at weight control (Faulkner, 2007). The concern of young women about this issue was graphically illustrated in research by Shucksmith and Hendry (1998), who noted the following quotes from girls: 'I think weight is totally important';

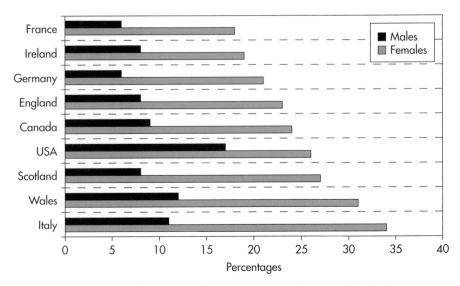

Figure 6.8 Proportion of 15-year-olds engaging in weight-controlling behaviours in selected countries in 2006.

Data from: Currie *et al.* (2008).

Source: Adapted from Coleman and Brooks (2009).

'Fat is a worry. It worries you'; ' I'm too heavy, probably getting too fat'; 'I'm trying to keep a constant weight, making sure I'm not overweight' (pp. 32–34).

Obesity has already been mentioned as one of the anxieties of adults concerning the health of children and young people, and as can be seen from the statistics shown in Figure 6.9 there is some justification for this concern. It would appear that in Britain the numbers falling into the category classified as obese have risen significantly over a ten-year period from 1995 to 2004. More recent studies do show a slight modification of this trend, possibly because of the higher profile given to healthy eating during this decade in the UK (Coleman and Brooks, 2009). However, the apparent increase in obesity among young people has to be seen in the context of wider population trends. It is not just adolescents that are showing increased weight, but those in all age bands. Possible reasons for increased weight among those in Western countries could include genetic factors, the likelihood of a decline in physical activity already discussed, increased food intake or increased intake of particular foods such as those having certain types of fats. This is not the place to enter into a detailed discussion of nutrition, but there is no doubt that the trend towards increased weight has significant and worrying health implications.

Finally in this section some mention should be made of eating disorders such as anorexia and bulimia. A good review of these phenomena may be found in Faulkner (2007), who sets out the diagnostic criteria and the possible aetiology of the disorders. The characteristics of anorexia include a significant weight loss, a morbid fear of becoming fat, a distorted body image, and the cessation of menstruation.

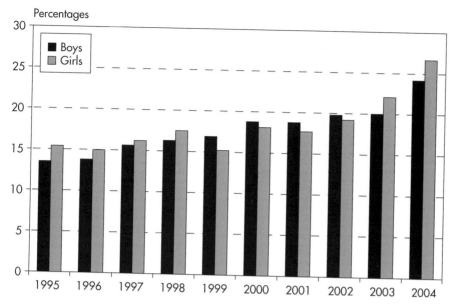

Figure 6.9 Obesity prevalence among 11–15-year-olds in England 1995–2004.

Data from: Health Survey for England 2004. The NHS Information Centre.

Source: Coleman and Schofield (2007).

Bulimia by contrast includes binge eating and a lack of control over eating behaviour. Anorexia is the more common disorder, and when it occurs can be of significant concern during adolescence. The dividing line between dieting and anorexia is often unclear, and this can cause anxiety and a preoccupation with the young person's eating behaviour on the part of parents and other carers. Females are far more likely than males to experience anorexia, and Vostanis (2007) reports that the gender ratio for this disorder in adolescence is 11:1. Various types of treatment are available, ranging from cognitive behaviour therapy to different forms of psychotherapy (see Gowers and Bryant-Waugh, 2004; Fonagy *et al.*, 2005). Eating disorders pose serious threats to mental health, and it is appropriate therefore to move now to the next section of this chapter, which is concerned with that topic.

Mental health

'I had a very difficult year last year, and I went and got counselling at that point, which was good. I'd never considered doing anything like that before because I kind of thought it was a soft option. Like "I can deal with this, and I don't need counselling. It's not like my life has fallen apart". But actually it was useful at the time. It was just a mess basically. My friend had tried to kill herself, and I was in the middle of my exams when that happened, and my parents had separated that year, and my cat was dying (laughs), and my Mum is chronically ill as well. When it's one or two things I think I can cope, but when it gets that big it's just you sort of lose the ability. . . .'

(17-year-old girl)

The very term mental health has different meanings for different people. For some, this term refers to good health, and is sometimes known as emotional health and well-being. On the other hand for other people mental health is the term used to describe disorder or illness. In the present context it will be argued that the two meanings of the term should be kept separate, and thus attention will be paid in this section of the chapter to both illness and well-being. A significant number of those who struggle during the adolescent stage of development are affected by mental illness or disorder, and thus it is essential to understand something about this topic in order to make sense of these difficulties. As was noted in Chapter 1, early theories of adolescence suggested that the stage itself could be considered to be a traumatic time, and the term 'storm and stress' was used to describe this period of life. Today these notions are no longer prevalent, but there is still debate about what proportion of young people are affected by mental illness. Whilst large-scale surveys appear to indicate that around 10 per cent have a psychological disorder, studies of depression or stress might lead one to conclude that a much higher number of young people experience problems during this stage of their lives.

This leads on to the question of what constitutes mental ill-health during adolescence. According to Vostanis (2007) the term disorder refers to a clinically recognisable set of symptoms or behaviours, linked with distress or interference with personal functions of at least two weeks duration. However, clearly mental health is a continuum, operating on many levels. A young person may be experiencing difficulties in one area, but functioning perfectly well in other areas. For this

reason no single aspect of behaviour can be described as 'normal' or 'abnormal', but rather the behaviour will need to be judged against a number of criteria including its duration, severity, the coexistence of other signs of distress, and the impact of the behaviour on the young person and on the family.

Whilst these criteria apply to everyone, there are special challenges when trying to establish the 'normality' of some aspects of adolescent behaviour. This is because of the wide range of emotional and social changes occurring during adolescence, and the fact that some behaviour caused by these changes can appear odd or peculiar to the outside world. If for example a young person is shy, withdrawn, uncommunicative, or depressed, how can this be distinguished from mental ill-health that requires treatment? The answer usually lies in the criteria mentioned above, such as the length of time the behaviour continues, how serious it appears, and most importantly, what the impact is on the young person and on those caring for him or her. Further information on these questions can be found in Goodman and Scott (2005) and in Bailey and Shooter (2009). In this section of the chapter there will be a discussion of

- emotional health and well-being
- the incidence of mental ill-health in this age group
- suicide and self-harm
- depression and other disorders
- a short review of interventions.

In recent years there has been a significant increase in the interest paid to emotional health and well-being. There are a number of reasons for this. In the first place publications such as that of Daniel Goleman (1996) on emotional intelligence have raised awareness of emotional health, and have chimed well with the growing interest in brain development. A world-wide concern over the possibility of increasing rates of mental disorder in young people (Rutter and Smith, 1995) has also played its part in emphasising the importance of mental health promotion. Thirdly there has been a gradual movement towards seeing the school as a suitable place for education on this topic. Thus programmes have been developed to address the stigma of mental ill-health, as well as for the promotion of well-being (Ogden *et al.*, 2009; Coleman, 2009).

Whilst it would be helpful to be able to suggest a clear definition of emotional health and well-being, there is unfortunately no agreement on the exact scope of this concept. For some it refers to emotional literacy, defined by Katherine Weare as follows:

> The ability to understand ourselves and other people, and in particular to be aware of, understand, and use information about the emotional states of ourselves and others with competence. It includes the ability to understand, express and manage our own emotions, and respond to the emotions of others, in ways that are helpful to ourselves and others.
>
> (2004, p. 2)

For Weare this definition is useful in that it allows her to go on to define a range of competencies relating to emotional literacy, thus putting the concept into operational terms. Not all writers on this topic take quite the same view, as can be seen in Coleman's (2009) review. For some authors emotional health and well-being refers to having resilience and coping skills, whilst others prefer to look at concepts of happiness or something similar. Research which considers the effectiveness of mental health promotion programmes indicates that such work is still at an early stage of development. What is clear, however, is that outcomes of such programmes depend on having clearly defined goals, having well-trained practitioners delivering the programmes, and most important of all, having young people involved at all stages in both the planning and delivery (Coleman, 2007).

The link between well-being and mental ill-health is complex, but important to understand. The most helpful way to conceptualise it is as a continuum from good to bad health, with well-being at one end and disorder at the other. It is now time to turn to the end of the continuum concerned with poor health.

Mental ill-health carries with it a significant degree of disadvantage extending to almost all aspects of development. Writing in a major survey of mental disorder in Britain, Green *et al.* (2005) pointed out that those with such disorders were likely to miss more school, have fewer friends and a more limited social network, and that their problems were likely to impact on other family members. Mental health problems are not equally distributed across society. One of the most striking findings in the survey by Green and colleagues (2005) is that mental ill-health is strongly associated with poverty and disadvantage. Rates of disorder are twice as high in young people being brought up in lone-parent families as they are in young people living in couple families, and also very much higher in families with a history of parental unemployment. These factors link with other indices of deprivation, such as low family income, poor housing and physical ill-health.

In terms of actual rates of disorder, the survey by Green *et al.* (2005) found that nearly one in ten children and young people in England and Wales could be classified as having a disorder. However this figure is an average taken from a number of different statistics, so that fewer boys than girls have a disorder, and the numbers for both genders increase with age. Boys are more likely to have conduct disorders, whilst girls are more likely to have emotional disorders, including depression and anxiety. The question of whether disorders are increasing has already been mentioned, and it is of interest to note that the survey by Green *et al.* (2005) can be compared with a similar survey five years earlier (Meltzer *et al.*, 2000). This reported a similar rate of disorder to that found in 2005, allowing the conclusion that there had been no change between these two time periods. However, this finding is in contrast to that reported by Collishaw *et al.* (2004), which investigated a range of disorders over 25 years. The results of this study showed that between 1974 and 1999, among both boys and girls in the UK, there were increases in conduct disorders and in emotional problems. There results are illustrated in Figure 6.10. Various explanations have been put forward for the results, including higher levels of exam stress, the changing employment market, and increasing alcohol and substance misuse. More research is clearly needed in the investigation of time trends, but for the present it can be said that there were changes during the 1980s and 1990s, but that the rates of disorder may have levelled out during the period from 2000 onwards.

Turning now to suicide and self-harm, in the field of adolescent mental health this is possibly one of the most difficult subjects to deal with. As one young woman expressed it: 'Nobody knows anything about death, suicide. . . . Suicide is probably the most frightening thing. If you mention it to somebody they don't want to talk about it. That's it, they close up. They don't want to know because it's too scary' (Coleman, 2004). It is important to understand that completed suicide differs from self-harm. During adolescence completed suicide is very much more common in males, whilst self-harm is twice as likely to occur in females as it is in males. There is a substantial literature on the differences between these two types of behaviour (e.g. Alsaker and Dick-Niederhauser, 2006; Windfuhr *et al.*, 2008). Self-harm encompasses a range of behaviours, including self-poisoning and various

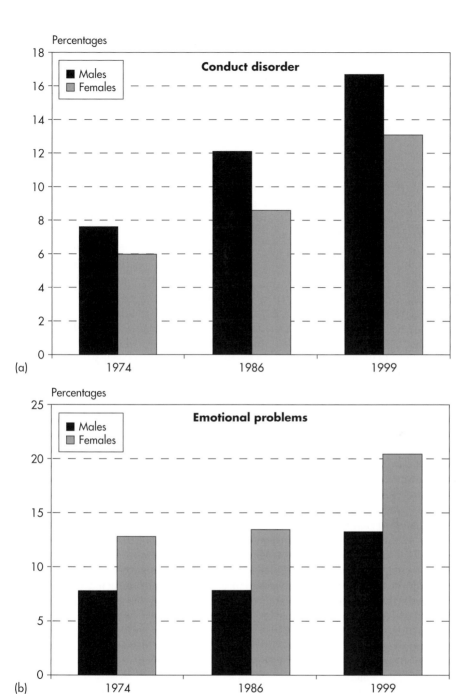

Figure 6.10 Proportions of 15–16-year-olds in Britain with conduct (a) and emotional problems (b), by gender and cohort, 1974–1999.

Data from: Collishaw *et al.* 2004.

Source: Coleman and Schofield (2007).

types of mutilation and self-injury. Many young people who self-harm do not intend to kill themselves, whilst the majority who use methods such as hanging, shooting or jumping off high buildings are obviously serious about taking their own lives. Parents as well as professionals often find self-harming behaviour extremely puzzling, since it is difficult to understand why young people should cut their wrists or take an overdose of pills if they have no intention of dying. It is for this reason that such behaviour is frequently termed 'a cry for help'. Whilst there is some truth in this, it may be too simplistic to explain the wide range of self-harming behaviours seen in young people. Serious self-mutilation, for example, may be a reflection of the pain felt by the individual as a result of sexual abuse or other overwhelming trauma.

In terms of the numbers of young people who complete suicide, research shows that in Britain, among young men, the rates have fallen since the mid-1990s (Windfuhr et al., 2008; Coleman and Brooks, 2009). To be more specific the rates for males between the ages of 15 and 25 were 18 per 100,000 in 1993, whilst they had fallen to 10 per 100,000 in 2006. This is a highly significant reduction, and it is far from clear why this has occurred. A reduction in rates of youth unemployment over this period may be one explanation, with another being the increase in funding that has gone to mental health services. Interestingly there has not been a similar decrease in rates of self-harm, as these have remained relatively constant in recent years (Hawton et al., 2003). Rates of completed suicide in most other European countries have not fallen either, although there are very large differences between the rates in different countries (Alsaker and Dick-Niederhauser, 2006). Russia, Finland and Ireland have the highest rates, whilst Portugal, Spain and Greece have low rates of completed suicide among males between the ages of 15 and 19. Many studies have considered the factors that might predispose a young person to take their own life (e.g. Gunnell, 2000; Bridge et al., 2006). Although there is no one pattern or set of factors that applies in all cases, it can be concluded that the following are some of the most common risk factors: having a family history of suicide, being close to someone who has committed suicide, suffering from serious depression or other psychological disorder, and a previous history of self-harm. Suicide is associated with alcohol and substance misuse, and is more common in particular groups such as those who have been abused or those who are in custody.

There is a close link between depression and suicidal behaviour. It is undoubtedly the case that long-standing depression and hopelessness underlies much self-destructive behaviour. However, many young people have times when they feel depressed, and indeed some would argue that periods of depression are almost inevitable as part of the journey through adolescence. Of course this all depends on how depression is defined. There is a critical difference between, on the one hand, a state which includes low mood, sadness and brief periods of misery, and on the other a state of chronic depression which includes bodily dysfunction, a sense of worthlessness, and hopelessness about the future. Studies show that between 30 per cent and 50 per cent of young people at some time experience the first state, but that only a small group experience the latter state.

In an important article entitled 'Is there an epidemic of child or adolescent depression?' Costello et al. (2006) were able to show, after carrying out a meta-analysis of 26 different studies, that rates of depression among young people in developed countries had not risen in 30 years between 1965 and 1996. There is no reason to suppose that this has changed in the past decade. In this study, using a generally accepted diagnostic measurement, Costello *et al.* (2006) reported that 5.9 per cent of girls and 4.6 per cent of boys between the ages of 13 and 18 could be said to have a formal diagnosis of depression. An alternative view is that put forward by West and Sweeting (2003), who argue that levels of stress and emotional disorder among 15-year-old girls in Scotland have risen significantly over a ten-year span, with over 30 per cent currently falling into this category. They put this down to increased pressure at school, linked to the culture of assessment and the excessive emphasis placed on testing. The explanation for the differences between the studies no doubt lies partly in the definitions of emotional disorder, but also possibly in the particular situation in schools in Scotland. Galambos *et al.* (2004) carried out a longitudinal study of depression in young people in Canada over a six-year period. They showed that levels of depression gradually increased from early to late adolescence, with gender differences (higher levels of depression in girls) becoming more marked with age. Over time increases in depression were linked with decreases in social support and with increases in smoking. Such findings have implications for intervention and treatment programmes, and lead neatly on to the next area of discussion.

To conclude this section some brief mention of intervention in the mental health field is necessary. Clearly there is a wide range of literature on this subject, and only the shortest note will be possible here. Useful introductions can be found in Fonagy *et al.* (2005), and in Ogden *et al.* (2009). Both reviews distinguish between the following things:

- whether the intervention is medical or non-medical, and in particular whether psychotropic medication is used;
- the theoretical basis of the intervention, i.e. whether it is cognitive-behavioural or psychodynamic;
- the location of the intervention, e.g. whether it is based in the family, the school or the community.

Since there are such a variety of conditions that may require treatment it is inevitable that many different approaches are available, and decisions about the choice of approach will depend on the severity of condition, the professional background of the therapist, the referral process and the interventions available in the young person's environment. Two issues of particular interest will be addressed here: first, the evidence base for different interventions, and second, some recent trends in intervention research.

As far as the evidence base is concerned, there has been much debate about the effectiveness of psychotherapy and other psychodynamic approaches, and these are often compared unfavourably with cognitive-behavioural approaches. However, these latter approaches usually have more easily defined outcomes, and more limited treatment goals, so the comparison may be unhelpful. As Fonagy *et al.* (2005) argue, different interventions may be appropriate in different circumstances, and indeed there is often a case for a multi-modal approach to adolescent disturbance. In summarising their work Fonagy and his colleagues draw a number of important conclusions, which include an emphasis on the developmental characteristics of adolescence, the need for a clear and explicit rationale for any treatment choice, the importance of having well-defined goals for any intervention, and the necessity to recognise the contribution of all professions, rather than prioritising the medical approach.

A number of new trends in the intervention literature relevant to adolescents have become apparent in recent years, and some of these are documented in Ogden *et al.* (2009) and in Stattin and Kerr (2009). Firstly there is a growing emphasis on prevention, and this has important links both with the topic of emotional health and well-being discussed earlier in this chapter, as well as with the changing role of the school and its place as a site for mental health promotion. To take some examples Giannotta *et al.* (2009) report on an Italian school-based intervention programme for social relationship problems, whilst Wenzel *et al.* (2009) are able to show the effectiveness of a German life-skills programme for the prevention of substance abuse. Another interesting trend has been the growth of parenting programmes, and the impact of these on the mental health of young people. This topic was covered in some detail in Chapter 5, but it certainly has a place here, not least because of the work of Gerald Patterson and the Oregon Social Learning Centre (Dishion and Patterson, 2006). Finally the development of programmes such as Multisystemic Therapy (MST), which includes intensive assessment and both family therapy and behavioural techniques, may be mentioned as evidence that clinicians and researchers are thinking of new ways to approach what have seemed to be intractable problems. Because of its expense, MST has until recently been used primarily in the USA. However, Ogden and Hagen (2009) report on a programme in which Norway is offering MST on a country-wide basis, and other European countries may well follow suit.

Health promotion

'School basically teaches you about anything you need to know. We have citizen lessons, and when we were in Year 7 they went through, like, sex education, and all the girls had a talk about periods. They basically tell you everything, and it was good. It made us all feel it was, like, normal.'

(15-year-old girl)

It is appropriate to end this chapter on health with a short section on health promotion. This is seen as a key role for the school, but in addition there is a growing interest in the part that can be played by youth workers and other professionals, as well as by the internet and other media. However, health promotion for young people has associated with it a number of contentious questions. What is the role of the family, particularly in relation to sex education? What approach should be taken regarding the use of such things as illegal drugs? Is the 'Just Say No' approach the right one, or is it better to recognise that young people will experiment, and opt for a harm minimisation approach? Is it best to have adults delivering the health promotion messages, or can peer mentoring be more effective with adolescents? In this section there will be a discussion of why health promotion is important, where it should be done, who is best to carry out health promotion, the role of adult and peer mentoring, the importance of digital technologies, and finally a note on the best way to put across health messages to young people.

As was noted at the beginning of this chapter, the views of adults and young people on health matters are not always the same. In spite of this, the adolescent stage is a critical one for health promotion. In the first place young people are in fact curious and interested in health matters at this time of their lives. Whilst they may not be interested in the long-term consequences of health behaviour, which is seen as an adult concern, they do want information on topics of importance to them. As is illustrated in Macfarlane and McPherson (2007), adolescents are concerned, among other things, about stress and depression, the size and shape of their bodies, cancer and other illnesses, skin and hair care, and about various aspects of sexual development. The number of hits on websites such as www.teenagehealthfreak. org (Figure 6.11) are testament to the need for information at this age. A second reason for the relevance of health promotion during adolescence is that, although

Figure 6.11 A page from the Teenage Health Freak website.

Source: The website Teenage Health Freak www.teenagehealthfreak.org. By permission of Dr Aidan Macfarlane.

in general young people have good health, there are a minority growing up in poverty and deprivation who have very poor health. This group do not find it easy to access conventional health services, which is all the more reason why health promotion can play a significant role here. A third reason for the importance of health promotion is that health risks associated with drinking too much alcohol or using cannabis can be reduced through the provision of good quality information. As long as this information is put across in a non-judgemental fashion it can play an important role in helping young people learn how to stay safe.

With regard to the question of who is best to undertake health promotion, and where it is best carried out, it can be noted that the school is the pre-eminent site for this activity. However, as emphasised by Mackinnon (2007), the media, digital technologies and the community can be important partners in this endeavour. There are many advantages to be gained in making use of the school setting for the purpose of health promotion (Young, 2004). More young people can be reached in this way than in any other setting, there is the likelihood of well-trained professionals being available, health promotion can be linked to other topics being covered in the curriculum, and parents are generally positive about the role of the school for this purpose. However, those who are disaffected or who are absent from school may miss out, and teachers are not always the best people to deliver adolescent-friendly health messages. It is for these reasons that it is essential to support community facilities such as youth clubs in becoming involved in health promotion, as it is only in this way that young people who are out of school or who feel marginalised may gain access to health promotion information (Mackinnon, 2007).

There are some who take the view that young people are more likely to listen to messages delivered by those of their own age than to messages put across by adults. This has led to a growing interest in peer mentoring or peer-led health education (Milburn, 1995; Cowie et al., 2004). There are some obvious advantages to be gained from this approach to health promotion. These include:

- Peer education makes use of existing social connections and networks.
- It can provide the opportunity to reach vulnerable groups.
- Young people may be seen as credible sources of information.
- Peer educators are seen as less likely to break confidences.
- Such activity can assist in the development of skills in the peer educators.

Whilst these advantages are attractive, research has also shown that there are pitfalls which should not be ignored. In the first place, peer mentoring or education will only work if young people receive appropriate training beforehand as well as support on an ongoing basis. Secondly it is essential to ensure that the goals of the adults are in tune with those of the peer educators, as conflict between the two groups will undermine any health promotion activity. Lastly it will normally only be possible to reach small numbers with this approach, so that if programmes are to reach out to a wider audience this can become a very expensive option (Eden and Roker, 2002; Mackinnon, 2007).

A perspective on the key elements of effective health promotion will be a useful way to conclude this section. Based on research in this field (Mackinnon,

2007) it may be suggested that there are three features of health promotion that will contribute to its effectiveness. These are:

- That it is communicative, rather than moralistic or didactic.
- That it is empowering.
- That it is participative.

In the best of circumstances, of course, these three elements should work together. Taking communication first, health promotion should have the intention of imparting information in an objective and easily accessible manner. How this is done has a significant impact on the way the information is received. Topics to do with health have the potential to be highly value-laden, in particular information to do with sex and relationships, smoking, alcohol and drugs, and even such seemingly neutral subjects as cancer prevention. Prevention of skin cancer through sensible protection from sunburn is a good example. Because this is a topic that is related to holiday behaviour, if warnings about this risk are put across with an 'adult knows best' approach they can be construed as 'kill-joy' and 'anti-fun'. This is obviously an even greater problem where topics such as sex are discussed within a moral framework. Thus health promotion programmes, if they are to be effective, will seek to avoid any hint of an underlying or unspoken message. They will work hard to create trusting relationships with young people, and to show that their role is to communicate information which is seen and understood to be accurate and objective.

Empowerment is the second principle of effective health promotion. By this is meant health promotion which gives young people a sense of control over their own health and well-being. There are various ways in which this can be achieved, partly of course through good communication and well-planned activities, but also through opportunities for participation. This is the third principle, and is of course closely linked to empowerment. Participation in this context refers to programmes which allow young people to understand how health services are run and to play a part in developing and monitoring such services. As Mackinnon (2007) notes, creating empowerment in relation to health promotion is not as easy as it may appear. Youth consultation can simply be a tick-box exercise, and in spite of much greater interest in this topic in recent years there is still a shortage of well-trained professionals who understand the principles of empowerment and participation.

One of the most influential concepts relating to participation has been Hart's Ladder of Participation (Hart, 1997). In this Hart shows how there are many different ways in which adults can offer what looks like participation to young people. These can range from opportunities that are essentially tokenistic, where for example young people's voices are used to carry adult messages, through to what is set out as being the top of the ladder, where activities are initiated by young people, with adults providing support and endorsement where necessary. Hart's Ladder is shown in Figure 6.12. Eden and Roker (2002) carried out research with a number of organisations where participation of adolescents was the central objective. Eden and Roker showed that, where adults left young people alone to get on with things, they rarely flourished. On the other hand where adults took the lead, young people soon lost interest. The organisations which were the most

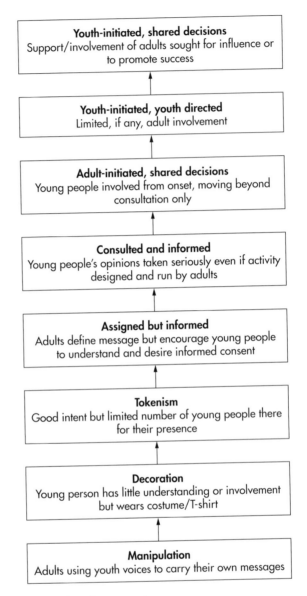

Figure 6.12 Hart's Ladder of Participation.

Source: Coleman *et al.* (2007).

successful were ones where adults offered support, allowed young people to take the initiative, and stood back, only becoming involved when asked. This is nothing less than a model of good parenting! What is clear is that, if health promotion is to be effective, adults have to think carefully about their role. What is required is not just good communication, but an attitude which facilitates both empowerment and genuine participation.

Implications for practice

1. In some respects the adolescent population is a healthy group compared with other age groups. However, that fact takes no account of the health inequalities that apply to young people living in disadvantaged circumstances, and nor does it acknowledge that all young people worry about their health and want access to good quality information and appropriate health services.

2. It is important to recognise that young people have a different understanding of health from most adults. While adult concerns have to do with what is seen as 'risk-taking', and with a deterioration in indices of young people's health, adolescent concerns are very much to do with the need for good quality information, and with the here and now of managing social situations. Young people worry about aspects of health such as diet and nutrition, stress and emotional health, hair and skin care, and sexual health matters, and it can be seen that these are subjects that affect their everyday lives. Young people are very concerned about health matters, but if this concern is to be harnessed then it is important for adults to understand the differences between the generations in attitudes to health.

3. One of the areas of health concern for young people relates to mental health. It is clear that a minority, but a significant minority, of adolescents do experience some difficulty in this domain, and yet there is too little support available to deal with these issues. In particular problems with bullying, conflict at home or with close friends, feelings of depression or even suicidal thoughts – all these do occur among adolescents, especially among those suffering disadvantage, or among those in vulnerable situations such as being in care or in custody. There is too little opportunity for discussion of these issues, and too much stigma still associated with mental health problems. The more that can be done to address the problem of stigma where mental health is concerned, the better.

4. Health promotion with adolescents is an important aspect of health provision. In this chapter the following three aspects of good health promotion have been noted: the communication of good quality, credible information; the empowerment of young people where their health is concerned; and the provision of opportunities for participation. If these aspects of health promotion can be emphasised, then young people will be well served by professionals working in this field.

5. Lastly where health services and interventions for young people are concerned, it is still the case that too little attention is paid to young people's views on what is best for them. Services are often planned with little thought given to matters of access, confidentiality, and the needs of young people. Where resources exist which have been planned jointly with young people there is always a much higher rate of service use. Involving young people in planning and service delivery is not always easy, but when it is achieved it pays handsome dividends.

Further reading

Coleman, J and Brooks, F (2009) *Key data on adolescence*, 7th edn. Young People
    in Focus. Brighton. www.youngpeopleinfocus.org.uk
A compilation of statistics about young people, with a strong focus on health issues.
Four of the seven chapters deal with health matters.

Coleman, J, Hendry, L and Kloep, M (Eds) (2007) *Adolescence and health*. John
    Wiley. Chichester.
This book includes a series of chapters dealing with various issues to do with
adolescent health. All the authors are British, and the book deals with health
delivery as well as basic research.

Fonagy, P, Target, M, Cottrell, D, Phillips, J and Kurtz, Z (2002) *What works for
    whom? A critical review of treatments for children and adolescents*. Guilford
    Press. New York.
An excellent book describing therapeutic interventions relating to mental health,
with summaries of the evidence base for each treatment approach.

Graham, P (2004) *The end of adolescence*. Oxford University Press. Oxford.
Although this is a general book about adolescence, it has a strong health slant.
There are chapters on moods, eating, sex, alcohol and drug use. It is easy to read,
and very informative.

Sexual development

'I think kissing is the furthest any of my friends has gone, but there are people in my year that think they're older than they are! They do kind of get into that kind of thing. My friends are kind of like enjoying life as they go along, and not trying to be older than they are.'

(14-year-old girl)

'I find it hard, because I have a boyfriend now, and if I say, I'll come round to your house, and then we'll be like "OK we've got to do homework as well", because we've got so much to do, but then it just turns into we just talk the whole night, and the homework's just left there!'

(17-year-old girl)

Sexual development is a central strand of all adolescent experience. Underlying this is the biological maturation which starts at the outset of puberty. However, sexual development involves not only biological change, but also growth and maturation in the social and emotional worlds of the young person. In this chapter some of these changes will be documented, and consideration will be given to how the experiences of adolescents interact with and are affected by the context in which they grow up. Adolescent sexuality is influenced by a range of factors; these may be internal, as for example the rate of pubertal maturation, or they may be external, such as the type of family and neighbourhood, as well as the political and cultural climate of the time. The developing sexuality of the young person may be a source of considerable anxiety, both to the teenagers themselves, and to the adults responsible for their care and education. This is especially so where young people appear to be at risk of unwanted pregnancy or sexually transmitted infections. In the course of the chapter some consideration will be given to safe sexual practices, as well as to changing patterns of sexual behaviour, the context and timing of sexual activity, romance and intimacy, gay and lesbian sex, teenage pregnancy, and effective sex and relationships education.

Changing patterns of sexual behaviour

'There's definitely a sense that it's all much younger now. Even from when I was first in secondary school, it's got younger again for my brother, and people start having relationships at primary school, and you don't know what you're doing at that age, do you? Like for me at that age I thought boys were horrible, and they were smelly (laughs)!'

(17-year-old girl)

The era of the 1960s is usually held up as the height of sexual permissiveness, but in fact patterns of sexual behaviour continue to change and evolve. Evidence from four studies carried out in the 1960s, the 1970s, the 1990s and in 2002 indicates just how much change there can be over a 40-year period. As can be seen from Figure 7.1, increasing numbers of both young men and young women report becoming sexually active by the age of 16 over this time period. Another very interesting feature of this chart is the decreasing gap between the two genders in

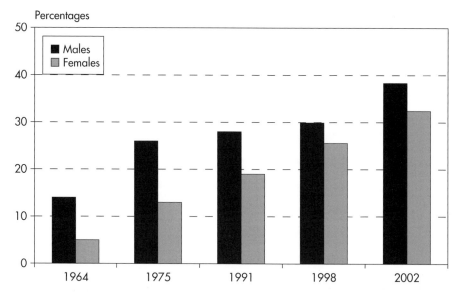

Figure 7.1 Reported first sexual intercourse before the age of 16, by gender, in Britain from 1964 to 2002, based on Schofield (1965), Farrell (1978), Johnson *et al.* (1994), Wellings *et al.* (2001) and Currie (2004).

Source: Coleman and Brooks (2009).

reporting of sexual activity. Whilst in earlier studies far more males than females reported having sex by the age of 16, by 2002 young men and young women were much closer together. It is not clear whether this change is because of actual behaviour, or because of changing social norms which make it more acceptable for women to report being sexually active.

This question of the validity of data on sexual behaviour is a key feature of any research in this area. Savin-Williams and Diamond (2004) set out the difficulties of investigating sex in young people, identifying a number of problems in the field. In the first place there is the issue of defining sex. What does 'having sex' mean to different people? Most agree that intercourse involving vaginal penetration is sex, but what other activities, such as masturbation or anal sex, might be included here? Clear definitions are essential, and researchers have to be careful to be inclusive, and to cover the range of sexual behaviour, both heterosexual and homosexual, if any survey is to be considered valid. Another problem discussed by Savin-Williams and Diamond (2004) is that of recall. Since very little research in this area is done with those under the age of 16, it is frequently the case that participants are being asked to remember past events. A number of studies show that young people do not report their sexual behaviour in a reliable manner. To take one example, research by Upchurch *et al.* (2002) indicated that only 22 per cent of young people aged 16 to 18 who were sexually active were consistent in their reporting. The great majority changed the date of their first sex when re-interviewed at a later date.

The evidence illustrated in Figure 7.1 indicates that, whatever the problems of carrying out research in this area, it is hard to dispute the existence of a trend with

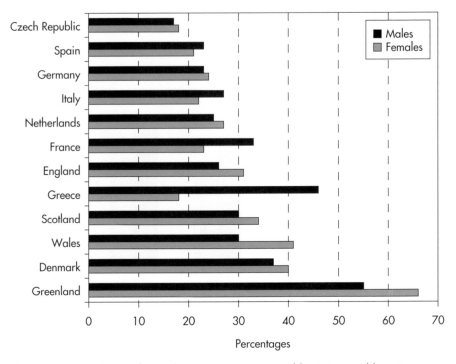

Figure 7.2 Experience of sexual intercourse as reported by 15-year-olds in Europe in 2006.

Data from: Currie *et al.* (2008).

Source: Coleman and Brooks (2009).

more young people becoming sexually active at an earlier age. The data in Figure 7.1 are from Great Britain, and they show that in 2002 somewhere between 30 per cent and 35 per cent of young people reported having sex by the age of 16. Information in Figure 7.2 puts this picture into an international perspective, and shows a similar picture, with England and Scotland being somewhere in the middle of the range. These figures are based on a survey carried out in 2006, and as far as the UK was concerned, involved only England and Scotland. Here it can be seen that again around 30 per cent of young people reported having had sex by the age of 16.

Apart from the increase over time in the numbers reporting sexual activity, another historical change noted by many commentators is the possibility that young people are engaging today in a wider range of sexual behaviours. The possibility of anal sex has already been mentioned above, and there have also been reports of a much greater number of young people engaging in oral sex. It would appear that formerly negative attitudes to what might be called less conventional sexual practices are shifting, with a greater acceptance today of a wider range of sexual behaviour. Moore and Rosenthal discuss this possibility in their book *Sexuality in adolescence: current trends* (2006), and they specifically include a section on 'variety of practices'. In this context they also note that 'solo' sex should

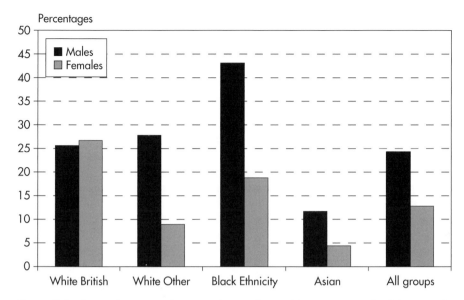

Figure 7.3 Proportions reporting experience of sexual intercourse under 16 years of age, by ethnicity, in Britain in 2005.

Data from: Testa and Coleman (2006).

Source: Coleman and Brooks (2009).

not be ignored, since, as their research indicates, this clearly gives many young people pleasure and gratification. This serves to reiterate the question posed earlier: 'What does having sex mean to different people?'

In considering this question two particularly important factors are gender and ethnicity. Numerous books and publications have indicated that sex does not mean the same for men and women, and in the context of adolescence this is manifestly a matter of some significance. More will be said about this in later sections of the chapter. Looking at ethnicity, research has shown that, as might be expected, there are marked differences between cultural groups. To take one example, research by Testa and Coleman (2006) in England indicates that substantially more Black males report being sexually active at 16 than do other ethnic groups, with Asian young people reporting the lowest levels of sexual activity at this age (Figure 7.3). Steinberg (2008) outlines a broadly similar pattern of ethnic difference in the USA, with African-American young people becoming sexually active at an earlier age than other groups. Moore and Rosenthal (2006) report two interesting cultural differences in the Australian context. Research in that country shows young people of Chinese background reporting less sexual activity than other groups, whilst the greatest discrepancy between what young men and young women report is to be found in the Greek community, with significantly more boys than girls reporting being sexually active. A consideration of these patterns of behaviour leads on to a discussion of some of the factors that are influential in the context and timing of adolescent sexual development.

The context and timing of adolescent sexual behaviour

'Yes, most of my friends, they all have boyfriends and stuff. We've all had boyfriends and stuff, but it's like stayed that way, it's not gone any further for sex and stuff. There's people higher up in the school and they're kind of more pressured to do stuff with their boyfriends, but people in our year at the moment they don't want to. . . . But I think in the next coming year people will be more pressured to do stuff.'

(14-year-old girl)

It may appear self-evident, but it is important to state that the sexual behaviour of young people takes place in the context of adult attitudes and behaviour. In much public debate about this subject commentators give the impression that they think young people are somehow cut off or detached from what is going on in the rest of society. Adolescents are blamed for having permissive attitudes, or for indulging in casual sex without considering the consequences. The fact is, however, that the sexual development of young people is affected in a fundamental sense by what is taking place around them. Today we live in a society which is remarkably open about sexuality. Many of the taboos which operated thirty or forty years ago have disappeared, and as a result sex is pervasive in our lives.

Young people see sex on the television, on film, on advertising hoardings and in the print media. More importantly they know about adults around them, whether in the family or the neighbourhood, who are having sexual relationships outside marriage. They can see that adults pursue sexual gratification without always considering the consequences. They can see that adults place sexual satisfaction high on their list of personal goals, and not surprisingly they are influenced by such experience. To believe that adolescents live in a world of their own is both unrealistic and unhelpful. Adolescent sexuality cannot be understood without recognising the context in which it occurs and acknowledging the major influence of adult sexual behaviour.

Of the range of social factors impacting on the sexuality of young people it is perhaps the family which should be considered first. Writers such as Crockett *et al.* (2003) and Moore and Rosenthal (2006) have outlined the ways in which parents and other family members influence young people in this sphere. First, parents themselves have attitudes about sexuality. These may be to do with the body and its functions, with privacy, with pleasure, with shame and guilt, and of course with the nature of intimate relationships. Parents will also have attitudes about gender, including such things as sex roles, power distribution, and communication between men and women. All these parental attitudes will be influential in determining how a boy or girl develops sexually. In addition to attitudes, parental behaviour also offers role models for young people. Thus, the way the mother and father relate to each other, the way they deal with decision-making, the way they treat each other, and the way they behave sexually will offer powerful models which will undoubtedly influence their sons and daughters.

One obvious example of this is the substantial body of research showing that young people in families where parents have divorced or separated are likely to become sexually active at an earlier age than those living in intact families. In one study Crockett *et al.* (1996) compared the effects of living with a single parent to other variables such as socio-economic status, pubertal timing, school performance, sibling behaviour and so on. These authors showed that, of all the variables, parental circumstance was the most significant factor influencing sexual debut, for both boys and girls. Many other researchers have shown similar findings (e.g. Davis and Friel, 2001). A variety of explanations have been put forward for this result, including exposure to permissive sexual norms, as well as reduced parental monitoring and supervision. Moore and Rosenthal (2006) use the words of a young woman to illustrate one possible explanation.

> 'If your parents are divorced or separated, and your Mum or Dad brings home different people on weekends and each night of the week and stuff, then you sort of think that (having sex) is no big deal. It is not special or anything like that. But if your parents are married and stuff like that, you sort of see it as a big deal, and should only share it if you love the person.'
>
> (2006, p. 101)

There are many different ways in which parents can be influential. In some circumstances parents may be the most effective sex educators, especially if they are open without being intrusive, and willing to deal with the young person's agenda, rather than with their own. As noted above, parents can offer monitoring and supervision, assisting teenagers to delay involvement in sexual activity. Alternatively they may leave adolescents to set their own boundaries, and make their own decisions about the pace of their sexual development. In one longitudinal study carried out in Scotland (Wight *et al.*, 2006) results were clear that in situations where parental monitoring was low there was a greater chance of early sexual behaviour in both boys and girls. Among girls low parental monitoring was also associated with multiple partners and less condom use.

Many studies have looked at the role of communication about sex between parent and adolescent, but the results are far from clear-cut. Aspy *et al.* (2007) report results indicating that the more parents discuss matters with young people in the family, the more likely it is that young people will delay sexual activity, or will use appropriate contraception if they do become sexually active. On the other hand Steinberg (2008) reviews a number of studies indicating that it is not so much the discussion that matters, but rather it is the attitudes and values that are communicated within the discussion that are crucial. If attitudes and values are congruent with those of the young person, then there is a greater likelihood that communication between parent and teenager will have an impact on behaviour. Solomon *et al.* (2002) make a nice point when they note that there are some important tensions within the concept of communication. As these authors note, while both adults and young people may subscribe to ideas of openness and honesty, in fact they come to this from opposing points of the compass. For parents, openness means having more information about what young people are doing, and thus retaining power and control in this vital area. On the other hand for young people withholding information, especially about something as important as sex, means that they gain privacy, identity and power.

The contortions that parents get themselves into when trying to discuss sex are illustrated by this young woman's reminiscences about her mother.

'It must have been when we were having stuff at school on it, and one day I remember I was walking along the track, and Mum says to me: "So you know how to do it now then?" So I said well I knew already, you know, because I did. Then she said: "You know properly now, and all this lot." And I was getting really embarrassed, and I was saying yeh, like this, and I was trying to get on to a different subject. And she was saying: "So you know how to make a baby, and how to look after a baby" and all this rubbish. So I goes "Yes, Mum", and I was trying to get off the subject all the time.'

(Coleman, 2001, p. 23)

A different approach to this issue is exemplified by the important work of Udry and his colleagues (Udry and Billy, 1987; Udry, 1990). Udry has been concerned to distinguish between social and biological influences on sexual behaviour. By measuring the levels of different hormones during adolescence, as well as sexual behaviour and the attitudes of friends and parents, Udry has constructed

a model of social and biological interaction. Using this model he is able to show that social factors are far more important in influencing girls' involvement in sexual activity than in influencing boys' activity. Although increases in the hormone androgen lead to an increased interest in sex among girls, whether this interest is translated into behaviour depends on the social environment. Girls who have high levels of androgens will only become sexually active if they have friends who are similarly inclined, or if they have parents who are permissive. If such girls are in a less encouraging environment then they are less likely to be sexually active.

These social controls to do not appear to act in a similar way for boys, in whom high levels of androgens are likely to lead to sexual activity, regardless of the social context. To explain these gender differences Udry argues that boys develop in an environment which is generally more tolerant and encouraging of male sexuality than of female sexuality. As a result the stimulus given to boys by the changes in their hormone levels is quite sufficient to instigate sexual behaviour. For girls the situation is more complex, where social controls may be more influential in determining behaviour. Savin-Williams and Diamond (2004) discuss the gender differences in a similar manner, agreeing that female sexuality is more contextual than male sexuality. As they say, it is almost considered conventional wisdom now to believe that boys experience sexual desire because of biological processes and a physical need for sex, whereas girls, on the other hand, experience sexual desire because of interpersonal relationships associated with romantic love. These differences may be important, but they should be approached with some caution, especially since they over-simplify what is of course a many-faceted picture. There are major individual differences within both males and females where sexual desire is concerned, and numerous other cultural and contextual variables will play their part in determining sexual behaviour. Since romance has now been mentioned, it is time to look more closely at this feature of adolescent sexual behaviour.

Romance and intimacy

'I don't know, I think it's good that people are free to have boyfriends and girlfriends if they want to, as long as there's no pressure that they have to. I don't have one, and I don't particularly feel. . . . Well, there's no-one I want to be with, there's no pressure to have a boyfriend for the sake of having a boyfriend. I think there's some people in my friendship group for whom being in a relationship is an absolutely key thing, they have to because it's their way of feeling wanted, like if someone cares what they are doing each weekend and stuff like that.'

(17-year-old girl)

'The thing about being in school, being in a relationship, you get judged by your friends in a way, you have to deal with your friends as well. So if your friends don't approve . . . well . . . like, if the person you are going out with isn't approved by your friends, and because your friends would normally approve it on looks, it depends on looks a bit more than it does when you're an adult.'

(15-year-old boy)

One of the criticisms that is sometimes levelled at academic researchers engaged in studying sexuality in young people is that there is far too much emphasis on behaviour (on who has done what at which age), and not enough interest in the meaning of sexual relationships. It is important therefore to pay some attention to ideas of love, romance and intimacy. This is especially so since it is evident that an experience of passionate love, or an all-consuming involvement in an intimate relationship can become the most important thing in a young person's life.

As commentators have frequently noted, falling in love is an integral part of the adolescent experience. Both Zani and Cicognani (2006) and Moore and Rosenthal (2006) draw on the ideas of Erikson, and suggest that falling in love is part of the search for identity or self-definition. As they point out, for Erikson the resolution of

the identity crisis depends partly on the ability to experience intimacy. According to Erikson intimacy involves openness, sharing, trust and commitment. Thus an experience of intimacy contributes to the development of identity, and maturity, through opportunities for self-exploration. The intimate relationship enables the young person to hold up a mirror to herself/himself, even if it is a distorted one, as well as to experience a sense of extraordinary closeness with another which must, in some way, echo the contact between mother and child in infancy. It is perhaps for this reason that falling in love in adolescence has an intensity that is different from that experienced in adulthood.

Until recently there has been little research in this area, but since the late 1990s an increased interest in the topic of romantic relationships has become apparent. One perspective has been outlined by Brown (1999) who identified four stages in the development of romantic or intimate relationships during adolescence. These stages are as follows:

- *Infatuation.* In this stage the young person is in love with 'being in love'. There is as much focus on the self as on the other person, and any actual romantic relationships tend to be short-lived.
- *Status.* Here the young person is looking at the romantic relationship from the point of view of how it will affect their status in the peer group. There is much concern with 'dating the wrong person', and this is a period when relationships are as much about reputation as they are about closeness and intimacy.
- *Intimacy.* It is in this stage that close relationships begin to be formed that are founded in mutual interests and feelings for each other. Although young people are still learning about themselves, they are developing the ability to share emotions, to develop trust, and to explore their needs in the context of intimacy.
- *Bonding.* Here concerns about commitment come to the fore. How long is the relationship going to last? Where is it going well, and where not so well? At this stage care and loyalty are of equal importance as pleasure and passion.

The suggestion of such a stage process has proved helpful and has generated some interesting research. For example Seiffge-Krenke (2003) carried out a study to look at whether the stages identified by Brown are pertinent in the European context, and broadly speaking it appears that they are. Other researchers have been interested in differences between cultural groups, and in the experiences of gay and lesbian young people, a topic to be considered at a later point in the chapter. Other studies, such as that of Feiring (1996), considered the experiences of romance among 15-year-olds. This study showed that at this age dating relationships were of shorter duration than stable same-sex friendships. The mean length of romantic relationships was between three and four months, compared with a year or more for friendships. However, the contact involved in romantic relationships was much more intense, as might be expected. Young people reported spending hours talking to each other face to face, or on the telephone. Of course today the internet would also be used. Thus it is likely that at the age of 15 many are in the Status stage rather than anything more developed. Another interesting perspective has to do with why relationships break up at this age. Connolly and McIsaac (2009) applied a developmental perspective, looking at a large group of adolescents aged between 14 and 18 and asking how many had relationship break-ups and why these occurred. Approximately 25 per cent of the sample had such experiences within a one-year period, most because of what the authors describe as 'unmet intimacy needs'. Finally a theme that has begun to appear in the literature has to do with the role of the internet, and the characteristics of those who form intimate relationships online. Wolak *et al.* (2003) studied this question, concluding that those who turned to the internet had more troubled relationships with both parents and peers. This topic will be discussed in more detail in Chapter 8.

Close relationships of a sexual nature at this stage of development have a high degree of impact on the young person's adjustment. As has been noted, such relationships have a major role to play in the gradual, sometimes painful, construction of a coherent identity. While they may be short-lived, these experiences may shape future choices as well as perceptions of self-worth. If the adolescent manages a break-up of a relationship without too much stress, and emerges as a wiser person, then the next step may be more developmentally mature. On the other hand if the loss is too painful, and the experience not fully integrated into other aspects of growth, then it may take some time before new learning can take place. In any event the significance of intimate relationships should not be underestimated. For the adolescent sexual experiences at this stage have the potential to be hugely pleasurable as well as deeply wounding. Adult support, where possible, can make a big difference.

Young people and safe sex

'My friend met this guy on a forum, and now she's dating him. She'd never met him and then she went up to London to meet him and now she's dating him, and he's 22 and she's 16. It's really weird, like when we would talk about stuff she would look down her nose at us, and then she's turned round and does that, and loses her virginity to him. . . . And we're like: "What are you doing?"'

(16-year-old girl)

From the perspective of the 1980s and 1990s the predominant issue when considering safe sexual practices was the problem of HIV/AIDS, and how to raise awareness among young people of its terrible effects. However, today HIV/AIDS is seen by

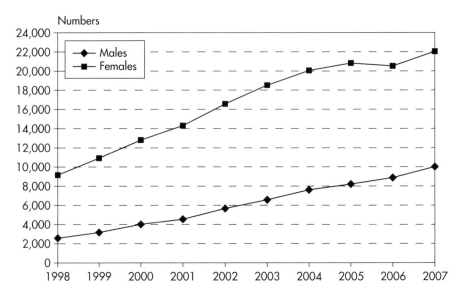

Figure 7.4 New diagnoses of Chlamydia infection among 16–19-year-olds in Britain from 1998 to 2007.

Data from: Selected STI diagnoses made at GUM clinics in the UK: 1998–2007. HPA.

Source: Coleman and Brooks (2009).

young people in Western countries as a problem for the developing world, rather than as a problem for them. Whilst it is still the case that certain groups, in particular intravenous drug users and gay young people, are threatened by HIV/AIDS, this particular sexually transmitted infection (STI) is relevant to a much smaller number of adolescents than other STIs such as Chlamydia and herpes. Indeed a few years ago hardly anyone outside the medical profession had heard of Chlamydia, yet today it is a key indicator of poor sexual health, with potentially serious long-term health consequences, especially for young women. As can be seen in Figure 7.4 the incidence of Chlamydia infection in the UK has more than doubled over a ten-year period up until 2007. A similar picture can be found for genital herpes and genital warts (Coleman and Brooks, 2009). Importantly these figures do not just apply to the UK. Moore and Rosenthal (2006) report a threefold increase in rates of Chlamydia infection in Australia over the period 1991 to 2001. This global trend poses significant challenges for those in the public health field, as well as raising the question as to what lies behind such findings. It seems most likely that young people are engaged in higher levels of sexual activity, starting at a younger age. A relatively small group may be taking more risks, with unsafe sexual behaviour being linked to other risk behaviours such as substance abuse.

In trying to understand the increase in STIs among young people, one spotlight needs to focus on contraceptive use. Research over the years has shown that there has been a steady increase in the use of contraception at first intercourse. To some extent this has come about due to the high profile of HIV/AIDS, and the amount of publicity that has been given to the importance of using a condom. Today, as might be expected, condoms are used more often than other methods, with 60 per cent of 15-year-olds reporting using this method in their first sexual experience (Coleman and Brooks, 2009). With increasing age more and more young people report using the pill, so that the NHS Information Centre in the UK publishes statistics showing that 40 per cent of 16-year-olds and over 50 per cent of 17-year-olds are using the pill when having sex. What reasons can be given for a young person not using contraception when having sex? We know that the older the adolescent is when he or she first becomes sexually active, the more likely they are to use contraception. It is also the case that those from poorer backgrounds, those with less motivation to stay on in school, and those with lower levels of parental monitoring are all more at risk of not using contraception when they are having sex (Henderson *et al.*, 2002; Wight *et al.*, 2006).

The easiest way to understand how unprotected sex can occur is to consider the requirements for the use of a condom. First they have to be purchased, and to be available at the right moment. Next it has to be acceptable to both partners to admit that one of you has planned to have sex. It is also probably necessary to be able to discuss the use of a contraceptive, and to feel confident enough with each other to risk interrupting sexual arousal. In addition of course all this assumes that at least one partner is sober and rational at the beginning of the encounter. When you are young, at the beginning of a relationship, and not at all sure of the other person it is hardly surprising that in some situations not all of these conditions are met!

Apart from lack of confidence, and all the other anxieties that are an inevitable part of growing up, the most significant factor that has to be considered is that of gender difference. There have been a number of important discussions on the topic of gendered constructions of sexuality in the UK (e.g. Lees, 1993; Thomson and Holland, 1998). Hillier *et al.* (1998) get to the heart of the matter with their article entitled: 'When you carry condoms all the boys think you want it'. As many of these writers make clear, a double standard operates in the sexual arena, whereby sexual prowess for men is something to be proud of, while for women it is something to keep quiet about. Indeed young women who are known to be sexually active are often called the most derogatory names within the peer group. These issues are closely linked to questions of power between men and women, and relate directly to how decisions about contraception are taken in relationships between young people. This is an absolutely central topic for effective sex and relationships education, and something that will be addressed later in the chapter.

In previous editions of this book the discussion of safe sex has focussed primarily on sexually transmitted infections and on contraceptive use. Today two additional topics in this sphere are receiving attention: these are sexual exploitation, and violence in dating relationships. Turning to sexual exploitation first, Pearce (2007, 2009) has written widely on this subject. She sets out three types of influence that might create routes into sexual exploitation. These are:

- *Individual.* Here the young woman is likely to have very low self-esteem and to be highly vulnerable to the influence of an older adult. In this situation it is the young woman's own fragility and her individual needs that play the largest part in leading to her being sexually exploited.

- *Family.* In this case it is the family situation which plays the largest part, either because of domestic violence, sexual abuse or because of intolerable family circumstances which cause the young woman to run away from home and to end up on the street.

- *Environmental.* It is not uncommon that environmental factors add to other risk factors, so that poverty or deprivation, interrupted schooling, placement into care, and/or limited access to support services all may contribute to making the young woman vulnerable and therefore open to exploitation.

Violence is closely linked to sexual exploitation, with many young women reporting violence in the home, or violence in their relationships with pimps or clients. However, there has also been a recent surge in research reports which look at violence in dating relationships, most of which originate from the USA. Studies indicate that somewhere around a quarter of all adolescents experience some form of abuse in a dating relationship, but this abuse can include a range of behaviours from physical and psychological abuse to sexual aggression. Work by Sears *et al.* (2007) showed that, whilst there was often co-occurrence between these behaviours, the use of psychological abuse was more common in girls, and the expression of sexual aggression was more common in boys. Most studies link dating violence or aggression to the parenting experiences of those involved. Thus, for example, Pflieger and Vazsonyi (2006) explore how low self-esteem acts as a mediator between parenting practices and abuse in a dating relationship. Those young people with low self-esteem and abusive parenting were more likely to express or experience violence or abuse in a dating relationship. In one of the few UK studies on this topic Barter *et al.* (2009) included 1,200 young people between the ages of 16 and 18 in a survey, reporting that 10 per cent of young women and 4 per cent of young men had experienced some form of serious violence in an intimate relationship. These authors corroborated Pflieger and Vazsonyi's finding that violence in a dating relationship was closely linked to experiences of domestic violence in the family. This is a topic which will no doubt continue to receive attention in research studies of adolescent sexuality.

Lesbian and gay sexuality in adolescence

It is generally recognised that no discussion of adolescent sexuality would be complete without some consideration of those who are lesbian, gay or bisexual. In the USA this group is known as sexual minority youth. As Savin-Williams and Diamond (2004) state: 'We use the term sexual minority rather than gay, lesbian and bisexual reflecting our view that adolescents with desires for or experiences with same-sex partners deserve systematic attention regardless of how they label their sexual identity' (p. 197). This statement raises questions about the term sexual identity, and as many writers have pointed out, it is important to distinguish between the following terms:

- *Sexual identity.* Sexual identity refers to how a person describes his or her sexual self, and how that self is described to others.
- *Sexual orientation.* Sexual orientation describes a person's underlying sexual preferences, and relates to a consistent pattern of sexual arousal towards persons of either the same or the opposite gender.
- *Sexual practices.* These are sexual acts engaged in by an individual, and these may involve both same and opposite sex partners, especially in adolescence when sexuality is assumed to be more fluid than in later life.

The important point about this distinction is that these different aspects of sexuality may not always match. Usually sexual identity will be an expression of a person's underlying sexual orientation, but this is not always the case. A young adult may believe that they have a heterosexual identity, but gradually find that their sexual orientation is gay, or lesbian. On the other hand during adolescence when there is a considerable degree of uncertainty about sexual identity, a young person might find that they have many different experiences, moving back and forth between different identities. Young people's descriptions of their personal journey towards a defined sexual identity are often very moving, as can be seen here.

> 'I suppose I started having sexual feelings – I didn't categorise them in any way – from the age of 11, and these feelings carried on until I was 14 or 15. It was only then, through watching television and talking to friends, that I would categorise some of them, not all of them, as gay thoughts. The actual process of realising that I was one of those "poof" things that everyone had been talking about at school, was a very long process. It didn't really finish till I was 16 or maybe 17, very late on really. I just thought they were ordinary sexual feelings, which in fact they were. It's just through images in the media, and social pressures, that our sexual feelings get channelled in one direction or another, and in mainstream society one of those feelings is good and okay and normal, and the other types are bad and to be got rid of and evil.'
>
> (20-year-old man quoted in Coleman, 2001, p. 124)

This statement raises the question of the process of the establishment of a sexual identity. A number of writers, such as Troiden (1989), have explored this issue, suggesting that there are four stages in the identity development process. First there is the stage of 'sensitisation'. During this stage the young person begins to be aware that he or she may be different from others. He or she may have different interests, and may begin to recognise sexual feelings that are not the same as those experienced by others of the same gender. The second stage is that of 'identity confusion'. Here the individual experiences an altered awareness of the self. Sexual arousal may be associated with those of the same gender, and there is a growing consciousness of the stigma linked to gay or lesbian behaviour. The third stage is that known as 'identity assumption'. Here the young person begins to take on the identity of someone who is gay, lesbian or bisexual, and is able to express that identity at least to close friends. Finally there is the stage of 'commitment'. At this point the individual can make a commitment to an intimate relationship with someone of the same gender, and is also able to disclose to family and other important people.

It is important to recognise that the notion of a stage process has some important limitations, as Coyle (1998) points out. First the idea of stages implies that all individuals go through the same processes in the same sequence, and this is manifestly not the case. Also it will be evident that there is great variability in the way young people come to the realisation of their gay, lesbian or bisexual identity. Some may know from an early age, whilst others will remain confused and uncertain throughout adolescence. It is sensible to consider the stages outlined above as examples of the tasks and issues faced by young people who may be gay, lesbian or bisexual, rather than seeing them as a fixed framework for identity development.

One question that has been included in many surveys of adolescent sexual behaviour has to do with sexual orientation. One study in Australia, for example, reported between 9 per cent and 11 per cent of young people growing up in rural areas who did not define themselves as exclusively heterosexual (Hillier *et al.*, 1996). Another larger study of high school students reported a somewhat lower figure in the region of 8 per cent to 9 per cent stating that they had had same-sex romantic experiences (Smith *et al.*, 2003). In the USA the study most often quoted is that known as the Add Health Study, which indicated that 8 per cent of boys and 6 per cent of girls reported having same-sex attractions or a same-sex relationship (Russell and Joyner, 2001). These figures should be treated with caution of course, as even in confidential surveys the fears and uncertainties associated with gay or lesbian sexuality will inevitably affect the response rates. As Savin-Williams and Diamond (2004) emphasise, more young people will admit that they have had a same-sex attraction than will admit that they are gay or lesbian. These authors also point out that the number reporting this type of sexual orientation increases with age, as adolescents become more confident about their sexual identity.

There is no doubt that there has been a substantial shift both in public policy and in attitudes to gay and lesbian sexuality over the past decade or so. Whilst in the 1990s there was much emphasis on the risk factors, such as poor mental health, associated with homosexuality (e.g. Coyle, 1993; Rotheram-Borus *et al.*, 1994), today there is a much greater stress on the normality of different sexual orientations and experiences. Thus Savin-Williams and Diamond (2004) have a section entitled 'Positive sexual development', and Moore and Rosenthal (2006) in their chapter on 'Gay and lesbian issues' include some paragraphs headed 'Creating change'. The intention of all these commentators is to underline the positive and functional aspects of sexual development, irrespective of whether individual adolescents become heterosexual or homosexual. Hillier and Harrison (2004), for example, report that 60 per cent of gay or lesbian young people say that they feel 'pretty good' about their sexual identity, and other studies have emphasised the same message. Hillier and Harrison (2004) discuss the strategies that gay and lesbian young people use to help them in developing their sexual identities, stating that many who adjust well: 'find, create or inhabit safe spaces in which they feel comfortable'. This may involve the use of the internet, or sports facilities, as safe spaces to work through issues relating to sexual identity. Although it is important not to ignore the fact that there are clearly some young people for whom sexual identity represents a serious challenge, nonetheless the change in policy and in emphasis is greatly to be welcomed. All of us should work to ensure that this shift in emphasis is translated into effective sex education programmes.

Teenage parenthood

'It just feels great when you have a child following you around, telling you they love you. I think that it's quite selfish, really, but that's one of the reasons I became a Mum, because I wanted someone, you know, who . . . "love them to bits" sort of thing. It's not just your child who's the centre of the world – the parents are the centre of the child's world, and that feels great. Yeah, it's brilliant, it's fantastic, you've got to do everything for the child, and it just feels great to be depended on.'

(17-year-old girl)

Early parenthood is both an emotive and a complex topic. In the first place it is misleading to talk of early parenthood as a general concept. It is apparent that parenthood for an 18-year-old that is planned and thought through is completely different from parenthood for a 14-year-old that results from a failure to use contraception. Unfortunately there is too little recognition of the significance of the developmental stage of the young parent. A second problem has to do with the stereotyping that has clouded any sensible policy discussion about this topic. It is of no help to anyone to see this group of young people as irresponsible youth trying to jump the housing queue, or as a drain on the state. To use these images creates a climate of resentment which makes it impossible to plan effectively for the needs of this group of parents.

It should be noted that it is not only politicians and commentators who slip into negative stereotyping when discussing this issue. In much research on this topic there is an undue emphasis on the disadvantages of being a young parent, and the use of the deficit model of early parenthood is widespread. A good example of this approach can be seen in Adams and Berzonsky's *Blackwell handbook of adolescence* (2003). In this volume there is a section entitled 'Problem behaviours' and the first chapter here is one on 'Adolescent pregnancy and childbearing' (Miller *et al.*, 2003). Some of the research highlights the poorer outcomes for children of teenage parents, while other studies concentrate on the characteristics of young people who become parents at an early age. Such studies often compare the parenting skills of young people with older parents, almost always to the detriment of the teenage group. Whether implicitly or explicitly, the great majority of research

on this subject emphasises the disadvantages of early parenthood for both mother and child. It is clearly important to recognise the obstacles faced by young parents, particularly the likelihood of being in poor economic circumstances and of having to postpone opportunities for education and training (Hobcraft and Kiernan, 2001). Nonetheless the capabilities of young parents, and their resilience in the face of adversity, should not be ignored. To do so does a disservice to adolescents, as well as painting a one-sided picture of the situation (Dennison and Coleman, 1998).

This picture varies from country to country. In the USA there are high rates of teenage pregnancy, but the majority of those who get pregnant or who become young parents tend to be from minority groups, particularly from an African-American background. This is not the case in the UK, where only a small minority of young parents come from an ethnic minority background. However, in the European context Britain is the country with the highest rates of teenage pregnancy, and this has been a matter of considerable concern to governments and to policy makers. In 1999 the government of the time established the Teenage Pregnancy Unit (TPU), following a review of the situation in Britain by the Social Exclusion Unit (SEU, 1999). The TPU was given the remit of reducing the number of teenage conceptions and establishing better support systems for young parents. While there is debate about how much additional support has been made available, there is no doubt that the conception rate for the under-18-year-olds has been reduced, as can be seen in Figure 7.5. This is a remarkable achievement, given the multitude of factors that lie behind a young woman's pregnancy.

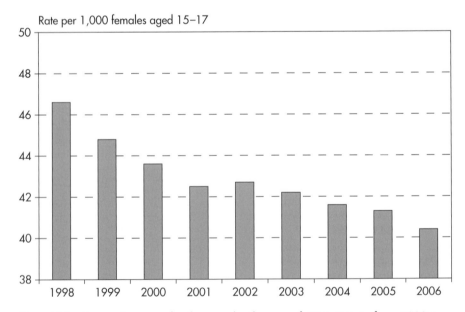

Figure 7.5 Conception rates for those under the age of 18 in Britain from 1998 to 2006.

Data from: Office for National Statistics and Teenage Pregnancy Unit, 2008.

Source: Coleman and Brooks (2009).

What are the factors that contribute to the likelihood of a young woman becoming pregnant in Britain today? First, conception rates are highest in urban areas, and several studies have shown a strong association between socio-economic status and the incidence of teenage pregnancy and maternity (Coleman and Brooks, 2009). In addition to these broad demographic factors there are other variables that play a part. Some commentators have noted an association between pregnancy in adolescence and similar experiences among the mothers of such women (Cater and Coleman, 2006). In addition it would appear that especially vulnerable young teenagers, such as those brought up in the care of local authorities, are more likely than others to become parents at an early age (Chase *et al.*, 2006). One young woman describes her motivation to become a parent as follows:

'I don't think I missed out on me childhood because I never really had a childhood anyway. Because I was kicked out when I was three, and my Mum walked out on me, and my Dad was beating me around, and I was sexually assaulted when I was five, so I never had a childhood of my own, so I don't miss it 'cos I never had it. And when I got to around 14 I was in a children's home, and all I felt was that no-one loved me, no-one ever loved me, no-one would ever love me, and that's when I decided I wanted me own family, and so that's what I done.'
(Young mother aged 16, quoted in Dennison and Coleman, 1998, p. 32)

There are some examples of studies of young mothers in the British context which have attempted to focus as much on the strengths as the challenges. Phoenix (1991) represents one of the earliest investigations of this topic. She examined the experiences of eighty young women who became pregnant between the ages of 16 and 18, and she found that they formed a heterogeneous group in terms of their ethnicity, education and employment, and in their reasons for wanting children. They were, however, all linked by a common experience of poverty, and a determination to do the very best for their child, often in extremely difficult circumstances. Phoenix argued that, in comparison with older women in similar economic circumstances, these young women were coping just as well. Their opportunities and life chances had, in any event, been limited, so that becoming a parent could be seen as a realistic and constructive path to choose.

A more recent study by Rolfe (2005) came to very similar conclusions. As she says: 'When alternative routes to adulthood are blocked, motherhood can be a route into adulthood. However young mothers' attempts at social inclusion are rejected by adults, and they are pushed further into social exclusion' (p. 243). Rolfe's work underlines the impact of negative perceptions of early parenthood on the part of the adult world. She quotes one young woman who said: 'You're expected to fail: end of story!' Yet the young women in this study reported many rewards and gratifications as a result of their status as mothers. They documented a range of adaptive strategies to ensure that their children got the best possible parenting, whilst also recognising that, in spite of the obstacles, they needed to engage in training and be able to stand on their own feet economically. One other study is worth mentioning, and that is one carried out by Cater and Coleman (2006), who looked at a group of young women under the age of 18 who had planned their pregnancies. In their conclusions the authors underline how important it is to distinguish between wanted and unwanted conceptions among this age group. As they note, whilst every effort should be made to reduce unwanted conceptions, there are those who choose the option of early parenthood, and these young people should be supported rather than vilified.

As a final point on this subject, it is striking how little attention is paid to the role of the young father in studies of early parenthood. Most writers on this subject contribute to the overall impression that young fathers are either invisible or absent. That said, it is important not to underestimate the difficulty of involving young men in the research process. They may be suspicious of the purposes of the investigation, or lacking in confidence regarding their role as fathers. As a result it is commonly assumed that young men do not want to take any responsibility for, or play an active part in, the upbringing of their child. What little research there is does not support this view (e.g. Speak, 1997). Significant numbers of teenage fathers do maintain contact with their children, and do play a role in parenting. However, there are a number of obstacles, including housing difficulties, unstable relationships between the two parents, and the economic stresses of finding training or work. More research is definitely needed in this area, but it is important to recognise that not all stories paint a negative picture.

'Well, he was pretty positive. Yeah, really, because we were only 17 at the time. We saw our friends, but I thought, what'll he think of being tied down with a baby? His friends are going to give him hassle, and one day he might turn around and say: "I've had enough. I don't see my friends, I don't go anywhere, I'm just sat here with you and that baby". But he weren't out always with his friends. He was with them, but at the same time he spent quite a lot of time with me. He found time for us both. It has brought us a bit closer than we were. We might argue a bit of course, when she cries and that, and he is a bit rough with her, and then I start shouting, but I think we're closest we'll ever be.'
(Young woman aged 18, quoted in Dennison and Coleman, 1998, p. 62)

Effective sex and relationships education

'They went through this list – what are the main reasons for under-age people to have sex, and they went through this list that they'd made, and it was all peer pressure and to fit in and stuff like that, and they didn't mention once that people might just want to do it. They seemed to think that no-one just does things because they want to, everyone just does it to fit in. And they don't, you know, that hardly ever happens.'
(17-year-old boy)

It seems appropriate to end this chapter with a consideration of sex and relationships education (SRE), and to look at some of the ways it might be modified or improved to take into account the needs of young people. As will be apparent, there is some overlap here with the discussion on health promotion to be found at the end of the previous chapter. First it is clear that SRE cannot focus only on the biology. While biology must be an important component, it is those elements which concern the social context of sexuality, together with relationships and the ethics of sexual behaviour, which are most needed by adolescents. Teaching the biology of sex is relatively easy, but creating an SRE programme which allows young people to explore the decisions and dilemmas involved in sexual behaviour, and to develop the necessary relationship skills, is much more difficult. It is in this direction that good programmes should be oriented.

A second element of a good SRE programme has to do with the importance of addressing the needs of young men and young women, as well as those from minority cultures, and those who are gay, lesbian or bisexual. In terms of gender it is a fact that SRE programmes rarely consider the significance of good communication between men and women, nor do they give young people an opportunity to explore issues relating to gender roles (Galambos, 2004). Furthermore girls and boys almost certainly need somewhat different things from an SRE programme, so that for some of the curriculum there may be a need for single-sex groups in order that open discussion is made possible. As far as the needs of other groups are concerned, the key here is for SRE programmes to be proactive in recognising minorities, and valuing their experiences. The needs of these groups cannot be met unless such young people feel safe from prejudice and the possibility of harassment, whether of a racist or sexist nature. The responsibility to create a safe environment must rest with the professional adult.

A third factor which is essential for effective programmes is a recognition of the differing levels of knowledge among pupils. Young people show considerable variation in their knowledge of sexuality. Both age and gender are factors to be taken into account, but equally important is the finding that pupils are more knowledgeable about some aspects of sexuality than about others (Coleman and Roker, 1998). Thus young people's understanding of fertility, for example, appears to be relatively poor in contrast to their understanding of some sexually transmitted infections such as HIV/AIDS. Information such as this should inform SRE programmes, and should emphasise the need for proper evaluation of programmes with a focus on both knowledge and attitudes.

A number of writers (e.g. Mackinnnon, 2007) have made the point that we do not need health education programmes that pre-empt decisions that young people are likely to make in relation to their health. Sex and relationships education should not be prescriptive, nor should it give a moral message about what is right and wrong. The most effective SRE programmes will be those which provide young people with information as well as interpersonal skills, so that they can make informed choices about what is right for them. Of course this viewpoint is not shared by all who take an interest in this topic. As Steinberg (2008) points out, since the beginning of the 1990s in the USA many SRE programmes have taught abstinence as the right way forward, and in some cases as the only means of protection against pregnancy. The promotion of these programmes has been supported by government funding. Such an approach has not been evident in the Australian or European context, although there are certainly pressure groups which are influential in some school settings and which promote a moral message on contraception and abortion.

To conclude it is necessary to make the point that, however effective school-based SRE programmes are, they cannot reduce teenage conception rates or improve adolescent sexual health without additional support from the community. The role of the family cannot be ignored, but in addition teenage-friendly sexual health services need to be in place. Resources have to be directed to the provision of appropriate professionals, sited in accessible clinic facilities, so that young people know where to go for sexual health advice and treatment. One of the important messages that the UK's Teenage Pregnancy Unit has been promoting is that a number of different strategies have to be in place if Britain is to reduce the teenage conception rate. Good SRE programmes have to work hand in hand with community services, and strong leadership is required from those in the relevant professions, such as nursing, youth work and teaching, if any real improvement is to be achieved in the sexual health of young people.

Implications for practice

1. There have been profound changes in the sexual behaviour of young people over the last decades. Most important of these changes is the increase in sexual activity among those in early and middle adolescence. This change is closely linked to changes in the pattern of adult sexual behaviour, and cannot be seen in isolation from other social trends. It does, however, have particular implications for parents and for educators, and underlines the crucial importance of timing of effective sex and relationships education.

2. The impact of HIV/AIDS on young people has been considerable, in spite of the fact that today there is less concern among adolescents in the Western world about this sexually transmitted infection (STI) than there is about other STIs such as Chlamydia and herpes. The phenomenon of HIV/AIDS has led to an emphasis on 'safer sex', including an interest in young people's knowledge about sexual matters, their attitudes to contraceptive practice, and the acceptability of condom use.

3. There has been a growing recognition of the circumstances which affect young people who develop as gay, lesbian or bisexual during adolescence. In particular attention has been paid to distinctions between sexual orientation and sexual identity, as well as to the stages of identity development among this group. Many writers have pointed to the difficulties faced by sexual minority young people, but in recent years there has also been a focus on the resilience and adaptive capacities of adolescents who develop a gay, lesbian or bisexual identity.

4. Teenage pregnancy and parenthood has received a high degree of attention, especially in the USA and in the UK, where conception rates are higher than in other countries. While some research concentrates on what might be called 'the deficit model' of early parenthood, comparing young parents unfavourably with older parents, such research overlooks the resources and commitment of adolescent parents. Given appropriate

support young people can be effective mothers and fathers, and it is essential that practitioners concentrate on strategies that facilitate parenting skills among young parents, rather than emphasising their limitations.

5. The concluding section of this chapter has been devoted to effective sex and relationships education (SRE). It is essential to recognise that SRE cannot be seen as a subject on its own in the school curriculum, nor can it be seen as a strategy isolated from other sexual health services for young people. To be effective, SRE has to be conceptualised in a holistic manner, incorporated into a 'healthy living' curriculum in schools, and integrated into other health provision in the community. If there is one lesson to be learnt from research into adolescent sexuality, it is that young people need relevant and unbiased information, together with the opportunity to explore interpersonal issues in a non-judgemental environment.

Further reading

Burtney, E and Duffy, M (Eds) (2004) *Young people and sexual health: individual, social and policy contexts*. Palgrave Macmillan. Basingstoke.
Good reviews of a variety of topics relating to sexuality and young people, with an educational slant.

Moore, S and Rosenthal, D (2006) *Sexuality in adolescence: current trends*. Routledge. London.
This is a second edition of a very popular book. The authors have an accessible style which makes the book easy to read, and there is excellent coverage of many aspects of adolescent sexuality.

Savin-Williams, R and Diamond, L (2004) Sex. In Lerner, R and Steinberg, L (Eds) *Handbook of adolescent psychology*, 2nd edn. Wiley. New York.
A review chapter by two leaders in the field. There is a strong emphasis on varieties of sexual experience, and on gay, lesbian and bisexual young people, or sexual minorities, as they are called in North America.

Adolescence and education

'It's quite difficult when you start to pick your options for GCSE course work, and all the teachers are saying you've got to choose what you want to do, and it's much easier if you know what you want to do, but it's quite hard when you're first choosing because I didn't know what I wanted. . . . I think you start picking them when you're 13 or 14, and I hadn't thought about anything like that when I started doing it. And I still don't really know, and I think it's quite hard to make a decision. Then, say you make your choices that you want to do at the time, and then you change your mind, and you don't really want to do that. It's quite a big decision to make.'

(16-year-old boy)

In thinking about adolescent development, the environment of the school or college cannot be ignored. Throughout this age period a significant amount of time is spent in some form of education, and the question of how this impacts on young people, and on their personal development, is a critical one. In this chapter it will first be necessary to consider briefly the broader educational situation in the UK and in other European countries. Following that there will be a review of transitions into secondary education, classroom climate and school ethos, stress at school, the role of the school in promoting health and well-being, and finally a consideration of how the educational environment facilitates or hinders adolescent development.

The context of secondary education

The first question to be considered is: what is the role of the secondary school? Clearly its function is to educate its pupils for a transition either into further or higher education, or into the labour market, but even these straightforward goals may be interpreted in many different ways. Furthermore in the twenty-first century there are a range of other objectives that have come to be seen as the responsibility of the school, such as life skills education, the promotion of well-being, some forms of health provision such as counselling and sexual health advice, involvement in sports and the arts, and in some cases continuing education for parents. In a review carried out by the Carnegie Corporation, quoted by Flammer and Alsaker (2006), five major goals for adolescents completing secondary education were noted: these were to be intellectually reflective, to be a good citizen, to be able to engage in work, to be healthy and to be an ethical person.

Few would disagree with such goals, but the question of how to achieve them is more complex. The process of deciding what is the appropriate role of the secondary school is complicated by a number of factors including the practical realities of the changing labour market; the huge financial burden on the state of providing good quality education for all; the range of individual needs of young people from different backgrounds and differing ability levels; and the impact of different political beliefs on educational policy. Pring et al. (2009) note that, in the UK, relatively low levels of attainment, high rates of attrition in secondary education, and a wide variety of types of schooling all contribute to a situation where there is an urgent need for a redefinition of the meaning of learning for this age group.

These authors ask the challenging question: what counts as an educated 19-year-old in this day and age (Pring *et al.*, 2009, p. 12)? They then break the question down into various constituents. First, what is meant by education? There are important differences between knowledge, skills and attitudes. Second, what sort of 19-year-old is envisaged here? Different students have varying interests and capabilities, so these need to be taken into account. Third, what do we mean by 'in this day and age'? The labour market is changing, so different types of preparation are needed. There is major social change, such as a more gender-equal labour force, and there are rapidly changing technological circumstances such as the growth of the internet and information and communication technologies. Bills (2009) argues that we need a broader vision of learning, with a greater value

placed on experiential and practical learning. This leads on to a more flexible approach to assessment, together with a revised curriculum for the twenty-first century.

These ideas link well with the notion of 'late modernity' discussed by Wyn (2009). She points out two key features of our world today which underline the need for some new thinking about secondary education. These are, first, a greater complexity of pathways for young people in their transitions from education to work. As Wyn notes, the options open to those from the age of 16 onwards in most developed countries are complex and hugely varied. If these pathways are to be assessed and negotiated, new skills will be required. In addition the boundaries between education and employment have become blurred, so that young people in many countries experience a stage of being both worker and student. The second point Wyn makes is that adulthood is achieved incrementally, with some aspects of maturity (e.g. sexual behaviour) achieved earlier than in previous generations, whilst other aspects (e.g. financial independence) may come much later. Again this characteristic of the early twenty-first century demands a more flexible approach to secondary education.

These thoughts prompt a reflection on the school leaving age, and how this has altered over the last century. In 1918 in Britain attendance at school was made compulsory up the age of 14. This was extended after the Second World War to 15, and then in 1972 the age was again raised to 16. Interestingly the law in Britain, identifying the age of 16 as the school leaving age, has been out of step with many other countries in Europe and North America, where 18 has been the norm. Recent legislation in the UK has altered this situation, and after 2014 all up to the age of 18 will be required to be in some form of education or training. In tandem with these changes there has been a drive to get more young people into higher education, with a goal in the UK of having 50 per cent of those aged 18 to 21 being at university or college. Furlong and Cartmel (2009) describe this trend in a chapter entitled 'Mass higher education'.

These facts raise interesting questions about the relation between the nature of the labour market and the education sector. Is education a good to which more and more young people should have access? Or is it that the labour market is shrinking, with fewer employment opportunities for the population as a whole, so that education and training are provided by the state as an alternative occupation for the younger age groups? It cannot be denied that, as new skills are demanded of workers, additional education and training will be required. If there is competition between different economies, there will be a concomitant drive to have a better qualified workforce. On the other hand, it is undoubtedly true that there is less demand for those in manual occupations, and examples of automation – from agriculture to heavy industry – can be seen everywhere. This leads to a reduction in the workforce, and so both younger and older age groups find it more difficult to find work.

Looking at the way different countries organise their secondary education can be instructive. There is a general view in Britain that this country suffers from high drop-out rates and low levels of attainment. Yet in Australia nearly 25 per cent of young people leave secondary education early (Wyn, 2006), a figure which is comparable with the UK. Raffe (2009) draws comparisons across developed countries, showing that a key distinguishing feature of secondary education is the way in which vocational education is integrated into the system. This author argues that there are two types of approach. In the first place there are countries that are highly standardised, with a large vocational sector closely linked to the needs of the labour market, offering occupationally specific training. Secondly there are countries which have more open education and training systems, with weaker links between education and occupation. Germany is the clearest example of the first type, with the USA being the most distinct example of the second type. Other countries fall somewhere along the continuum between the two extremes.

It comes as no surprise to find that, for young people in the first group of countries, transitions are faster and smoother. Importantly vocational qualifications are highly valued in these countries, and there is a tight structure with relatively little room for manoeuvre. Young people in the second group of countries have more flexibility, but on the other hand vocational qualifications are less highly valued and there is a less well-defined match between the needs of employers and the process of education and training. In a country such as Britain, where there is an emphasis on academic qualifications, and where vocational qualifications are not given particular prominence, there has been a constantly changing array of possible options for those who are less academic in the 16–18-year age group. This has created a far from ideal situation, clearly described by Pring et al. (2009), in which many struggle to find appropriate routes through the options available in further education. It has also meant that, because of fall-out rates and disaffection, a significant number become what is described as NEET (not in education, employment or training). In spite of numerous government initiatives, it has proved difficult to reduce the proportion of 16–18-year-olds falling into this category.

In concluding this introductory section it is important to point out that not all young people have equal access to adequate secondary education. There are major inequalities associated with education and training, and these play an important part in determining the individual's life course in the transition to adulthood. Inequalities may occur as a result of race and ethnicity, social class, gender, or the historical or geographical context in which the young person grows up. One interesting example of this latter type of inequality is illustrated in Petersen *et al.*'s (1993) research looking at the circumstances of young people in the former East and West Germany, and then at those attending school after re-unification in 1989. Young people experienced significant change in the opportunities available to them once Germany became one country. Contrasting experiences of education for Catholic and Protestant adolescents in Northern Ireland offer a further example of inequality associated with place of growing up. A third example of inequality, this time between countries, is given by Eurydice (1997), who, in a cross-European comparison of secondary schooling, shows that adolescents in Iceland attend 750 lessons a year whilst those in Austria and Switzerland attend 1,100 lessons a year!

Whilst the ideal may be to have equal access for all, the reality is that numerous forms of disadvantage operate to influence the type of secondary education experienced by different young people. In Britain there have been intense debates over the performance of boys and girls in state examinations, fuelled by a historical trend in the results showing continuing improvement in performance on the part of girls. What factors influence such a difference, and does it reflect some manner of disadvantage for boys? In Britain social class too plays a major part in all types of education, even in higher education. In their analysis of trends in higher education Furlong and Cartmel (2009) argue that social class differences operate just as strongly at this level as they do at secondary level, with far greater opportunities for access to university being available for those from middle class backgrounds. Thus it will be apparent that inequalities among young people are among the most important factors determining their experiences of education. Having looked at some of the factors that provide a context for secondary education, it is time now to turn to the transition from primary to secondary school.

Transition to secondary education

'Yes, going to secondary school, that was the big change. I remember feeling like, in Year 7 or 8, being sort of worried. . . . Suddenly, when you go to secondary school, you are put in a group with a much wider group of people, who you've never met before, and you see a vast range of people and you see how some people have, or appear to have, grown up much quicker than others. Like, I don't know, wearing make up, or the kind of clothes people wear, and you sort of go "Oh my God! People have started caring about this already, time to catch up!"'

(17-year-old girl)

All young people experience some form of school transition, or transfer, in the early stages of adolescence. In the UK the most common system is one in which the individual moves at the age of 11 from a small primary to a large secondary school. A minority experience what is known as a three-tier system, with a middle school providing a bridge between the ages of 11 and 14, but this system is only available in a small number of localities. From an international perspective the three-tier system is the predominant one in use in the USA and in several European countries. It is also widely used in Australia and New Zealand. The two systems clearly have differing implications for young people, since it could be argued that a three-tier arrangement allows for a more gradual shift from the intimate and informal to the large and impersonal type of school environment. On the other hand the more transitions there are, the more disruptive the process is likely to be. An alternative argument would be that having only one transition, although a major one, is likely to offer a smoother pathway for educational achievement and developmental progress than having two transitions.

In order to understand the process of transition to secondary education it is important to rehearse the main features of adolescent development at or around the ages of 11 and 12. In the first place the great majority of young people will be at some stage in the pubertal process. Some may be at the beginning, perhaps just starting the growth spurt, whilst others may be well advanced. Girls, as noted in Chapter 2, are likely to be a year or more in advance of boys at this stage. The physical changes associated with puberty may, in some cases, lead to uncertainty, lack of confidence, self-consciousness and anxiety. It should also be remembered that, because of changes in the brain and in the hormonal balance around this age, young people are likely to experience rapidly shifting emotional states. The regulation of emotion is particularly difficult at this age. Early adolescence is also associated with a need for greater autonomy from the family, and with an increased focus on the importance of the peer group. Finally this age is also one where significant change occurs in thinking and reasoning, as described in Chapter 3.

Turning now to the characteristics of the transition from primary to secondary school, it is possible to describe a number of areas of potential challenge for the young person. These may be identified as follows:

School work. There will be greater expectations from teachers, with more work in school and more homework.
Teachers. Instead of having one teacher the young person will have to make relationships with a large number of teachers.
Environment. The school will be large and initially confusing. Different lessons will be in different places, and it will take time to get used to new buildings.
Peers. It will be necessary to make a range of new relationships with a different peer group. There may be threats of bullying and greater pressure to conform to peer group norms.

In setting out both the developmental features of early adolescence, together with the possible risk factors associated with a move to a much larger and more formal educational system, it becomes clear that this may not be the ideal arrangement for the individual. However, an alternative argument could be advanced to claim that it is precisely at this stage that a move to a wider social environment and a more demanding educational regime is both necessary and beneficial, in view of the developmental changes that are occurring in early adolescence. Much research has been carried out to assess whether and in what degree young people are disadvantaged by this transition, and there is also a body of research looking at whether there are particular characteristics of either the individual or the school which hinder or facilitate the transitional process. Before looking at the research evidence a brief review of some theoretical perspectives will be helpful.

One possible viewpoint might be that which stems from anthropology, identifying the need for a 'rite of passage' at the beginning of adolescence. In societies that were studied by anthropologists such as Margaret Mead there was reported a ceremony designed specifically to identify a transition point in the individual's development. This could involve having to carry out an especially demanding challenge, or being cast out in the wilderness for a short period. These rituals clearly marked, for both society and for the individual, the point at which childhood ended and adulthood commenced. Commentators have noted the absence of such a ceremony in Western societies, so that the Jewish 'bar mitzvah' or the passing of a driving test are sometimes offered as pale examples of a 'rite of passage' for adolescents today. Could the transition from primary to secondary education be seen in this light, as suggested by Measor and Woods (1984)?

A second theoretical perspective is one which derives from life course theory, identifying continuities and discontinuities during development. Thus it could be argued that, while features of the individual's environment such as the family and the community remain constant, or continuous, at this age other features will undergo change, or discontinuity. These discontinuities are necessary to facilitate development, prompting the individual to acquire new skills and to extend social horizons. Transition to secondary education could be one such discontinuity. Overall adaptation depends on how well the individual adjusts to the discontinuities that are experienced. Discontinuities are sometimes known as turning points, or milestones, and some writers have suggested that the individual's adaptation will to some extent be dependent on how many turning points are experienced at any one time (see Chapter 1). Thus, for example, if a young person experiences parental divorce, which in turn necessitates a move from one community to another, at the same time as having to change school, then the outcome is likely to be more problematic than if the turning points are experienced one at a time.

One further theoretical perspective that may be mentioned here is that known as 'stage–environment fit' (Eccles, 2004). In this viewpoint it is assumed that, as individuals mature, they will have changing cognitive, emotional and social needs. Thus, in the context of school transition, Eccles and her colleagues have argued that the school system needs to change in ways that suit the changing developmental needs of the young person. If young people are to remain motivated to learn then the secondary school (the environment) should be constructed to fit the stage (early/middle adolescence). In particular adolescents will need to be given increasing opportunities to control their own development, and over time be allowed more room to extend their cognitive skills, and be shown clearer evidence of the purposes of education. If schools do not respond to these changing developmental needs then the conclusion is that young people will become progressively more disenchanted with the educational system (Zimmer-Gembeck *et al.*, 2006). Since much of the research shows that the early stages of secondary education involve tightly controlled learning and teacher-dominated classroom activities, this is an interesting perspective from which to explore the empirical evidence.

Broadly speaking, research suggests that most pupils adjust fairly readily to a change of school. Whilst many children report anxieties about the transition during the last year in primary school, these anxieties appear to be short-lived. In the 1970s Youngman and Lunzer (1977) found that approximately 80 per cent of pupils had positive experiences at transfer, while more recently Evangelou et al. (2008) found that 75 per cent of pupils indicated that they had adjusted well by the end of the first term in the transfer school. However, it is clear that a small minority do not do so well. Galton and Wilcocks (1983) state that about 12 per cent of pupils continued to have a dip in attainment once reaching secondary school, and others have reported somewhere in the region of 10 per cent having persistent problems. The problems reported by those who continue to struggle include poor relationships with peers, including worries about bullying; difficulties associated with harder school work and more homework; and difficulties in relationships with teachers, either because of having many different teachers or because the teachers are stricter and more demanding than the young person can cope with (Hargreaves and Galton, 2002; Caulfield et al., 2005). Some research has concentrated on what might be called the protective factors which assist young people to cope with this transition. Flammer and Alsaker (2006) summarise the findings by describing three main factors which are helpful at this stage – having supportive parents, having a group of friends who make the transition together, and finally having a primary school that prepares the individual beforehand. A proactive approach on the part of the school and the family can make a substantial difference to the outcome of transition.

Not surprisingly educational policy makers have been concerned about changes in attitudes to school subjects following transfer. Before looking at individual subjects, however, it is important to emphasise that attitudes to school generally change once young people have made the transition, with pupils showing less favourable attitudes to school as they grow older. Studies show that attitudes to school decline in most developed countries, and that the sharpest decline in attitudes occurs after the first term in secondary school (Galton et al., 2002). Results from the HBSC study (Currie et al., 2008) showed only 25 per cent of 15-year-olds in the UK reporting high levels of satisfaction with their school experience. Some studies have shown that more able pupils have more positive attitudes, but this finding is not consistent across the board. Turning now to individual school subjects, findings are again consistent in showing that the decline in attitudes is least marked in relation to the native language of the country, but is more marked in relation to maths. However, the sharpest decline in attitudes is reserved for science, which becomes significantly more unpopular with age, and this is especially true for girls (Galton et al., 2003).

In conclusion it can be seen that research evidence throws some light on the theories outlined earlier. In the first place many pupils report positive feelings associated with being able to cope with the transition to secondary school. The ability to manage the transfer reflects a sense of being more grown up. Thus for some pupils the transition is acting in a sense as a 'rite of passage'. Of course this is not the case for everyone, and some research has looked at those who find this transition hardest. Not surprisingly Evangelou *et al.* (2008) identified those with special educational needs as being especially vulnerable at this stage. In terms of 'stage–environment fit' the evidence is not particularly encouraging. With young people's attitudes to secondary school deteriorating over time in most developed countries it can hardly be claimed that the school is meeting the developmental needs of the pupils. However, this is not just an effect of age. Other factors will play their part as well, and it is now appropriate to examine evidence regarding classroom climate and school ethos.

Classroom climate and school ethos

'The teachers sometimes, they don't really listen to students. Things like with the school, they tend to just do it. They put out a survey, and then they do the opposite to what we say. Throughout the year they've done things like that. They ask but then they do the opposite of what we say. I can't really be bothered with getting involved.'

(16-year-old boy)

In this section of the chapter there will be a focus on some of the school-based factors that have been identified as contributing to the adolescent's engagement with education. As Eccles (2004) has argued, understanding the impact of schools on adolescent development requires a conceptual framework which allows one to think simultaneously about the young person's needs as well as the characteristics of the school environment. This is the perspective described above as the 'stage–environment fit' theory. It has been suggested that within the educational environment both classroom and general school factors can be distinguished. As far as classroom variables are concerned, these include teacher expectations, teachers' general sense of efficacy, teacher–student relationships and classroom climate. Second there are broader factors that concern the school as an institution, with school ethos being a particular example of this. Each of these factors will be briefly reviewed.

Teacher beliefs have received considerable attention in educational research, and it is not difficult to see how important these might be for young people. Looking first at teacher expectations, many readers will be aware of the classic study by Rosenthal and Jacobsen (1968) entitled *Pygmalion in the classroom*. In this study the authors showed how artificial manipulation of the teacher's beliefs about the ability of pupils impacted on those pupils' classroom attainment. In this study the pupils were in primary school, but subsequently other studies have shown similar effects in the secondary school. While today it would be considered unethical to manipulate a teacher's beliefs about the ability of pupils, studies have looked at differential treatment accorded to students as a result of gender, race and social background. Results are clear in showing a small but consistent undermining effect of low teacher expectations. These are apparent on girls in maths and science, and on African-American pupils and on those from poorer backgrounds in all school subjects (Jussim *et al.*, 1996; Ferguson, 1998). An interesting study looked at teacher expectations of Asian students, finding that Asian students believe that

teachers expect them to perform well, and that this expectation actually leads to higher levels of achievement when ethnicity is evident in the classroom (Shih *et al.*, 1999).

The teacher's sense of self-efficacy is another factor which has been of interest to researchers. Again results are clear, showing that when teachers have a sense of self-worth and a belief that they can reach even the most difficult students, this is communicated to the students. The teacher's attitude thus enhances the student's own self-confidence about their ability to tackle academic work (Roeser *et al.*, 1998; Lee and Smith, 2001). In contrast studies have also shown that, where teachers have low confidence in their teaching efficacy, this also affects student performance. It has been reported that such attitudes on the part of teachers reinforce feelings of incompetence and alienation in students, possibly leading to anger, resentment and disengagement among adolescents in school (Jackson and Davies, 2000; Lee and Smith, 2001).

Both the variables discussed above are closely linked to the nature of the relationship between teacher and pupil. It is self-evident that high quality teacher–student relationships facilitate academic achievement, and make a substantial difference to broader psychological variables such as self-esteem, well-being and self-confidence in young people. If teachers are able to show respect for their students, and provide emotional support in the classroom, then this will have a marked influence on pupil behaviour. In line with the findings noted above concerning a deterioration in attitudes to school in early adolescence, a number of studies have shown that, following the transfer from primary to secondary school, there are declines in the students' perception of both emotional support and a sense of belonging in the classroom. As Eccles and her colleagues point out, these are worrying findings, since they illustrate a serious mismatch between the needs of young people and the organisation of secondary education (Eccles *et al.*, 1996; Eccles and Roeser, 2003).

In terms of classroom management the evidence suggests that there are a wide variety of teacher behaviours that impact on the functioning of the classroom. These include the ability to organise the class in relation to order, structure and smooth running, as well as the choice of type of instruction and the general teaching methods employed. Eccles (2004) outlines two notions that can be seen to relate to student performance. The first of these concerns goal theory, distinguishing between young people whose goals are to do with mastering the academic material, and those concerned with doing better than other students. It is claimed that students with differing goals will need different teaching methods in order to achieve well. Aspects of classroom management such as the assessment procedures used and the way feedback is organised will determine the way individual students respond and perform. Evidence would appear to suggest that pupils perform better in schools where mastery is emphasised as having a higher value than coming top of the class (Midgley, 2002).

A second and related aspect of classroom management has to do with whether teaching is organised in a cooperative or competitive manner. The work on girls and maths is one example of a situation where this becomes important. Research on this subject (Eccles and Roeser, 2003) indicates that girls do better in maths and science if teaching is organised on a cooperative basis, if it is taught from an applied rather than an abstract point of view, and if the teacher avoids sexism in all its forms. Eccles (2004) uses the term 'girl-friendly classrooms' to describe this form of classroom management, and as she notes, the findings are an excellent illustration of the 'person–environment fit' perspective. Where teaching is organised to coincide with the personal or developmental needs of the young person, it is not surprising to find that performance will be enhanced. Thus teacher behaviour in all its aspects can play a part in determining whether adolescents thrive or drift in the secondary school.

Turning now to the broader factors relating to the school generally, it is of importance to consider the school ethos. Numerous studies have explored the impact on young people of school ethos at the secondary level, and the findings reported by Michael Rutter and colleagues in the classic study *Fifteen thousand hours* (Rutter *et al.*, 1979) remain valid today. In this work the authors showed that, when comparing twelve secondary schools in South London, there were noticeable differences in such things as the way students' work was exhibited, the way young people were involved in school decision-making, and in the quality of teacher–pupil relationships. Of greatest interest was the finding that school ethos was related to such things as the level of truancy and the extent of pupil's involvement in anti-social behaviour outside school hours. As the authors say:

> Factors as varied as the degree of academic emphasis, the availability of incentives and rewards, good conditions for pupils, and the extent to which children were able to take responsibility, were all significantly associated with outcome differences between schools.
>
> (1979, p. 178)

Since the publication of this research many other studies have shown similar results. Bryk *et al.* (1993) explored differing attitudes to academic achievement by comparing Catholic and non-religious schools in the USA. This study illustrated how the culture of the school clearly affects both academic motivation and performance. West and colleagues (2004), in a large-scale investigation of Scottish secondary schools, were able to show that school ethos was related to a variety of health behaviours including the use of alcohol and tobacco. In Australia the Gatehouse project (Bond *et al.*, 2004) investigated whether making changes to the ethos of the school could lead to enhanced levels of social inclusion and a reduction in problematic behaviours such as early teenage pregnancy. As Bonell *et al.* (2007)

point out, interventions such as this show that, by improving school ethos, pupil behaviours that are not directly related to academic attainment can be affected in a positive direction. To conclude, therefore, this section of the chapter has illustrated how classroom and school factors contribute both to academic performance and to pupil engagement with school. With that in mind it is appropriate to look now at the broader issue of the role of the school in the promotion of pupil well-being.

Schools and well-being

'Doing exams and things was pretty stressful, the last couple of weeks was just like nuts, because you've got so much course work in the last month or so. You've got loads of course work to hand in, you've got loads of exams, and the exams are pretty stressful, you've just always got something to do, like you can't relax, it's pretty stressful. I think however much support they give you, you're going to find it stressful doing loads of exams. Like I found it quite annoying the amount they talked about it. Like they were giving us loads of booklets, and we had a whole day about preparing for exams, it just gets too much!'

(16-year-old boy)

As notions regarding the role of the school have gradually evolved, there can be discerned a growing interest in pupil well-being. Various strands of both research and policy have contributed to this trend. In the first place the writings of Goleman (1996) and others on the topic of emotional intelligence have been influential in encouraging educators to concern themselves with the emotional aspects of learning. Secondly there has been an international movement developing ideas to do with mental health promotion in the school setting (Coleman, 2007). Various interventions in countries such as Canada and Australia have looked at ways in which schools can mitigate the stigma of mental ill-health as well as enhance universal well-being among young people (Sawyer et al., 2010). Thirdly there has been widespread concern over the possibility that emotional disorders among adolescents are on the rise. This has led some to take the view that, if say teenage depression is on the increase, then schools have a place in tackling this problem. This concern is linked with cross-country comparisons, such as those contained in the UNICEF report on child well-being in rich countries (2007), and in the HBSC study of young people and health (Currie et al., 2008). Both these publications have shown young people in Britain to be doing poorly on indicators of emotional health when contrasted with their peers in other countries.

One of the problems with the trend towards seeing the school as an agent in the promotion of well-being is that there is no clear definition of this elusive concept (Coleman, 2009). For some well-being may equate to a notion of happiness, so that schools are expected to explore notions of the 'good life'. For others the idea of well-being is linked to the positive psychology movement, which focusses on characteristics of resilience and on effective coping (Seligman et al., 2009). Other writers have attempted to identify skills or competencies that could be associated with emotional literacy (Weare, 2004). These include such things as self-understanding, the management of emotions, and the ability to respond appropriately in social situations. Finally well-being for some writers is associated with the absence of mental ill-health, thus leading to the belief that schools have a role to play in addressing risk factors related to emotional disorders. As will be apparent, if there is no clear definition of the concept, there are significant problems for schools in deciding how to meet the objective of promoting pupil well-being.

In addition to problems of definition there is also the interesting question of how much influence the school is able to exercise when it comes to a variable such as well-being, however that is defined. There are two possible views on this. In the first, it is believed that schools vary in the effects they have, and that therefore interventions to improve schools will have the desired effect on pupils. The research on school ethos outlined above would lead to this conclusion, so that, for example, the study by Rutter and colleagues (1979) suggested that there are key differences between schools which impact on pupil outcomes. An alternative point of view is suggested as a result of research by Torsheim and Wold (2001). These authors explored outcomes amongst a sample of Norwegian adolescents, and showed that differences in schools only accounted for just over 2 per cent of individual variance in health complaints. A study in the UK among younger children showed similarly low levels of variation in health and well-being as a result of school differences (Gutman and Feinstein, 2008). Thus it may appear that differences between individual young people are likely to be greater than differences between schools when it comes to the promotion of well-being.

A further challenge in relation to this topic is that of assessment. How are schools and those responsible for inspecting educational regimes expected to identify whether pupil well-being is being effectively promoted? At the time of writing this is a matter of concern in Britain, and proposals currently under discussion have put forward a two-tier method of assessment (Coleman, 2009). The first tier is one which relates to the school's performance on measures of general well-being, as for example overall attendance rates, the proportion of persistent absentees, truancy rates and policies relating to exclusion from school. A second level of assessment depends on information originating from the individual pupil, and concerns such things as:

- whether the young person feels safe in the school;
- whether the school provides teaching on emotional health and well-being;
- whether the school actively discourages smoking, the use of alcohol and other risky behaviours;
- whether there is an appropriate system of pastoral care in place.

It is argued by Alsaker and Flammer (2006) that there are two aspects of the school environment which contribute as much as anything to pupil well-being. These are a genuine attempt on the part of the school to address the problem of bullying, and a concern with levels of pupil stress and feelings of pressure over school work and examinations. Considering bullying first, there is clear evidence that of all the difficulties that young people face when they move to secondary school, the threat of being bullied is one of the most worrying. Countries vary considerably in how much bullying occurs in secondary schools (Currie *et al.*,

2008), with a range of between 10 per cent and 20 per cent of adolescents reporting being bullied within the previous school term. Steinberg (2008) states that about one-third of pupils in high school in the USA experience harassment or bullying at some time in their school careers. Many writers have pointed out that bullying creates a vicious circle, in which the initial teasing or rejection has an effect on the individual's self-confidence and peer relationships, leading to an even greater sense of being an outsider, and thereby encouraging further bullying.

It is also the case that being bullied undermines the adolescent's sense of academic competence, leading to poor performance and thence to disengagement with school. The consequences of bullying can therefore be extensive and have a long-term impact on the individual's adjustment beyond the stage of secondary education. A number of studies have looked at those who bully as well as those who are bullied, and an important finding is that a significant proportion of those who are bullied are also ones who bully others.

This group, which accounts for approximately 25 per cent of those who are bullied, are among the most vulnerable, and as might be expected, they report more adjustment difficulties and mental health problems than others who fall into the group who are bullied (Haynie et al., 2001; Pellegrini and Long, 2002). In concluding these comments on bullying it is critical to underline the point that schools can do something about this. The evidence is clear that active anti-bullying policies and strong leadership from senior staff, together with schemes such as peer mentoring, can have a significant influence on reducing the incidence of bullying (Cowie et al., 2004). In this sense schools play a critical part in determining the well-being of pupils.

The other factor that Alsaker and Flammer (2006) mention as being central to well-being is the level of stress or pressure experienced by pupils in relation to homework and exams. A small amount of stress may be beneficial, in that it acts as a motivating force, but clearly high levels of stress are not consistent with an environment that is promoting well-being. One study compared Swiss and Norwegian young people, looking at levels of stress generated by homework (Alsaker and Flammer, 1999). Interestingly they found that in both countries there was a group of about 10 per cent for whom homework created significant levels of stress. However, in this small group it was not just homework that was creating problems, but other difficulties were also likely to be present, including poor relationships with teachers and lack of peer support. In the study reported by Currie et al. (2008) the numbers of young people in Britain reporting feeling pressure from schoolwork rose from 40 per cent at 11 to 50 per cent at 13 and then to 60 per cent for boys at 15 and 70 per cent for girls. These are worrying findings, especially as figures for young people in other European countries are, on average about 15–20 per cent lower than in the UK. Such results corroborate the UNICEF (2007) findings which showed children and adolescents in Britain having poorer emotional health than their peers across Europe.

As Coleman (2009) points out, there are many problems with the application of the concept of well-being to schools. Should teachers be expected to teach on topics such as emotional health, resilience, and the development of coping strategies? Should schools be expected to address the wider ills of society? Furthermore, as Webb *et al.* (2009) ask, what is the point in promoting pupil well-being if schools do not at the same time promote teacher well-being? On the other side of the argument, some aspects of well-being are clearly the responsibility of the school. Bullying and stress are obviously related to school performance, and thus need to be addressed within the school setting. Schools should undoubtedly have good pastoral care systems in place, and should pay attention to the quality of relationships and the academic motivation of their pupils. There is a strong case to be made for schools to address the psychological needs of young people, so long as those needs relate to the educational outcomes for which they are responsible. In the final section of this chapter the relation between schools and adolescent development will be explored.

Schools and adolescent development

'I think when you get to secondary, because there's so many different subjects to choose from, it's when you discover what you're good at. Like I never knew what I was good at before, now I've sort of discovered I'm good at cooking for instance. I never used to be good at PE (physical education), but now I'm okay. You change quite a lot at secondary school.'

(14-year-old girl)

'I think like, sometimes with your parents, like, you can't put your say in what you want, and they won't let you have your say in some things, but like now at school you sort of get to have your say in more things, like in lessons, and you can say what you like, and in school council and stuff.'

(14-year-old girl)

It is appropriate to end this chapter with a short discussion of the role of the school in facilitating or hindering adolescent development. It could be argued that large organisations, characterised by formal relationships between adults and pupils, strict timetables of activities, and inflexible means of assessing progress are hardly likely to offer an optimal environment in which young people can flourish and mature. However, it is also clear that some schools do better than others in this respect, and indeed it is also evident that young people themselves use their skills and resources to make the most of their educational environment. Adolescents are not passive recipients of whatever the school offers them, but are active agents in assessing, filtering and utilising the opportunities to be found within the school.

One important point to make is that schools are not simply academic institutions. Schools provide a wide range of experiences, and in terms of adolescent development they provide a setting for progress on multiple fronts, not just in terms of academic learning. One study asked young people to list their best and worst things about school (Brown *et al.*, 1992). What was liked best? 'Being with my friends'. 'Meeting new people'. What was liked least? 'Homework' 'Tests and exams'. In discussing the key part that schools play in facilitating development Rutter *et al.* (1979) made the following claim. 'Schooling does matter greatly. Moreover the benefits can be remarkably long-lasting. Schools are about social experiences as well as scholastic learning' (p. 197). It is clear therefore that schools enhance development not just because they provide a vehicle for the attainment of educational goals, but because they offer a range of other, often informal, settings for social development to take place.

In the course of this chapter this point has been substantiated with a range of examples. School ethos and classroom climate clearly make a big difference. The behaviour and attitudes of individual teachers are critical, and adolescents are only too well aware of how important these relationships can be.

> 'Yes, well certain adults, like responsible adults you know, like the normal sort of . . . cool, like good people, rather than . . . you know. There's a lot of muppets who are grown ups! A couple of my teachers are quite cool, which is quite nice to have some teachers you can have a joke with and stuff, which is better than the really horrible ones.'
>
> (16-year-old boy)

Transition at the beginning of the secondary school experience as well as transition out of schooling and into training or employment play a major part in affecting the course of development, and the brief review of well-being has highlighted ways in which schools can influence the emotional health of each individual within the system.

In thinking about what makes a good school in the context of adolescent development, Steinberg (2008) underlines three key elements which need to be in place. First, the school should demonstrate commitment to its students, and provide a good deal of flexibility about how the curriculum is delivered so that individual needs can be accommodated. Second, Steinberg argues that good schools constantly monitor their progress. Rather than seeing audit and inspection as an intrusion, a good school actively engages with such a process and makes use of all the feedback that is provided. Third, a good school would be one that is engaged with the local community. Parents would be involved with school activities, and the school would reach out to the community through strong links with local industry, local services and interested professionals.

Thinking about what makes a good school is one way to consider the developmental needs of the young person. Another way to consider this question is to imagine what would be needed to empower young people through education. Philip Graham, in his book *The end of adolescence* (2004), offers a perspective on this issue which takes empowerment as the criterion of success. In Graham's view there are a number of ways in which schools can empower adolescents. These include:

- the use of teaching methods that give adolescents some degree of autonomy;
- making the curriculum more relevant to 'the real world';
- providing feedback on teacher performance;
- offering opportunities for adolescents as they get older to teach younger pupils;
- involving students in the organisation of the school;
- involving students in the prevention of bullying;
- using technology in a way that makes sense to young people.

As will be apparent many of the features being suggested here are linked to what is known about the developmental needs of young people. These could be described as the need for gradually increasing responsibility and autonomy, the need for more equal relationships between adults and young people, the need for some element of individual choice in relation to academic learning, the need for rules and activities to have a clearly perceived rationale, and the need for opportunities that offer space for the young person to demonstrate maturity. There are examples of secondary schools that take these developmental needs seriously, and recognise that academic targets will be more readily met if the needs of young people are incorporated into the school's objectives. Much more could be done, however, and there is still a long way to go before all schools demonstrate their understanding of adolescent development.

Implications for practice

1. The context of education is changing rapidly. Young people are facing more uncertainty about the 16–19 stage, and about the transition into the labour market. There is also uncertainty today about higher education, and questions over which route to take in terms of the best option for a future career. This means that choice of subjects is critical, and guidance for young people becomes especially important. Research shows that parents play a key role here, but also that good support from schools and the recognition of the individual needs of pupils all contribute to better outcomes.
2. There has been greater recognition in recent years of the importance of transitions. The transition between primary and secondary school is of especial importance, and much has been learnt about how to mitigate some of the possible negative effects of moving from a small intimate school to a much larger more formal institution.
3. Research has shown that there are a number of factors that influence pupil engagement at the secondary level. These include school ethos, classroom climate, styles of teaching and teacher attitudes and behaviour. Much can be done to enhance the involvement of young people with learning and with the aims of the school, but this depends on recognition of some of the characteristics of adolescent development. One feature of this is an awareness that young people can easily become disengaged if they are not shown respect, and offered opportunities for autonomy and personal growth within the school setting.
4. Schools can promote the well-being of pupils, but there are many questions over how much teachers should concentrate on the emotional life of the young person as well as the teaching of the curriculum. There is no debate that adolescents will learn better if they feel safe in the school environment, and if they believe that the school will offer support when it is needed. Strategies to combat bullying are necessary, as is an appropriate and positive life-skills or personal, social and health education (PSHE) curriculum. Schools have many different expectations imposed upon them, but research

shows clearly that young people achieve better when the school ethos is aimed at creating an environment which is inclusive for all pupils, and in which pupils feel a sense of ownership and pride.

5. Schools can help or hinder adolescent development. It as well to remember that young people are not simply passive recipients of knowledge. On the contrary they assess the type of education on offer, and filter the information they are receiving from adults in ways that suit them. There are many things schools can do to facilitate adolescent development, and that in itself is an unusual message for many teachers to hear. What is known about adolescent development underlines the message that young people will need increasing amounts of autonomy as they move up the school, as well as opportunities to use their capabilities to make the most of their education. It is to be hoped that there are some ideas here that will be of interest and of value to the teaching profession.

Further reading

Eccles, J (2004) Schools, academic motivation and stage-environment fit. In Lerner, R and Steinberg, L (Eds) *Handbook of adolescent psychology*, 2nd edn. Wiley. New York.
Eccles is an original thinker who has done ground-breaking research on young people and education. This is an excellent review of key findings in the field.

Flammer, A and Alsaker, F (2006) Adolescents in school. In Jackson, S and Goossens, L (Eds) *Handbook of adolescent development*. Psychology Press. Hove.
A chapter outlining the main issues relating to schooling for young people, with an emphasis on a Europe-wide perspective.

Graham, P (2004) *The end of adolescence*. Oxford University Press. Oxford.
Although a general book about adolescence it has a chapter on schools and schooling entitled 'Schools: the solution or the problem?' This is a breath of fresh air when considering questions of education for young people.

Pring, R, Hayward, G, Hodgson, A, Johnson, J *et al.* (2009) *Education for all: the future of education and training for 14–19 year-olds*. Routledge. London.
An outline of a major five-year research programme to identify the way forward relating to education for older adolescents in Britain. Challenging and interesting.

Friends and the peer group

'I usually go to town with my friends on Saturday, and then probably stay the night round someone's house, and on Sunday do something round their house, and come back. Xbox, computer, pizza, just relaxing really. I used to go to youth club, but then I came out of it. I just found it boring. I realised they weren't really my kind of friends. I kind of hang out with normal people, not really chavs, normal people. Really, like at the youth club, they were kind of chavs, geeks and stuff.'

(14-year-old boy)

Peer groups are not unique to adolescence, nor do they first appear in the teenage years. Nevertheless they do have a special role in adolescence, and in this period of the lifespan they receive great attention from the adult world. This is partly because there is a sense of threat when groups of young people gather together, and partly because much of the negative stereotyping of adolescents is linked to behaviour in peer groups. In this chapter various aspects of friendship and the peer group will be considered, together with other social networks and settings in which young people meet and interact. Since the previous edition of this book was written in the late 1990s the use of digital technologies has become an integral part of 'social networking', and there will be a section in this chapter devoted to the topic.

In one of the classics of the literature on adolescence Dunphy (1972) first wrote about peer groups following his study of Australian youth. He suggested that youth groups form in societies where families or kinship groups – groups we have little or no choice in joining – cannot provide young people with the social skills or the roles they need in order to function in the wider society. Dunphy maintained that participation in youth groups was necessary in order to become self-regulating and for the construction of an adult identity. In this way adolescents become embedded in a complex network of relationships which include best friends, close friends, acquaintances, peer groups, crowds and intimate relationships. These groups all allow the young person some degree of choice in whether to join or not. In this chapter there will be sections covering the genesis of adolescent social relationships, the dynamics of friendship and of peer groups, the interaction between families and friends, the role of digital technologies, and finally the problem of isolation and rejection.

The genesis of adolescent social relationships

'Friends are definitely important in giving you more confidence and feeling sort of secure and safe. And sort of they're stability. I mean I've had some bad experiences with best friends, and when it all falls apart it's a horrible experience to have to go through, but when you have a lot of good friends around you just feel secure. Like they wouldn't really care what you came in looking like, they'd still be your friends. And also for discovering new things, and finding out new things, they can open you up to new experiences, whether it's like going out, or where they shop, or things like that. And new music that you get to hear, all helps you with finding out your identity.'

(17-year-old girl)

Two theoretical notions can be helpful in understanding the genesis of social relationships in adolescence. These are attachment theory and social identity theory. Both these theories give some insight into why friendship and the peer group assume greater significance in adolescence than in childhood. As far as attachment theory is concerned, psychoanalysts have argued for nearly a century that adolescence is a time of gradual separation from parents and a turning towards a wider social environment. While parents gradually fulfil less of the individual's emotional needs, friends step forward to fill the gap. As part of this process the attachment patterns learnt very early in life will be transferred to the close friends and intimate relationships that are formed during adolescence. Attachment theorists believe that people have mental models of relationships, models that are learnt in the earliest contact between the infant and his or her parents. These are known as attachment representations, and as Carlson and colleagues (2004) note: 'These representations carry forward previous social experience and provide structure for subsequent encounters with the world' (p. 67). The behaviour of young people with their friends illustrates this process. Indeed the young woman quoted above talks of security and stability, two key attributes of early attachments. Another is proximity-seeking, again illustrated by the need of adolescents to keep constantly in touch with their friends, and to remain close through texting, telephoning and messaging. Attachment theory argues that the shape and texture of young people's relationships with their friends are based on earlier attachment experiences (Cotterell, 2007).

Turning now to social identity theory, this arose initially as a result of research into prejudice and stereotyping. Tajfel (1978) and others talked of a group identity, and of the interpersonal benefits that may be derived from a shared world view and a shared set of attitudes and opinions. This is especially true where individuals are experiencing major transitions, where they feel vulnerable in respect of their identity, or where they feel under threat from other groups. In the case of adolescence this threat may be perceived as coming from adults or from other groups of young people. Tajfel (1978) suggested that the value of belonging to a group is dependent on its status relative to other groups. People, especially those who are vulnerable for one reason or another, make distinctions between in-groups and out-groups, and then denigrate or find fault with the out-group, thus boosting their own status. It is not difficult to see how this theory may be applied to adolescent social relationships!

In terms of the process of friendship formation, it is usually during early to mid-adolescence that personal needs and social pressures direct young people towards at least one friendship group. Work by Ryan (2001) showed that 75 per cent of 13-year-olds belonged to a friendship group, with a small number having only one friend, and about 15 per cent having no friends at all. Although friends typically live in the same neighbourhood and are similar in ethnic and socio-economic backgrounds, friendships sometimes cross boundaries in terms of gender, race, age and social background. Friendships frequently begin in school, while time outside school strengthens the bond. Some young people find it difficult to establish out-of-school friendships because they lack confidence or the necessary social skills. How well adolescents get on with friends partly reflects what they have learnt about close relationships at home, not only because of very early attachments, but because everyday family life provides children with many learning opportunities around self-disclosure, trust, loyalty, conflict resolution, compromise and respect (Cotterell, 2007). Race, gender and age differences, as well as lack of transportation, are all potential obstacles to out-of-school friendships, and it appears that friendship networks become more exclusive with increasing age (De Goede *et al.*, 2009).

Compared with younger children, who are normally more flexible and less self-conscious, many adolescents feel awkward about meeting strange peers and joining established groups. This may be partly due to the fact that adolescents have links to a range of groups, for example having a school-based friendship group, a neighbourhood group, and one built around a hobby or sports activity. It is also very much to do with social identity, the importance of conformity, and the existence of rigid codes of behaviour within one group or another. More will be said about this in a later section. Different groups have different norms and expectations, and it is not always easy for newcomers to understand these, sometimes arcane, rules (see Scholte and van Aken, 2006). One of the key social skills that most young people develop during adolescence is the ability to make contact and interact with strangers, in other words to form new social bonds. Whilst in childhood these social bonds tend to be relatively intimate and to occur in small groups, complexity and differentiation increase during adolescence so that it is usual to expect a young person of 15 or 16 to be able to function socially in a number of social groups, both large and small.

The dynamics of friendship and the peer group

'Recently I've made loads of new friends at school. I've changed a bit, like I care more about what I look like and stuff. I used to hang around with a load of other people, but I didn't really get on with them very well, so I started hanging around with one other person, and then met all her friends. The old group, they care a lot about their school work, and they're not very sociable and stuff, but like my friends now, we're like every Friday after school we go into town, see people and have sleepovers and stuff. It's made me much happier, because I've met loads more people from them, and its made me meet others as well, it's good like that.'

(14-year-old girl)

The manner in which social relationships operate through the adolescent age period is of great interest, but before looking more closely at this it is important to differentiate between friendships and relationships with the wider age cohort. One useful distinction is that outlined by Brown (2004) between cliques and crowds. Cliques are small groups – of between three and ten people – defined by common activities and shared interests. Teenagers are likely to call these their 'friendship groups'. Crowds on the other hand are larger groups, defined by age or class in school or neighbourhood. These groupings are also known as peer groups. Of course this picture is too simple, since within the peer group there will be sub-groups, sometimes given names such as chavs, druggies, geeks, nerds, brains and so on. Nonetheless the distinction between the small, intimate group and the larger crowd is useful, and in this section we will first consider friendship, and then move on to look at the dynamics of the wider peer group.

There has been much discussion in the literature on the function of friends during adolescence, and a useful starting point is the work of Mendelson and Aboud (1999), who defined six functions of friendship. These are:

- companionship
- a reliable alliance
- help
- intimacy
- self-validation
- emotional security.

As noted by Cotterell (2007) these attributes describe key elements of friendship, such as being available, providing someone to share things with, being loyal and trustworthy and offering assistance in times of difficulty. Cotterell argues that there are two factors here underlying any categorisation of the functions of friendship. These are, firstly, that relationships with those of the same age offer a route for integration into a social network, and secondly that they offer reassurance of worth through validation by one's age cohort. These ideas can be subsumed under a general notion of belongingness, since they describe social processes that include 'fitting in' and 'feeling accepted', as well as social identification and well-being. Many studies have shown that those who become friends share common interests. Thus Steinberg (2008) points out that motivation towards school, interest in a particular sport or hobby, orientation towards teenage culture, or anti-social behaviour are all dimensions which might differentiate friendship groups. Crosnoe and Needham (2004), for example, showed that friends tend to have similar academic grades, and to choose similar subjects to study in school.

Being popular is highly valued by everyone, but it is of particular significance during adolescence. As has been noted, having a friendship group, and being able to remain within the group, are factors which relate to self-esteem and to the development of a coherent identity. The chief determinant of popularity is whether the individual is socially skilled or not. Those who are popular act appropriately in the eyes of their peers, they are able to recognise the needs of others, and are confident without being conceited. In addition athletic prowess for boys and attractiveness for girls also play their part in determining popularity. However, these are generalisations, and there are many different routes to popularity. One study (Rodkin et al., 2000) identified two distinct popular groups among a population of boys aged between 12 and 15. These researchers described the two groups as 'model' boys and 'tough' boys. While the 'model' boys were sporty, competent, friendly – fitting the stereotype of popularity – the 'tough' boys, who were equally popular, were physically strong, aggressive and not particularly friendly. Thus it is important to recognise that popularity can be determined by many different factors. It is also worth noting that those who are not especially popular in school may have a well-developed friendship network outside school. A study by Kiesner *et al.* (2003) noted that the disadvantages of having few friends in school were buffered by having a friendship group away from the school environment.

Turning now to the dynamics of the larger peer group, one of the key themes here has to do with the question of peer influence, or peer pressure. Are all adolescents susceptible to peer influence, or is this true only of certain individuals? The answer is closely linked to the issue of social acceptance. Where the need for acceptance is high, peer influence will be more powerful, and there are two variables that affect the need for acceptance: one is age and the other has to do with individual differences. As far as age is concerned, studies have shown clearly that conformity to peer group norms or influence is at its height in early to middle adolescence – i.e. from about 12 to 15. It is at this time that questions of acceptance or rejection loom largest in the minds of young people, and thus they are more susceptible to the pressures that stem from peers. As they grow older adolescents are more able to make up their own minds and to stand up to any pressure that might originate from peers. However, it is also the case that individual differences affect susceptibility to peer influence. Some young people will be more autonomous than others, and thus personality factors will play their part too in determining acceptance or rejection of peer influence. One further factor that is significant is the degree of support provided by the family. More will be said about this later, but it is apparent that those who receive low levels of support from parents are likely to be more open to the influence of the peer group.

Brown (2004) makes the point that there are different types of peer influence. In his view direct pressure is relatively rare, but other types of influence include:

- modelling (where young people seek to emulate the behaviour of others);
- structuring of opportunities (where peers provide an arena for certain types of behaviour, such as taking drugs at a party);
- normative regulation (where peers work together to define the norms they are comfortable with, such as for example working out what is right and wrong in sexual behaviour).

Brown also emphasises the fact that influence works both ways. As has been noted at other points in this book, relationships are reciprocal, so that adolescents are both recipients and producers of influence. This leads on to the important question of whether peer groups are self-selecting, in that those with common interests are drawn together, or whether peer groups are socialising agents, exerting influence and changing the behaviour of those who belong. Research indicates that both selection and socialisation are at work in a variety of different areas, including school achievement, drug use, mental health and anti-social behaviour. Adolescents who drink or smoke are more likely than others to choose friends who do the same, but similarly spending time with such friends increases the

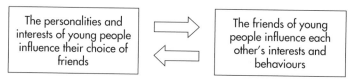

Figure 9.1 The interests and attitudes of young people both influence and are influenced by their choice of friends.

likelihood that the individual will take up these behaviours (Ennett *et al.*, 2006). The same goes for mental health, with depressed friends influencing each other (Stevens and Prinstein, 2005), and anti-social behaviour, where young people encourage their friends to misbehave, but are also influenced by them (Werner and Silbereisen, 2003). The question is often asked as to whether the peer group encourages certain behaviours, especially anti-social behaviour. Based on the research findings it would appear that this is too simple a question. Influence works both ways, as can be seen from Figure 9.1.

Parents and peers

'When things are really difficult I would say friends are the most important. I've got a really good friend, and basically I could tell her anything or trust her with anything. I'm the sort of person that if I can't say it, I get really aggravated about it. If you can't say something, or at least get it out or voice your opinion and get an opinion back it gets really hard to think what to do. Some people are close to their Mums or Dads or whoever. I tell my Mum a reasonable amount of stuff, but I'm not the sort of person who would be like, oh there's a problem I'll go straight to my Mum. I don't believe that she should know everything that's going on with me.'

(16-year-old girl)

As many writers have pointed out, friendships are based on a very different set of structural relationships than those with parents. Friendships are more symmetrical, involve reciprocity and are evolutionary through adolescence. While friendships are important to younger children, there is a change at the beginning of adolescence, with peers assuming greater salience and taking up more leisure time outside the family. During the adolescent years obvious alterations take place in relationship patterns and in social contexts. As has already been noted friends become companions, providers of advice, support and feedback, as well as models of behaviour and sources of comparative information concerning personal qualities and skills. Relationships with parents alter too, and there are changes towards greater equality, and more opportunity for negotiation and discussion. The process of autonomy development has been discussed in some detail in Chapter 5.

The central question in considering family and peers has to do with whether parents or friends are more influential during this stage of life. In early writings this was known as the 'parent–peer issue'. This is a matter of major importance for parents themselves, as well as for society generally. The idea that somehow young people create their own society, one that is separate from the adult world with values that are antithetical to those of adult society, is a scary notion. James Coleman wrote a book called *The adolescent society* (1961) which gave some prominence to this view, and more recently much publicity was given to a publication entitled *The nurture assumption* (Harris, 1998), which argued that parents matter little, and that in reality the development of young people is largely determined by their friendship groups. These ideas go hand in hand with concerns about the decreasing time that adults spend with young people. This is partly to do with having more mothers in the labour market, but also reflects the possibility that a generation of adults may perhaps have less interest in spending time with their teenage sons and daughters. Indeed one writer (Marsland, 1987) spoke of 'auto-socialisation', meaning that today young people essentially act as their own socialisation agents, free from adult influence.

These ideas are understandable, but they are not borne out by the research evidence. It is clear, firstly, that the notion of an either–or situation is far too simple. It is not a question of whether parents or peers are most influential, but rather a case of both being influential in different circumstances. The second point to make is that peers fill a vacuum when parents are not engaged or involved with their sons and daughters. It is only when parents are not playing a role that friends assume greater significance, and may in such situations become more influential. Looking first at the either–or question, the evidence shows that in general parents remain important in future-oriented domains such as education and career choice, whilst friends are more influential where social dilemmas, fashion and leisure activities are concerned (Hendry *et al.*, 1993). Some studies have shown that adolescents are more influenced by parents than by peers in core values (Cotterell, 2007), whilst others have argued that in many situations young people will in fact consult both parents and peers before making important decisions. In terms of whether parents or peers are seen as more supportive, the evidence is clear that as young people move through adolescence friends assume greater and greater significance. Interestingly, however, a study carried out in the Netherlands by Scholte *et al.* (2001) indicated that although support from parents gradually declined and friends played a bigger role as providers of support, friends never surpassed parents.

It is easy to see how young people would turn to friends for support. Friends are less likely than parents to coerce, criticise and lecture, and are more willing to give each other personal validity when it comes to making difficult decisions. Nonetheless virtually every piece of research that has been carried out underlines the major role that parents play in affecting outcomes for young people. One good example of this can be found in Liza Catan's (2004) report based on 19 different studies which were part of the British ESRC 'Youth, citizenship and social change' programme. As she says:

> Studies in the programme moved towards a view of families of origin as the co-ordinating site for many different types of resources central to young people's futures, both economic and material, and social/cultural, as in the

studies which highlighted the importance of parental aspirations, parental involvement in children's education, and support for school and college work. . . . For the majority some level of family support lasts throughout their twenties, and provides fundamental personal and material resources, without which the transition to adulthood is highly risky and stressful.

(pp. 24 and 25)

From this it is clear that whether parents are involved or not, and whether young people can look to their parents for support at critical junctures, at 'turning points' as Graber and Brooks-Gunn (1996) called them, is absolutely vital for future development. Thus friends have a key role to play, but without parental support adolescents will find it much harder to progress in a functional manner towards adulthood.

This links closely to the point about friends and peers filling a vacuum when parents are not available. The discussion about this notion has been framed in terms of whether support from one relationship can compensate for the lack of support in another relationship. This question can only be understood if a social network approach is taken, whereby all relationships are looked at simultaneously. Thus, for example, East and Rook (1992) found that those with low peer support received more support from siblings. In terms of parents, a study by Gauze et al. (1996) demonstrated that friendships have enhanced significance where support from the family is low. Further, research by Reicher (1993) looked at those with low parental support but high support from friends. This group had significant levels of problem behaviour, as well as having more anxiety and depressive symptoms. Of all groups of adolescents, these young people were most likely to be involved in anti-social behaviour, and to be least engaged with school and future career. Further research has shown that even where young people have anti-social friends, if they have support from parents this will make them less susceptible to their friends' negative influence (Crosnoe et al., 2002; Walker-Barnes and Mason, 2004).

Parents and peers cannot really be looked at in isolation, but need to be considered as two interconnected aspects of the social world of the adolescent. Indeed most of the characteristics that young people bring to their friendship and peer relationships will have their basis in what has been learnt in the home. During adolescence this pattern continues, with parental behaviour having an impact on the way young people manage their peer relationships. Durbin et al. (1993) showed that parenting style affected friendship choice. Those with indifferent parents chose friends who were indifferent to adult values, those with indulgent parents selected fun-loving friends, and those with authoritative parents chose friends who were engaged with school and community activities. It must not be forgotten, however, that young people will influence their parents too. Some adolescents will opt for friendship groups that mirror the values of the family, whilst others will choose those that annoy or irritate their parents. Some may even select friends who are the exact opposite of what their parents would like! As in all situations, parents and young people interact in a reciprocal manner, and this is as true of friendship and peer group choice as it is in other domains.

Rejection and isolation

'Yeah, you got to do stuff. It's not going to be much fun if you don't do stuff, or if you just do stuff with your Mum for the rest of your life. So you have to, like, get out there, or even just to go round to a house to play games or stuff, it makes it more sociable. Because you do see them types that is just not doing much, like people you know that just don't go out much, and then they're, like, cut off and just . . . well, sad.'

(15-year-old boy)

In view of the importance of friends and the peer group, it is as well to consider the implications for young people of being solitary, lonely or rejected by the social group which surrounds them. There are various questions here.

- Firstly, does it matter if a young person is without friends?
- Secondly, do lonely or rejected individuals share particular personality characteristics?
- Thirdly, is there anything that can be done to help such individuals?

As Goossens (2006b) points out, there are some important issues of definition that need to be noted before these questions can be addressed. Loneliness is an emotion, and is something that is felt by everyone at some time. To have experienced loneliness does not mean that the individual is without friends. The same goes for solitude. Everyone spends time alone, and during adolescence there are many positive aspects of being alone, such as time for reflection and opportunities for privacy. Difficulties arise when solitude is unwanted, when the individual seeks company but is unable to make friends or to keep them. In this chapter attention will be focussed on situations of unwanted solitude, leading to isolation or rejection.

Looking at the question of the impact of being without friends, there is very little research on this topic. Yet it is one that concerns parents and young people alike, and deserves greater attention. As already noted, research by Ryan (2001) showed that approximately 15 per cent of young adolescents are without friends. It seems probable that this group is not homogeneous, but will include within it a range of different young people. There are undoubtedly some who go through adolescence as solitary individuals, but who cope well with this situation. Among them will be those who get support from other sources, such as a sibling or other family member. A proportion of these individuals will go on to become more socially active and engaged as they mature. Another group here will be those who are withdrawn, who have social skills deficits or social anxiety. Lastly there will be others who are unpopular due to aggressive or inappropriate behaviour. Clearly the impact of being without friends will differ for each of these groups, but it is important to emphasise that not all adolescents who lack a friendship group are necessarily damaged or disadvantaged by this situation. Having said this, research findings do, in the main, report negative consequences for young people who are rejected by their peers. Steinberg (2008) lists a number of studies showing rejection to be associated with depression, anxiety, low self-esteem and poor academic performance.

The next question concerns the characteristics of isolated or rejected adolescents. Again there are different sub-groups here, and these will need to be discussed separately. Before doing this, a general point can be made about age. Goossens (2006b) has carried out extensive research on this topic, and he points out that age is an important variable here. Loneliness is experienced most often in early adolescence, but this may partly be because of the increased importance of the peer group at this developmental stage. As young people grow they develop strategies to cope with loneliness, and report fewer low moods as a result of being on their own. The author's own work, published as *Relationships in adolescence* (Coleman, 1974), was one of the first studies to document this. The developing cognitive abilities of the adolescent may be valuable in helping to manage solitude, but it could also be that for the older adolescent solitude is useful for self-reflection, emotional regulation and coping.

In considering the characteristics of isolated or rejected individuals most writers draw a distinction between those who are withdrawn and those who are aggressive. Studies by Dodge and his colleagues (Crick and Dodge, 1994, 1996) have shown that unpopular aggressive young people are more likely than others to think that other people's behaviour is deliberately aggressive, even when it is not. This characteristic has come to be known as *hostile attributional bias*, and it plays a central role in the aggressive behaviour of adolescents who are rejected by their peers. Crick (1996) has also made the point that when aggression is mentioned it is boys who are most often in the frame. However, girls can be just as aggressive, only their aggression is expressed in a different form. Crick calls this *relational aggression*, involving verbal bullying, trying to cause unhappiness, and manipulating social situations to upset or aggravate others. These young people differ from those who are unpopular and withdrawn. The withdrawn group consists of individuals who are likely to be excessively anxious and uncertain of how to behave when they are with others of the same age. Their lack of confidence and low self-esteem make others feel uncomfortable, and they become easy targets for bullying. They are often especially sensitive to being rejected, which in turn is likely to make the situation worse. Graham and Juvonen (1998) have called this a cycle of victimisation.

Bullying is an important consideration in any outline of rejected or isolated adolescents. There has been much research on this topic, and numerous surveys of young people's experiences of bullying. To take one example Eslea *et al.* (2003) surveyed over 40,000 young people in seven European countries, and reported that up to 17 per cent of all adolescents were bullies, 26 per cent were victims, and a further 20 per cent were bully/victims. This raises the question of how bullying is defined, and studies of this phenomenon have been plagued by definitional problems. Where the definition of bullying is more restricted, or where bullying is understood differently, the proportions reporting bullying are much lower, and this may partly explain the large inter-country differences. In the Eslea *et al.* (2003) study only 5 per cent of young people in England and Ireland report having been bullied, yet in Italy it was 26 per cent. Other surveys have been carried out by Olweus (1993) and by Smith *et al.* (1999).

As far as characteristics of the bullies and victims are concerned, research on this topic shows that victims tend to be more depressed and lonely than others, and to have lower self-esteem and more limited social skills (see Hawker and Boulton, 2000, for a review). Bullies on the other hand, while also having social deficits, differ in significant respects. They tend to be more aggressive and to display fewer pro-social behaviours such as cooperation and the ability to share. They are also more likely to be at risk for later problem behaviour (Olweus, 1993). There has been some debate in the literature about whether bullies are socially inadequate or not. Some have argued that bullies use bullying behaviour to obtain social goals such as dominance or social status, and thus cannot be described as socially inadequate. As Scholte and van Aken (2006) put it: 'These bullies may not lack social skills since they can accurately interpret social cues, but they use socially deviant strategies to obtain their goals' (p. 188). It is important to note that there is a small group who are both bullies and victims. Research by Smith *et al.* (1999) shows that these young people have more problems than those who are either bullies or victims. Bullying is a major problem for some young people, and whilst numerous strategies have been introduced in schools to tackle this, it is difficult to eradicate it completely. There will be more to say on this in the next section when what is known as cyber-bullying is considered.

Lastly in this section it is worthwhile to review what can be done to help young people who are isolated, rejected or the victims of bullying. A variety of programmes have been designed by psychologists to help develop social competence among this group of adolescents. Some programmes teach social skills, whilst others bring together popular and unpopular young people in group situations and help them to learn from each other (see Fonagy *et al.*, 2005). Many such programmes depend on the development of cognitive behavioural skills, teaching adolescents to get better at judging social situations and rehearsing acceptable ways of behaving with their peers. One good example of a social problem-solving approach is the PATHS programme, which stands for Promoting Alternative Thinking Strategies (referenced in Cowie *et al.*, 2004, and Steinberg, 2008). There is some evidence that this has been successful in raising self-confidence and reducing social anxiety, but further evaluations of such programmes should be a high priority (Coleman, 2007).

The digital generation

'Things are a lot faster, if I want to get hold of someone I'll just go on the computer, or if I wanted to talk I'd just, like, text. You sort of rely on it so much that you don't even realise it. Because I lost my phone today, so I haven't got it tonight, and even then I was just sort of coming home from school and I felt, like, completely vulnerable, and I was just, like, I haven't got anything to sort of, have! And it's just, like, what happens if I suddenly get lost, not that I would, you start to panic.'

(15-year-old girl)

'I don't like it when people, like, you go round to someone's house and spend time with people and they're texting someone else. People get too attached to their mobiles. And I don't really like Facebook. I recently joined because a friend made me, and I'm not really a fan. I don't know how people can get addicted to it. There can be loads of misunderstandings, and also being in contact with people that you don't really want to be in contact with. And you can't be anonymous because they can find you on Facebook. And all the competition around it, there's a lot of bitchiness over other people's photos, and what people are doing and stuff. It's a lot more hurtful because it goes there and it can stay there, and everyone can see it, whereas if two of my friends were just bitching about me that would be fine because I don't know about it, but there it seems much more serious and permanent.'

(17-year-old girl)

There have been major changes in the use of new communication technologies over the past decade, and the situation is changing so rapidly that it is difficult to paint a picture that will be relevant in the next decade. From 1999 onwards there was a dramatic increase in the use of mobile phones by young people, and in subsequent years the use of the internet, social networking sites and messaging through the computer has become the norm. In the early 2000s there was much discussion about access to the internet, with fears that impoverished or socially excluded young people would suffer a disadvantage if they could not make use of the internet. However, this situation is altering all the time, so that more and more homes are linked to the internet, the technology of mobile phones is changing and developing, and a wider range of community settings have computers available for public use. In this section there will be a short review of the use young people make of communication technologies, followed by a consideration of both the opportunities and risks for adolescent development associated with these technologies. It should be noted that young people use digital technologies not only for communication purposes, but for activities such as gaming, surfing, watching films and information-seeking. All these are features of screen-based activity, as described by Mesch and Talmud (2010), but there is not the space to consider them here. In this brief section the focus will be on communication.

The first point of note is that digital technologies have made keeping in touch with friends easier than ever before. If texting, messaging, emailing, using social networking sites and using telephones are all included, the potential for communication is immense. The desire to keep in touch with friends is hardly new. In previous generations it was common for parents to complain about the constant use of the phone, and to question why it was necessary for a young person to spend hours chatting to someone they had seen a short while previously. In that sense nothing has changed, but what is new, however, is the range of media available, and the potential to widen the communication network. A message that would in the

past have gone between two people is now frequently seen and shared by many. This has implications for notions of privacy, an issue we will return to below. Livingstone (2009), in her review of the use of the internet, makes the point that those who use many different digital media for communicating with friends are also in the main good face-to-face communicators. Many commentators have feared that, as young people turn to screen-based forms of communication, interpersonal skills will be lost, but the research does not support this contention. Valkenberg and Peter (2007) show that online communication actually fosters closer relationships between friends, providing wider opportunities for sharing and intimacy. It appears that for all but those who are already isolated, the internet facilitates existing social contacts rather than undermining them (Mesch and Talmud, 2007, 2010).

A second function of communication through digital media is the exploration of identity. Because both chat rooms and social networking sites offer the possibility of manipulating how the individual is presented to others, these have turned into ideal forums for trying on different identities. Erikson (1968) talked of adolescence as a time of social play, the successor to childhood play. Digital technologies have provided the perfect opportunity for this aspect of adolescent development to be facilitated. As Marwick (2005) puts it: 'Social networking sites enable people to codify, map and view the relational ties between themselves and others, a codification that requires constant revision' (p. 3). There is also the question of privacy and intimacy that is raised by these types of communication. Young people are making decisions about privacy all the time, in offline as well as online spaces, so it is not the case that new technologies have suddenly thrown up new challenges for adolescents. However, there are some important concerns, especially because of the potential for what appears to be anonymity on the internet. What young people post on their Facebook or Bebo sites has been the subject of much research, and there is no doubt that personal information is being shared with large numbers of relative strangers, as the UK Children Go On-Line survey showed (Livingstone, 2009). What it also showed, however, was that young people are very much aware of privacy issues, and would welcome discussions about this with teachers and other adults.

One of the most intense debates concerning the use of digital technologies by young people has to do with balancing the threats against the opportunities. There are some who take extreme views, so that commentators such as Palmer (2007) believe that technological advances undermine core values, destroy the family and take away childhood innocence. Not surprisingly there are others who see great opportunities for children and young people in the development of the internet and other communication technologies (e.g. Buckingham, 2007). Most writers take a balanced view, accepting that there are risks to young people, but that these must be acknowledged and addressed, so that the enormous potential of digital technologies for adolescents is not lost or restricted. The chart drawn up by Sonia Livingstone (2009) illustrating both risks and opportunities is shown in Box 9.1.

There are some obvious benefits for young people of new technologies. The possibility of communicating with friends and keeping in touch has already been mentioned. In addition the internet provides instant access to banks of information in a manner that was unknown to previous generations. It is important to note that

Online opportunities	Online risks
Access to global information	Illegal content
Educational resources	Paedophiles, grooming, strangers
Social networking among friends	Extreme or sexual violence
Entertainment, games and fun	Other harmful offensive content
User-generated content creation	Racist/hate material and activities
Civic or political participation	Advertising and stealth marketing
Privacy for identity expression	Biased or misinformation
Community involvement/activism	Abuse of personal information
Technological expertise and literacy	Cyber-bullying/harassment
Career advancement/employment	Gambling, phishing, financial scams
Personal/health/sexual advice	Self-harm (suicide, anorexia)
Specialist groups/fan forums	Invasions/abuse of privacy
Shared experiences with distant others	Illegal activities (hacking, copyright abuse)

Box 9.1 Risks and opportunities for young people posed by online activities.
Source: Livingstone (2009) by permission.

new technologies allow skill development, and they also offer autonomy to young people, by virtue of the fact that the online world is a world largely hidden from adult view. Two other facts should be mentioned. In situations where young people live in dangerous or severely deprived communities the internet can provide a route for learning and development that would be impossible in the offline environment. Further where young people might suffer prejudice or disadvantage the internet can provide a safe arena for identity exploration and for social development. Henderson *et al.* (2007) give examples of gay and lesbian young people who used the 'Gaydar' website to meet others and explore their identities, as well as young people with a disability who made contacts through the internet which would not have been possible in any other way.

No matter how positively these new technologies are viewed, the threats cannot be ignored. Three particular risks may be mentioned here. Cyber-bullying has already been mentioned. Research on this is sparse at present, and there is little clarity about either the scope or the harm posed by this type of bullying. Some believe that the use of phones or the internet is simply bullying by another means, and that such behaviour would be occurring anyway. Others argue that the type of bullying that is made possible by digital technology does increase the harm caused, particularly because of the anonymity afforded by online methods and because of the range of people that can be contacted through these means (Patchin and Hinduja, 2006). A second risk has to do with sexual harassment, grooming or exposure to unsafe relationships. This is an understandable adult fear, and a range of strategies have been put in place to address these concerns. Nonetheless this is a difficult problem, as Finkelhor (2008) points out. Research shows that a significant proportion of adolescents, both male and female, have exposure to erotic or sexual material on the internet (Livingstone and Bober, 2004). There is no

189

single answer or strategy to make young people safe online, but some part of the answer surely lies in better education for young people in the use of technology.

A third risk has to do with internet addiction and the possibility that adolescents' mental health will suffer if too much time is spent online. Again there is relatively little research on this subject, but Punamaki *et al.* (2007) report poor sleep patterns and waking tiredness among those who are habitual users of the internet, whilst Selfhout *et al.* (2009) find evidence of depression and social anxiety among heavy internet users. Thus it will be apparent that the development and increasing availability of digital technologies reflects a situation which poses some threats to young people, especially those who are already vulnerable because of poor mental health or social isolation. However, it is also a situation which has exciting potential for the enhancement of adolescent development. The costs and benefits of new technologies must be weighed dispassionately by all concerned with the welfare of young people, so that adolescents can be better prepared for the digital world in which they live.

Implications for practice

1. It is not always recognised by parents and other adults, but in adolescence friends and the wider peer group play an especially significant role as contributors to development. Friends are important in childhood, but they become much more central during the adolescent years as the young person seeks social support outside the family. In addition, the peer group provides an alternative set of values and opinions, and acts as a useful barometer of fashion and taste. Peers also offer an arena for the development of social skills, and assist in key areas of identity formation.
2. Issues of popularity and status in the peer group matter greatly during this stage of development. As a result, young people may appear to be conformist in their dress, their choice of music and leisure activities, and in their opinions. This conformity reflects the need to be accepted within the salient social grouping of the moment. As young people develop their own self-confidence and assurance, the need to be like everyone else will diminish, and more individualistic forms of behaviour will become apparent.
3. It is often believed that, during adolescence, the peer group becomes the most influential reference group, and that parents no longer have any part to play. Research shows this to be incorrect. Parents and peers are not necessarily in opposition to each other, but rather the two groups may be influential in different arenas. Thus, young people will listen to their friends when it comes to questions of fashion or social convention, but will refer to their parents over school issues, careers, morality and so on. It is also important to note that young people often choose friends who have views similar to those of their parents, even though it may be essential for them to deny any such similarities.
4. Because friendship and acceptance in the peer group are so important at this stage, those who are isolated or rejected are at a particular disadvantage.

Loneliness can be difficult to deal with, especially when everyone else appears to be part of a group. For practitioners these young people need special attention, and, as has been shown, there is a lot that can be done to assist those who find friendship problematic during adolescence.

5. Practitioners will be only too well aware of the risks posed by digital technologies. Cyber-bullying, grooming on the internet, and the activities of paedophiles are all very much in the public mind. It will also be important, however, for practitioners to be aware of the opportunities provided by new technologies. Whether it is using texting to remind a young person about an appointment, or finding ways for someone to access information on the internet that would not have been possible in any other way, it is essential to recognise both the positives and negatives where technology is concerned.

Further reading

Brown, B (2004) Adolescents' relationships with peers. In Lerner, R and Steinberg, L (Eds) *Handbook of adolescent psychology*, 2nd edn. Wiley. New York.
An authoritative survey of the field by one of the pre-eminent American scholars. Brown has carried out some of the key research in this area, and provides extensive coverage of the main topics relating to peer groups for this age group.

Cotterell, J (2007) *Social networks in youth and adolescence*, 2nd edn. Routledge. London.
Another of the popular books in the 'Adolescence and society' series, now in its second edition. Provides an excellent summary of research on the peer group, within a framework of social network theory.

Henderson, S, Holland, J, McGrellis, S, Sharpe, S and Thomson, R (2007) *Inventing adulthoods: a biographical approach to youth transitions*. Sage. London.
A good description of a qualitative research programme following young people through key transitions in four very different locations in the UK. The book has a strong focus on social relationships, and gives examples of how peer groups facilitate and moderate the transitional process.

Livingstone, S (2009) *Children and the internet*. Polity Press. Cambridge.
Despite the title this book is very much about adolescents as well as children, and provides a first class survey of the field as it stands at present by one of the leading researchers in the field. Very good coverage of the threats and opportunities afforded by new technologies for young people today.

Mesch, G and Talmud, I (2010) *Wired youth: the social world of adolescence in the information age*. Routledge. London.
The authors use social network theory to provide a critical analysis of research on the use of digital technology by young people. This is a stimulating and interesting book, offering a valuable perspective on the rapidly changing world of adolescents and technology.

Anti-social behaviour

'They sort of pick on a small minority of young people that cause trouble, but I mean there's probably just as much adults that cause the trouble. It's pretty unfair to lump us all together when it's only quite a small minority that's doing things that are particularly bad I think.'

(15-year-old boy)

'It's awful, isn't it? It's very much like one small group who are broadcast all the time, which makes it look like it's everyone. I remember we had to do citizenship classes and we were shown a quote about how young people are always destroying everything, and they were all yobs and whatever, and we were asked to date it. And it turned out that it was written three thousand years ago (laughs). This "young people are yobs" thing has remained through-out. . . . It's definitely an image that's pushed on young people. I'm not sure why, I'm not sure what we do because there's just as much crime within adult circles, but it seems to be "youth delinquents" that gets moved in on!'

(17-year-old girl)

As the quotes from the young people illustrate, adolescence is closely associated in the public mind with ideas about anti-social behaviour, and it would appear that this has been the case for as long as history has been recorded. This is truly unfortunate, and has many implications for young people, for their relationships with adults, and for public policy. For these reasons it is particularly important to include a short review of this topic here, covering issues such as the prevalence of anti-social behaviour, the characteristics of those involved in crime and other types of problem behaviour, the research evidence on the antecedents of crime, and a note on prevention and intervention. The last few years have seen significant advances in both our understanding of anti-social behaviour as well as the emergence of new approaches to dealing with this problem. The results of a number of key longitudinal studies became available during the 1990s, bringing a life course per-spective to this field and allowing a far clearer picture to emerge of the different trajectories of those who become involved in anti-social behaviour. Furthermore during the first decade of the twenty-first century, in Britain and in other countries, there has been a greater emphasis on prevention, as well as some new political initiatives aimed at dealing with young people engaged in this type of behaviour. Both these topics will be covered here.

It will be as well to say a brief word about terminology, since a number of different phrases are in use, and their meaning is not always clear. Terms which need to be distinguished are 'anti-social behaviour', 'psychosocial disorder', 'problem behaviour' and 'behaviour disorder'. In this chapter only the first of these will be considered. The term 'anti-social behaviour' is usually taken to refer to behaviour that is criminal, although it may not necessarily result in a prosecution. The terms 'offending behaviour' and 'delinquency' are also used to cover the same range of behaviours. It is important to note that children and young people below the age of criminal responsibility may engage in anti-social behaviour – an appearance in court is not necessary for behaviour to fall into this category.

Before moving on to consider the prevalence of anti-social behaviour a word about gender is in order. Since the great majority of youth offending is committed by young men, it is generally the case that discussions about this topic tend to focus on males. In the course of this chapter it will become apparent that trends for males and females are not necessarily the same, and there has been a growing concern in recent years that young women are becoming more involved in anti-social behaviour than has been the case previously. Hagell (2007) reports figures showing that the ratio of young men to young women in official crime statistics in the UK was 11:1 in 1957, 4:1 in 1977, and 3:1 in 1997. Gender differences will need to be borne in mind in the following discussion.

Prevalence of anti-social behaviour

'There's nothing different now, people just make it sound as if it's different. It's the media and stuff, people are making out that the younger generation is badder, so in like the newspapers they say that our ages are having babies and stuff, it doesn't make us sound that great, when the older generation do badder things as well, but they don't even take notice of that stuff. They make us sound really bad.'

(14-year-old boy)

Closely associated with the stereotype of adolescence as threatening or problematic is the notion that youth crime is on an inexorable upward trend. Public debates about youth frequently include references to phrases such as 'a rising tide of crime', and there is no doubt that this is a topic beset by prejudice and misinformation. All young people get tarred with the same brush, and statistics in areas such as anti-social behaviour have to be treated with great care. In Rutter *et al.*'s book *Anti-social behaviour by young people* (1998) the authors reported figures showing a fivefold increase in recorded offences in the UK over the period 1950–1990. Similarly Steinberg (2008) reports a steady rise in crime amongst those under 18 in the USA up to the year 1993, while Koops and Castro (2006) report on trends across European countries, showing that between the 1970s and 1990s there were generally increasing levels of youth crime.

The situation is complex, and there are a number of factors to take into account here. Most of the studies look at youth crime over long historical periods, and it seems clear that in the latter part of the twentieth century there was an increase in most countries, although the reason for this is still unclear. However, more recent evidence indicates that this is no longer the case. Indeed in Britain there has been a fall in the number of young men found guilty or cautioned for indictable offences between 1996 and 2006 (Coleman and Brooks, 2009). This trend is illustrated in

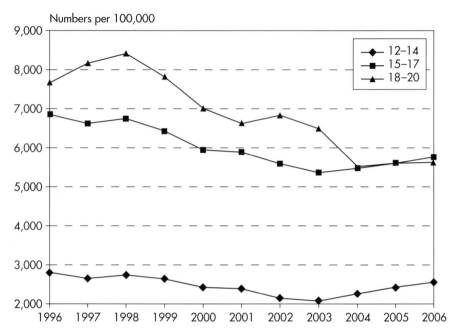

Figure 10.1   Males aged between 12 and 20 found guilty or cautioned for criminal offences, per 100,000 population, in England and Wales between 1996 and 2006.

Data from: Criminal Statistics 2006, England and Wales. Ministry of Justice. Nov 2007.

Source: Adapted from Coleman and Brooks (2009).

Figure 10.1. Steinberg (2008) notes a dramatic fall in juvenile offending in the USA since 1993, and Koops and Castro (2006) report that in many European countries there was either a reduction or a levelling off in youth crime from 1990 onwards. Thus it would appear that, although there were well-documented rises in male youth crime from the 1970s onwards, this trend has now either ceased or reversed. It is important to note, however, that this fall is not true of young women. Although they account for a very much smaller amount of youth crime, females, in Britain at least, show little change over the past decade, as illustrated in Figure 10.2. In addition to historical trends, the actual level of recorded crime is subject to variations in police procedures and in methods of data collection. It is certainly true that official statistics provide only a partial picture of anti-social behaviour among young people, and it is for this reason that researchers have turned to self-report data to present a more reliable picture of young people's behaviour in this domain.

It is perhaps not surprising that results from self-report studies show higher levels of anti-social behaviour than studies based on police statistics. A well-known study carried out in the UK (Graham and Bowling, 1995) reported that 55 per cent of males and 31 per cent of females between the ages of 14 and 25 admitted to having committed at least one criminal offence in their lives. Looking only at behaviour in the year of the study, 28 per cent of males and 12 per cent of females reported that they had committed an offence during this 12-month period. One of

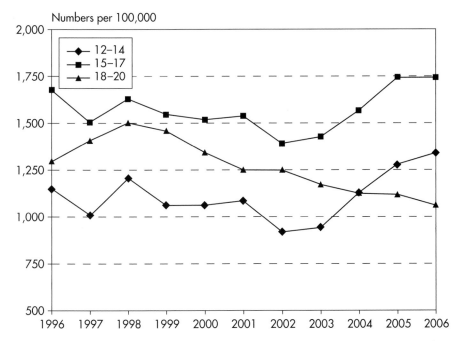

Figure 10.2 Females aged between 12 and 20 found guilty or cautioned for criminal offences, per 100,000 population, in England and Wales between 1996 and 2006.

Data from: Criminal Statistics 2006, England and Wales. Ministry of Justice. Nov 2007.

Source: Adapted from Coleman and Brooks (2009).

the key variables here has to do with the nature of the criminal activity, and it is important to consider the type of offence being reported. Thus in what is known as the Cambridge study of offending behaviour, Farrington (1995) notes that there is a strong correlation between self-report and official records when the more serious offences are considered. Looking at the worst offenders (by seriousness and frequency) in the Cambridge study, it can be seen that 62 per cent of those who reported serious criminal activity were also convicted of these offences in the courts (West and Farrington, 1977).

To turn now to some other features of anti-social behaviour, the evidence indicates that such behaviour is not equally distributed across age groups, nor is it equivalent in males and females. Most recent statistics show the peak age of offending to be 18 for males, and 15 for females (Coleman and Brooks, 2009). The statistics also illustrate a gender ratio of between 3:1 and 4:1, similar to that reported by Hagell (2007) as being the case for the year 1997. This age and gender distribution is illustrated in Figure 10.3, and the figures have given rise to a number of debates about the nature of anti-social behaviour. Why is it so closely associated with the adolescent period? Why does it decrease markedly as young people reach adulthood?

While there are no clear answers to these questions, numerous writers have advanced suggestions. Thus Emler and Reicher (1995) believe that processes in the

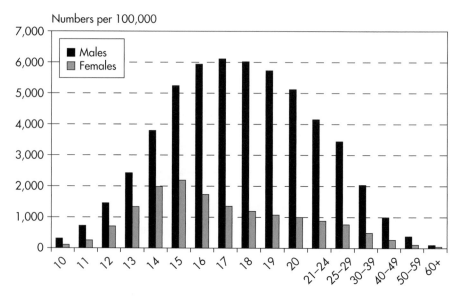

Figure 10.3 Male and female adolescents found guilty or cautioned for criminal offences, per 100,000 population, in England and Wales, by age and gender in 2006.

Data from: Criminal Statistics 2006, England and Wales. Ministry of Justice. Nov 2007.

Source: Coleman and Brooks (2009).

peer group in adolescence, especially what they call 'reputation management', underlie anti-social behaviour, whilst others such as Pitts (2008) look to the social circumstances in deprived urban communities which affect certain groups of adolescents as they grow up. Some commentators, such as Koops and Castro (2006), take the view that an understanding of the natural history of aggression is an essential part of any understanding of youth crime. There will be a more detailed discussion of risk factors for anti-social behaviour in the next section. Most writers agree that maturation and age play a key role in the trajectory of youth crime, as described in Schaefer and Uggen (2009). They argue that what is called desistance from crime, i.e. the time at which anti-social behaviour ceases, is a function of the processes involved in becoming an adult and assuming adult roles. Having a stable relationship, being in employment and becoming a parent all contribute to a developmental process operating in contradistinction to engagement in anti-social behaviour.

The evidence from longitudinal studies on the nature of anti-social behaviour was mentioned earlier, and this has enabled commentators to emphasise that there are many different types of anti-social behaviour or youth crime. Key studies (e.g. Moffitt, 1993; Stattin and Magnusson, 1996) drew attention to the fact that, based on large cohort longitudinal studies, it has been possible to distinguish between different trajectories for young people who were identified as being anti-social in adolescence. While a number of trajectories were described by these and other researchers who followed children from birth onwards, two particular trajectories are of most importance. These are:

- the life-course persistent group
- the adolescence-limited group.

On the one hand there appear to be a very small number who display serious problem behaviour from an early stage. Such children, predominantly boys, are hyperactive, have relationship problems and demonstrate aggressive behaviour from the age of three or four onwards. These individuals are known as life-course persistent as they commence anti-social behaviour patterns early, and continue with this behaviour through adolescence and into adulthood. The adolescence-limited group, as the term implies, start their anti-social behaviour when they reach adolescence and are the ones who desist from crime when they reach adulthood. Taking the Stattin and Magnusson (1996) study as one example, these Swedish researchers showed that males who were designated as life-course persistent represented 14 per cent of the sample who were at some time involved in anti-social behaviour. However, this group accounted for approximately 60 per cent of the crimes committed by the whole cohort, so they are clearly the most serious offenders. These findings have significant implications for intervention, and more will be said about this below.

Risk factors in anti-social behaviour

'There's been loads of graffiti around here. I think it was people around here, from my school, but I think it's down to boredom, there's not a lot to do.'

(15-year-old boy)

Research has indicated that anti-social behaviour can be shown to have associations with a number of variables. These include gender, family background, housing, schools and neighbourhoods, and anti-social peer groups. It is important to note a distinction here between a discussion of risk factors and one about causes of anti-social behaviour. These is still much debate about the exact reasons lying behind adolescent anti-social behaviour (e.g. France, 2009), and indeed, as indicated in the paragraphs above, it may be that different types of anti-social behaviour will prove to have quite different causes. For the present therefore it seems to be more sensible to avoid a discussion of causes, and concentrate rather on the risk factors associated with anti-social behaviour.

The trends illustrated in Figure 10.3 show two important features of anti-social behaviour. Not only is age an obvious factor influencing the prevalence of this behaviour, but in addition offences are committed much more frequently by males than females. Indeed gender is considered to be one of the key variables associated with the development of this behaviour. The great majority of crime is committed by males, and this raises a central question about its nature. Why should anti-social behaviour be so skewed in terms of gender? Many different explanations have been put forward to explain this phenomenon. Thus for example it may be that boys' and girls' peer groups function differently, with boys engaging in more risk-taking, competitive and macho behaviour, thereby facilitating anti-authoritarian and delinquent activity (Maccoby, 1998). An alternative view is that taken by Emler and Reicher (1995). They suggest four reasons for the gender imbalance. First, they believe that girls are less likely to be out and about on the streets where crime is committed. Second, the very fact that girls lead less public lives reduces the need to have delinquent identities for protection in unsafe environments. Third, girls will have fewer confrontations with authority, and thus have less need to demonstrate an ability to challenge that authority. Finally girls spend more time at home, leading to closer links with parents, and a greater opportunity for parents to know friends and monitor peer-group activities.

An entirely different explanation is given by those who believe that males are more aggressive than females, and that this characteristic is associated with criminality (Smith, 1995; Koops and Castro, 2006). In addition, as Rutter *et al.* (1998) point out, hyperactivity and conduct disorders are more common in boys, both of which are characteristics linked with at least one type of anti-social behaviour. Others have suggested that young men and young women are treated differently by the youth justice authorities, leading to higher rates of conviction for males. It is important to note that self-report studies show less of a discrepancy between males and females than is apparent in official statistics, and this may lead to the conclusion that the attitudes of magistrates and judges could play some part here. Graham and Bowling (1995) also explored the gender discrepancy in their self-report study, concentrating on desistance from crime. In their view, the fact that young women are likely to leave home earlier, and to make the transition to adult roles at a younger age, all contribute to the fact that not only do women commit less crime, but that they desist from this behaviour at an earlier stage in their development.

As will have been apparent, the longitudinal studies discussed in the previous section concentrated on boys as the main focus of their attention. More recently there has been growing interest in the anti-social behaviour of girls, and Fontaine *et al.* (2009) have asked the question as to whether similar trajectories can be identified for females as have been described for males. The question poses significant difficulties, partly because the numbers are so much smaller for girls than for boys, and partly because early problematic behaviour of girls is not so easily described or classified. The critical review of the literature carried out by Fontaine and her colleagues (2009) indicates that there may well be similar trajectories for females, but that because of the difficulties mentioned there is a need for further research before any firm conclusions can be drawn about this question. In considering girls and anti-social behaviour, there remains the issue of why this should have increased over the last decade. Hagell (2007) suggests that risk factors that apply to boys, such as poor parenting or the impact of anti-social peer groups, are likely to apply to girls as well. Another possible factor may be the rise in alcohol and substance misuse, which has increased significantly among females during the 1990s and the early part of the twenty-first century (Coleman and Brooks, 2009). Nonetheless it is remarkable that the great majority of the commentary on anti-social behaviour remains focussed on males, and there is a real necessity to keep gender in mind in future research.

Turning now to the role of the family, every study carried out on the subject of anti-social behaviour has identified family factors as being highly significant (see Lahey *et al.*, 2003). In a meta-analysis of a large number of British, American and Scandinavian studies Loeber and Stouthamer-Loeber (1986) outlined four ways in which the family might be associated with anti-social behaviour in young people.

First, they pinpointed the role of neglect, whereby parents spend too little time with their children for them to fulfil normal parenting roles. Two dimensions of neglect may be important here: parents may be neglectful in failing to supervise or provide structure and boundaries for their children, or they may simply be uninvolved or uninterested in the lives of their sons and daughters. The second point that Loeber and Stouthamer-Loeber (1986) make is that conflict in the home appears to be a key factor, either through direct aggression or violence, or through harsh and erratic punishment. Numerous studies have provided supportive evidence for this, including West and Farrington's (1977) Cambridge study, and Kolvin et al.'s (1990) Newcastle Thousand Families study.

The next variable to be considered is the behaviour or values of the parents themselves. Thus, for example, Hagell and Newburn's (1996) study of persistent offenders showed that one of the most significant predictors of whether a young person will acquire a criminal record is whether they have a parent who has been convicted. The fourth issue of note is what Loeber and Stouthamer-Loeber (1986) call the 'disruption paradigm'. By this they mean that neglect and conflict may arise in the family because of other factors such as parental discord, illness, or the absence of one parent. Again there is a wealth of evidence to support this argument, although many writers make the point that it is not the event itself – illness or trauma – which is associated with anti-social behaviour. Rather it is the consequences that flow from the event, such as parental neglect, or chronic conflict, which are significant here (Hill and Maughan, 2001).

The meta-analysis showed that, while all four factors were associated with anti-social behaviour in young people, it was the first of these – neglect – that had the strongest connection. In addition, there appeared to be a cumulative effect, so that the greater the number of family handicaps, the greater the chance of anti-social behaviour being in evidence. Before leaving this subject it is interesting to note that, just as family factors are significantly associated with the onset of anti-social behaviour, they also have a clear link to the desistance from anti-social behaviour. Thus, improved parental relationships can have a critical impact on anti-social behaviour, and there is some evidence in the literature that marriage or stable partnerships are associated with a reduction in anti-social behaviour. The title of a paper, 'I met this wife of mine and things got on a better track' by Ronka et al. (2002) illustrates this very well.

It is not necessary to spend too much time on the peer group at this juncture, since this is a topic which has been considered in some detail in the previous chapter. For the moment it is important to note that for many writers an association with a deviant peer group is a significant risk factor in explaining anti-social behaviour. However, the picture is not entirely clear, since it cannot be certain whether young people encourage each other, or whether it is simply the case that much anti-social behaviour tends to occur in groups rather than alone. Indeed there may be a third explanation, namely that young people with deviant attitudes tend to cluster together, so that those with similar behaviours and interests are drawn to each other, without anyone exerting an anti-social influence on anyone else (Scholte and van Aken, 2006).

That said, there is no doubt that there is a close association between the anti-social activities of a young person and those of his (or her) friends. In

Ogood *et al.* (1996) it was shown that having anti-social peers was one of the best predictors of self-reported offending behaviour. Similarly Moffitt (2006) concluded that the association was strongest for those who were most attached to peers, and who felt most peer pressure. As Farrington (1995) notes, however, there is still a problem of interpretation. If anti-social behaviour is a group activity, then anti-social adolescents will inevitably have anti-social friends. This does not mean that the peer group necessarily leads others to offend. It is safer to conclude that having friends who are engaged in anti-social behaviour is an indicator of such behaviour, rather than the cause of it.

It is now time to turn to the links between social and environmental factors and anti-social behaviour. While it used to be a common assumption that social class and anti-social behaviour were associated, today it is more common to point to other factors linked to growing up in disadvantaged circumstances. Thus, for example, it is probable that poverty and deprivation, rather than social class, are critical in affecting the behaviour and experiences of young people. First, when families live in impoverished neighbourhoods parents are less effective in providing support and structure for their teenage children (Sampson and Laub, 1994). Second, poverty undermines the social fabric of a neighbourhood, making it more difficult for adults to provide role models, leisure activities and other resources necessary for the transition to adulthood. This has come to be known as social capital (Bourdieu and Passeron, 1977), something which represents all the assets that belong to a community or environment and contribute to its develop-ment. Where social capital is lacking young people face multiple disadvantages, as described by MacDonald (2007) and White (2009). Third, poverty and unemploy-ment are closely related, and being without a job makes it more difficult for young men to find appropriate adult roles, as well as encouraging aggressive behaviour as a mark of status and power in the community (Fergusson *et al.*, 1997). Finally, there is a significant incidence of violence in communities which suffer high levels of poverty, and exposure to this, either in the home or in the community, has profoundly negative effects on the behaviour and adjustment of young people (Zinzow *et al.*, 2009).

In Hagell's (2007) review she points to three further possible environ-mental factors that need to be taken into account. The first is school effects. Research shows that schools can make a difference, not directly, but in the way they support the less able young people, and in the ethos they create. Where schools facilitate a sense of belonging and engagement they are likely to reduce the chances that vulnerable young people become involved in anti-social activities (MacDonald, 2007). The second factor mentioned by Hagell is the media. The way in which the media represent young people, and the way in which crime and other anti-social activities are reported does undoubtedly impact on the public view of adolescence, and this in turn is influential in determining policies at government level (France, 2009). Lastly there is the question of the availability of guns and other weapons, as well as alcohol and drugs. There is no doubt that access to weapons has an impact on criminal behaviour, as does the misuse of drink and illegal substances. All these factors are potentially influential in either encouraging or making possible anti-social behaviour by young people.

Youth movements. Social movements characterised by a distinctive mode of dress or other bodily adornments, a leisure-time preference, and other distinguishing features (e.g. punk rockers).

Youth groups. Comprised of small clusters of young people who hang out together in public places such as shopping centres.

Criminal groups. Small clusters of friends who band together, usually for a short period of time, to commit crime primarily for financial gain and may contain young and not so young adults as well.

Wannabe groups. Include young people who band together in a loosely structured group primarily to engage in spontaneous social activity and exciting, impulsive, criminal activity including collective violence against other groups of youths. Wannabes will often claim 'gang' territory and adopt 'gang-style' identifying markers of some kind.

Street gangs. Groups of young people and young adults who band together to form a semi-structured organisation, the primary purpose of which is to engage in planned and profitable criminal behaviour or organised violence against rival street gangs. They tend to be less visible but more permanent than other groups.

Criminal business organisations. Groups that exhibit a formal structure and a high degree of sophistication. They are composed mainly of adults and engage in criminal activity primarily for economic reasons and almost invariably maintain a low profile. Thus while they may have a name, they are rarely visible.

Box 10.1   Robert Gordon's six-point typology of youth groupings.
Source: Pitts (2008) by permission.

To conclude this section a word should be said about gangs, and their place in the genesis of anti-social behaviour. Pitts (2008) makes an important point when he notes that, although it has been generally assumed that gangs are an adult phenomenon, his own research in East London shows clearly that a small number of young people are involved in gang culture. However, he identifies a number of different associations between adolescents which are not necessarily criminal, and these are set out in Box 10.1. This is a point also underlined by Hagerdorn (2009), who distinguishes between groups of young people hanging out together for safety in a violent neighbourhood, those who become involved in gangs for economic reasons, and those who have literally no choice because of pressures from parents, older siblings or other relatives. The very title of Pitts' book *Reluctant gangsters* (2008) reflects the complex web of motivations that lie behind involvement in the gang culture. The most powerful point that this book makes is that it is to the communities themselves, rather than to the individual young people, that we need to turn if anything is to be done about reducing involvement in gangs and gang culture. It is appropriate therefore to consider now the question of interventions in relation to anti-social behaviour.

Interventions in relation to anti-social behaviour

'You see on the telly kids being stroppy at our age and, like, hidden away, but that's not most of us though. I've noticed it in some of my friends, they used to be all happy and joyful and now they're not really. Hoodies and stuff, loitering all around the place!'

(15-year-old boy)

'There's been a few times where I suppose I wouldn't have, you know, I wouldn't have done something. . . . Well, I suppose like it wouldn't be my idea to do that, but if someone's got the idea I've thought "Why not?" Like not really bad things, but getting in a few scrapes, being somewhere we shouldn't at like the wrong time and place sort of thing.'

(16-year-old boy)

The consideration of risk factors helps to point the way to interventions that might be effective in reducing engagement in anti-social behaviour. In particular the role of the family, the peer group and the community have all been identified as contexts in which interventions can be developed. Before looking at these, however, two other modalities in which treatment programmes have been located will be considered. There is substantial research to show that both impulsivity and having limited cognitive skills are risk factors for the development of anti-social behaviour (see Rutter *et al.*, 1998; Fonagy *et al.*, 2005), and some important interventions have been developed in these areas. First, in relation to impulsivity it has been clear for some years that young people involved in anti-social behaviour show deficits in interpersonal skills, and a variety of programmes have been tried out that address these deficits. Fonagy *et al.* (2005) call these programmes 'Social and problem-solving skills training'. These authors note half a dozen such programmes (e.g. Tate *et al.*, 1995). They report mostly good results, but note that none of the programmes can demonstrate lasting gains for young people over time. Fonagy *et al.* (2005) also review anger management interventions that have been developed in various settings, but again long-term effects are hard to identify. As they note, 'it is likely that anger, as a target for interventions, is not sufficiently central to problems of aggression for its control to be an appropriate goal on its own' (p. 167).

As far as cognitive and intellectual development is concerned, one of the most successful interventions to reduce the risk of offending has been the Perry Preschool project, carried out in Michigan and described in Schweinhart and Weikart (1980). This programme has become a model for numerous other interventions, including the UK's Sure Start programme. There is no doubt that early intervention can be of great significance, particularly for those children identified in longitudinal studies as being 'life-course persistent' where anti-social behaviour is concerned. However, there are of course enormous hurdles in identifying such children at an early age, and in targeting any intervention in an appropriate manner which does not stigmatise the families involved. The outcome evaluation of Sure Start in Britain is an object lesson in highlighting such difficulties, as Rutter (2006) makes clear. Whilst the Sure Start programmes were popular and well utilised, they did not demonstrate any significant improvements in the behaviour of children who were considered to be most vulnerable. This finding should not be used to criticise the development of initiatives such as Sure Start, but should help in identifying the challenges implicit in early intervention programmes.

Regarding interventions in the context of the family, there has been an explosion of interest in this field over recent years, as has been discussed earlier in Chapter 5. Where anti-social behaviour is concerned there have been attempts by governments, especially in Britain, to introduce parenting programmes and to facilitate parenting skills as a way to reduce youth offending. This has led to the development of many new programmes (see Barrett, 2003), but there is not the space to review these here. To choose one example, it is undoubtedly the case that programmes originating from the Oregon Social Learning Center have been at the forefront of work in this field, and so these will be briefly detailed. The Oregon model, based on social learning principles, has been tested most stringently in studies that included not only parent training, but interventions that focussed solely on the young people as a comparison group (e.g. Dishion *et al.*, 1992; Dishion and Andrews, 1995). Results were encouraging, particularly considering the high levels of problem behaviours being manifested by the young people involved. However, some of the effects were not maintained one year later, and this was most noticeable in the comparison group where the parents had not been involved. Further reviews of parent training programmes relevant to young people showing anti-social behaviour can be found in Roker and Coleman (2007).

The possible role of Multisystemic Therapy (MST) in work with young people having multiple problems has already been mentioned in the section on mental health in Chapter 6. In particular, evaluations by researchers such as Henggeler *et al.* (1998) have shown positive outcomes where this approach is applied to juvenile offenders. The basis of this type of intervention is that it 'fully recognises the multi-determined nature of serious anti-social behaviour' (Fonagy *et al.*, 2005, p. 201). As a result MST includes techniques drawn from family therapy, parent training, social perspective training and behavioural methods. As already noted it is an expensive option, but it remains the approach which is arguably the most promising for serious young offenders (Fonagy *et al.*, 2005).

Other areas in which interventions have been targeted include the peer group and the wider social environment. In relation to the peer group Botvin (1990) summarises the results of programmes aimed at increasing resistance to peer group pressure, and developing social skills. Findings show that adult teachers are rarely effective in such programmes, while same-age individuals have more success. Peers of high status may be used as role models, combined with the sort of interpersonal skills training already mentioned. In the view of Tobler (1986) such approaches are especially successful in reducing substance abuse, but less successful in relation to offending behaviour. Other strategies that have been used to reduce anti-social behaviour include modification of the environment, such as increased lighting on housing estates or the use of closed-circuit television, or the reduction of opportunity, such as paying wages by cheque or electronically, rather than with cash. In a review of such approaches Clarke (1992) notes some successes, but also sounds a warning note in saying that many offenders may simply move on to other environments where controls are less effective.

One important result of this review is the recognition that anti-social behaviour is not a single category of behaviour, but may have a variety of causes and include different developmental pathways. Interventions for those who may be classified as life-course persistent should be different from the interventions aimed at the adolescence-limited group. For some young people interventions are likely to be most effective if they are multi-modal, or if they target very specific behaviours. For others, however, addressing issues in the community such as pervasive deprivation and the lack of social capital will be likely to make the greatest difference to their lives. There is a lot to learn from the research on interventions that has been referred to here. Hagell (2007) summarises the findings from the research literature by saying that programmes to stop offending should be based on the following principles:

- They should target specific behaviours where possible, and should include social skills training and problem-solving.
- They should be clearly matched to the particular needs of the young person.
- They should be well structured and planned.
- They should be effectively supervised and monitored.
- They should have a clear theoretical model which explains how they are expected to work, and they should remain true to the original model.

To conclude this chapter, it is important to recognise that the early part of the twenty-first century in many European countries, especially in Britain, has been marked by a high level of concern on the part of policy makers about young people's anti-social behaviour. This has given rise to numerous new initiatives which, while positive in some respects, have had the unfortunate effect of increasing the negative perceptions of young people as a 'problem' or as 'youth causing trouble'. This of course links directly with the quotes from young people at the beginning of this chapter. As France (2009) notes, it is paradoxical that during a

period when levels of youth crime have been falling both government and the media have seemed to be preoccupied with this topic. In England and Wales the definition of anti-social behaviour has been widened, and various activities that were previously seen as minor nuisances, such as small groups congregating in public spaces, are now classified as criminal behaviour. This increases the ways in which young people are monitored and policed, as well as heightening the risk of a wider range of adolescents being sucked into the criminal justice system. It is to be hoped that more rational and research-based policies will be introduced in the future, and that the voices of young people can be heard when they emphasise the damaging effects of negative stereotypes.

Implications for practice

1. One of the most powerful findings to emerge from research has been the conclusion that there are different types of anti-social behaviour, with different developmental trajectories. In particular it is important to make a distinction between offending behaviour that is life-course persistent, and that which is adolescence-limited. The factors underlying these trajectories will not be the same, and thus interventions will need to be tailored to meet the specific needs of different individuals.
2. Young men are significantly more likely than young women to engage in anti-social behaviour, yet male youth crime has been falling since the early 1990s, whilst this is not the case for female youth crime. Factors associated with anti-social behaviour include having a family member involved in crime, as well as parental neglect, or harsh and erratic discipline. Environmental circumstances are also critical here, and poverty and disadvantage are of particular importance.
3. Much has been learnt about the possible interventions available for those involved in anti-social behaviour. Interventions include the development of social and cognitive skills, the enhancement of parenting strategies, the modification of disadvantaged environments, and the support of positive peer groups. Studies of interventions show that opportunities for employment are possibly the most powerful of all options, but that in addition those interventions which are multi-modal are more likely to be successful than those which concentrate on one modality at a time.

Further reading

Coops, W and de Castro, B (2006) Development of aggression and its linkages with violence and juvenile delinquency. In Jackson, S and Goossens, L (Eds) *Handbook of adolescent development*. Psychology Press. Hove.
A thought-provoking chapter reviewing research in this area, discussed from a European perspective. It includes a useful comparison across different countries in Europe, and explores possible reasons for some of these differences.

Hagell, A (2007) Anti-social behaviour. In Coleman, J and Hagell, A (Eds) *Adolescence, risk and resilience: against the odds*. John Wiley. Chichester.
A good review chapter outlining recent research as well as promising interventions for young people engaged in anti-social behaviour.

Pitts, J (2008) *Reluctant gangsters: the changing face of youth crime*. Willan Publishing. Tavistock, Devon.
This book has attracted much publicity, involving an important discussion of the growth of gangs in the UK. It includes a useful review of research on this topic, together with some suggestions for public policy initiatives.

Rutter, M, Giller, H and Hagell, A (1998) *Anti-social behaviour by young people*. Cambridge University Press. Cambridge.
Although some years old now, this remains a classic text. An outstanding review of research, combined with an excellent critical analysis of the main issues in this field.

Risk, resilience and coping in adolescence

'It's all been good. Well, overall it's been good, but there have been some not so good points, but there haven't been any really down parts of it. There's lots of people, I mean like close friends, who found this age as being a really tough time. To be honest that's part of the reason why I stopped being friends with them, because they went within themselves a bit, or withdrew from the world because they were not having a nice time as adolescents. But I haven't. . . . I mean there's been some bits when I've been annoyed, and I've been unhappy, but overall it's been good.'

(16-year-old boy)

To many people adolescence appears to be a stressful time. Commentators might point to worries about exams, peer pressure in relation to sex or drugs, anxieties about jobs and qualifications, and to a variety of other factors that might make life difficult for young people today. Yet communities and neighbourhoods are full of young people getting on with their lives, coping with problems that adults might find daunting, enjoying their leisure, preparing for and taking their exams, and doing their utmost to become independent and enter the adult world. Because of this there has in recent years been a movement, particularly in the USA, to focus on what is known as 'positive youth development' (Benson *et al.*, 2004). This approach has sought to emphasise a strengths-based model of adolescence, rather than a deficit model which highlights the problems and difficulties of this stage of development. Another term also used in this context is an asset framework (Flanagan, 2004), again emphasising the positive contributions that young people can make to society. Approaches such as these are interested in the building blocks that underlie healthy development. They are associated with concepts such as agency, competence, connectedness and resilience, ideas to which we will return below.

While it is extremely important to point out the adaptive abilities of young people, it would be wrong to underestimate the impact of stress and disadvantage, and to minimise the difficulties and obstacles faced by some adolescents as they move towards adulthood. As will be indicated below, there are a variety of types of risk which face young people, ranging from relatively minor daily irritants to acute risk, such as divorce or the death of a parent, or chronic risk such as poverty or long-term illness. Risks of this type affect young people in different ways, and although some may cope well, others will not. These adolescents may, as a result, become socially excluded, or develop emotional or physical disorders of varying severity.

Nonetheless the evidence that has accumulated on the resilience and coping skills of young people has led to a new way of thinking about adolescence (Coleman and Hagell, 2007). No longer is it seen as a 'problem stage'. Today writers and professionals are more concerned to identify risks, and to attempt to understand the processes of coping used by adolescents in their daily lives. Such an approach is especially important since it is a reflection of a perspective which emphasises adaptation rather than disorder. It is also a viewpoint that underlines the role of the young person as an active agent, and as a constructor of the environment in which development takes place. This perspective is integral to the focal model outlined in Chapter 1, and to the underlying assumptions of developmental contextualism. The perspective will provide a framework for the consideration of risk, resilience and coping during the course of the chapter.

The first topic to be explored will be the concept of risk. It should be noted that, in the present context, the terms risk and stress or stressor are interchangeable. In the main the word risk will be used here, but more will be said about stress below. Risk is a complex term, however, especially as it applies to young people, and it is essential to draw a distinction between various meanings of the word. Coleman and Hagell (2007) identified a variety of different uses, among which the following three are of greatest importance:

- *Risk* factors: as noted in the previous chapter on anti-social behaviour, these are factors that contribute to poor outcomes for young people. Some examples might include poverty, deprivation, illness, or dysfunctional family relationships.
- *Risk* behaviour: this applies to potentially harmful behaviour such as having unsafe sex, abusing substances, or taking part in anti-social activities.
- Young people at *risk*: this term is used to refer to those who are potentially vulnerable, such as those who are subject to abuse or neglect, or those in custody or care.

These three meanings of risk will now be explored in more detail, after which concepts of coping and resilience will be discussed.

Concepts of risk as they apply to adolescence

'I hope it's a lot more stressful than other periods of life, because it's been pretty stressful. You're constantly being tested all the time, you're in school and in education, and also all the new things that are coming at you, and you've got to make judgements by yourself, and not go too wrong. Because you can go wrong, you can afford to go wrong a bit, but if you make too many wrong decisions you end up lost. Yeah, it's pretty tiring, and just busy as well – hectic! There's so many things coming at you, that you have to get used to.'

(17-year-old girl)

As with any stage of human development, there are a wide range of risk factors that may impinge on an individual. Landmark studies of risk and resilience have considered the impact of poverty, war, natural disasters, long-term family disadvantage, health problems, abuse, neglect, and so on. These factors represent some but not all of the established risk factors that are known to be associated with negative outcomes for children and young people. Early studies of risk tended to focus on one factor only, such as poverty, but later studies have recognised that risk factors tend to cluster or to co-occur. Thus parents living in poverty are likely to have higher rates of depression and other mental disorders, as well as being less effective in their parenting behaviour. In such circumstances adult depression, parenting behaviour and financial hardship all impact on the young person in a cumulative fashion. In this way the impact of risk can multiply, and later studies have tended to look at what is known as cumulative risk, where risk indicators have been aggregated together (Masten and Powell, 2003). All writers in this field agree that, in general, the more risks the individual is exposed to, or the greater the risk gradient, the greater the likelihood of a poor outcome (Appleyard *et al.*, 2005).

Another approach to the understanding of risk factors is to consider them in terms of whether they are within the individual, the family or the community. Of course not all factors can be classified in this way, and many of these will interact with each other, but some of the following examples are useful.

- *Individual factors*: anxious temperament, low intelligence, poor health, hyper-activity, limited attention span, low frustration tolerance.
- *Family factors*: parental ill-health, parental conflict, parental involvement in crime, harsh or erratic discipline, loss of a parent due to death or divorce, disruptive siblings.
- *Community factors*: economic disadvantage, poor housing, quality of schooling and other services, crime rate, level of substance abuse, lack of community role models.

A different view of risk factors comes from the clinical literature, where risk is viewed from the perspective of studies of stress. The term 'stressor' deals with variables that are very similar to those described by other writers as risk factors. One important contributor to this literature is Bruce Compas (e.g. Compas, 2004). He notes that stress will vary along a number of dimensions, including whether it is normative or atypical, large or small in magnitude, and chronic or acute in nature. Compas goes on to distinguish three broad categories of stressor, the categories being generic or normative stress, acute stress and chronic stress. As can be imagined all young people experience some degree of stress as they move through adolescence. Such experiences will include changes of school, the loss of friends, daily hassles with adults, and so on. This is what is known as normative stress.

Compas, however, points out that some young people will experience more serious stressors, including some of the things already mentioned such as a bad car accident, or the death of a parent (acute stress). Alternatively an adolescent may grow up having to deal with racism, economic hardship, bullying, or other disadvantage (chronic stress). These distinctions are helpful, and yet there are other factors that need to be taken into account as well if a young person's adaptation to such adversities is to be understood. Two key factors include the timing of events, and the number of stressors experienced by the young person at the same time.

Looking first at the number of stressors, it will be clear that the more difficulty any young person experiences, the more resources will be needed to deal with these. This is particularly true during adolescence, when there may be both normative and non-normative stressors to manage. Thus, for example, if a young person has to deal with moving school, going through puberty, losing friends, as well as having an acute problem to deal with at home (such as parental illness), then this is going to be very different from someone who has only one stressor to deal with. This notion is similar to that of a risk gradient, mentioned above, where the example was given of poverty interacting with parental depression and parenting behaviour.

The number of events is also linked to the question of timing. The way normative and non-normative events cluster together is a key factor in determining the individual's ability to cope. If difficulties impinge on the individual all at the same time, this will obviously make things more difficult than if stressors occur one at a time. It will be apparent that these ideas are similar to those identified as features of the theoretical models discussed in Chapter 1. An interesting model of a mental health trajectory which incorporates many of these concepts is illustrated in Figure 11.1, where it can be seen that both timing and the number of stressful events contribute to the trajectory. This model also identifies a number of protective factors, including parent and peer support, coping responses and so on. These will be explored in more detail at a later stage of the chapter.

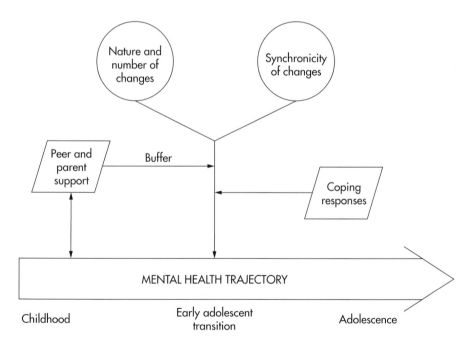

Figure 11.1 Model of developmental transition in early adolescence.
Source: Rice *et al.* (1993).

Up to this point we have been considering risk factors (or stressors), but as has been noted earlier, the concept of risk factors differs from the concept of risk behaviour. While risk factors are the variables that may contribute to poor outcomes, risk behaviour concerns those activities that are potentially harmful, such as drinking, smoking, using illegal substances and engagement in anti-social behaviour. A challenging question arises when these behaviours are considered.

● Is the engagement in risk behaviour a normative feature of adolescence? Do adolescents need to take risks in order to grow and develop, or is risk behaviour a threat to health and to social order?

Some reference to this question has already been made when considering adolescent health in Chapter 6. As was noted then, there is no easy answer to the problem. For some commentators a degree of risk behaviour is commonplace, and indeed beneficial, for young people. In this model adolescents need to learn how to drink alcohol safely. Such a learning process is seen as an essential part of growing up in a social world where alcohol plays a major part. As for illegal substances, research shows that between 30 per cent and 40 per cent of those aged 16 have experimented with cannabis (Coleman and Brooks, 2009), so that it makes little sense to describe cannabis use as a seriously harmful behaviour. On the other hand, there has to be a degree of moderation. Experimentation is one thing, but abuse is another. As is now known (see Chapter 6), frequent cannabis use can be damaging to health, as can the use of certain types of cannabis. It is also important to recognise that risk behaviours tend to cluster together. Binge drinking or serious alcohol abuse is often linked to substance abuse or risky sexual behaviour. Thus experimentation, which involves learning to stay safe, should be distinguished from behaviour that poses a threat to health or to safety.

One of the difficulties with the concept of risk behaviour is that it gives currency to a negative stereotype of young people. Thus, if adolescents are perceived as sexually promiscuous or as drug takers, then this allows adults to feel critical, even threatened, by this age group. This is a serious concern, and gets to the heart of the mutual misunderstanding that can be a feature of inter-generational attitudes and opinions. It is important to underline two facts:

● Not all adolescents engage in risk behaviours.
● Many of those who do engage in risk behaviours only do so at a minimal, non-harmful, level.

The third use of the term risk as outlined above is that to do with being 'at risk'. By and large these young people are likely to be those who have a high number of risk factors in their background. Studies show that such young people are significantly more likely than others to have poorer outcomes and restricted life chances. However, it is not always the case that those with a high number of risk factors in their backgrounds do badly. The major studies of risk and resilience (e.g. Werner and Smith, 1992; Fergusson and Horwood, 2003) point out that there are some who, despite being exposed to major adversity, appear to cope well and to show remarkable resilience in the face of huge odds. Why should this be so?

The key lies in the presence of protective factors. As John Bynner puts it:

Protective factors work on the more malleable components of development, reflecting the different kinds of resources that may help the child to resist adversity. They comprise the emotional, educational, social and economic influences on the child's life, operating singly, or more usually, in interaction with each other.

(Bynner, 2001, p. 286)

What are these protective factors? Many writers believe that it is helpful to draw the distinction, as has already been done with risk factors, between those that are individual attributes, those which originate from within the family, and those that depend on resources in the neighbourhood or community. This distinction was first described by two of the major writers in this field, Michael Rutter and Norman Garmezy (Garmezy and Rutter, 1983). In this paradigm, the following are some of the common attributes described:

- *Individual attributes*: good intellectual skills, positive temperament, positive views of the self.
- *Family attributes*: high warmth, cohesion, high expectations, parental involvement.
- *Community attributes*: good schools, neighbourhood resources such as sports facilities, low levels of crime, strong social networks, adequate housing.

Readers will be aware that this classification is the same as that which has been used to describe risk factors, and the relationship between risk and protective factors is one that inspires continuing debate. Further consideration will be given to this issue in due course, but for the moment it is time to turn to the major studies of risk and resilience, so that a picture can be gained of the key findings from these ground-breaking investigations. One of the most interesting challenges for social scientists working in this field has been to try to understand how it is that, even in situations where there is a high level of adversity, some children and young people manage to cope well, and to overcome the extreme risks to which they are exposed.

Two landmark studies are often quoted when considering this question. The first is one carried out in Hawaii during the 1980s by Werner and colleagues (Werner and Smith, 1982, 1992). In this research the investigators managed to track down over 500 individuals who had been studied as part of a large cohort when they were children. They found that out of the group who had experienced major risk factors (chronic poverty, parents lacking education, troubled family environments) two-thirds had developed serious problems by the age of 18. However, approximately one-third appeared to have survived well, and to be functioning effectively as adults.

This group was distinguished by high levels of achievement orientation, as well as by having alternative care-takers during middle childhood. Other factors that were prominent included sociability, good communication skills, a supportive neighbourhood and good peer relationships. Of considerable importance also was the presence or absence of additional stress factors experienced later on, especially in adolescence. Thus those who were exposed to a high number of risk factors in childhood, and who also experienced further stress as teenagers, did worst of all. As was noted earlier, when the risk gradient becomes steeper, the individual is at greater disadvantage.

The second study is that known as the Christchurch Health and Development Study, carried out in New Zealand. The lead researcher on this study is David Fergusson, although many other individuals have worked with him and contributed to the scientific excellence of the research. In essence this is a longitudinal study of an unselected sample of 1,200 children born in 1977. The cohort was studied at a number of points between birth and 21 years, and a particular focus of the research was to identify those children exposed to major risk factors. The study shows that, as with the Hawaii research, some who experience such risk environments do survive and overcome adversity.

Fergusson and others (Fergusson and Lynskey, 1996; Fergusson and Horwood, 2003) report that, with increasing exposure to childhood adversities, there were marked increases in mental health problems in adolescence. Yet not all individuals developed such disorders. Some showed a capacity to overcome the risk environment, and most of the protective factors already mentioned were present in those individuals who could be described as resilient. One particular protective factor highlighted time and time again by the researchers was the presence of one key adult during childhood and adolescence. This adult did not need to be a parent. It could be another relative, or even someone outside the family. However, the role played by one adult who cared about the individual, and who was available at significant turning points, appears to be absolutely central to the development of resilience in the face of adversity.

In recent discussions of the interplay between risk and protective factors (e.g. Olsson et al., 2003; Rutter, 2003) there is a strong emphasis on the importance of considering dynamic processes, rather than looking at a catalogue of static factors acting in a cumulative fashion. Rutter is keen to emphasise the role of gene–environment interactions, as well as the importance of biological factors such as the neuro-endocrine system and brain structures. He argues that the psychological variables, such as personal agency, coping mechanisms and so on interact with the genetic and physiological characteristics of an individual, and that all these variables contribute to an ongoing dynamic process of adaptation to adverse environmental circumstances.

One last point on questions of risk is that to do with the pre-eminence of early childhood experiences in determining outcomes for vulnerable young people. Are risk factors in childhood more powerful than those that occur at later ages? Is it the case that, as Bynner (2001) puts it: 'The earlier the disadvantage occurred, and the longer it has persisted, the lower the likelihood that these factors (the protective factors) would counter it?' This is an assumption that is generally accepted by social scientists and policy makers, and many of the results of the longitudinal studies on resilience do appear to support this conclusion.

In spite of this, the evidence is not entirely clear-cut, and it may be that there are some exceptions to the rule that the earlier the exposure to risk factors, the more difficult it is to alter the course of development. It is the case that, even for those who have suffered high levels of adversity at an early age, there are some protective factors that operate in adolescence and early adulthood. Studies of young offenders, as well as those who have been brought up in care, have shown that changes in relationships in adulthood, especially marriage to a stable partner, can act as a powerful protective factor (e.g. Sampson and Laub, 1993). There is also evidence that, during adolescence, involvement with positive peer groups, as well as the impact of a caring and supportive adult, can act to counter early exposure to risk factors (Luthar, 2003). One academic paper, already mentioned in the previous chapter, captures the point exactly. Ronka *et al.* (2002) gave their article the title: 'I met this wife of mine, and things got on a better track'.

Up to this point the nature of risk has been considered, as well as the role played by protective factors in modifying experiences of adversity. Various questions to do with risk and adversity have been explored, and the results of major studies in this field have been noted. The question has been considered as to whether there are protective factors that can be effective in adolescence and early adulthood, despite early disadvantage. It is now time to take a closer look at the literature on coping, and this will be followed by a discussion of the concept of resilience.

Coping in adolescence

'I wouldn't be like "I've got a problem, can we talk?" Because problems aren't like that. The way I see it is that if it is a practical thing, like work, then just, well, like, "just do it!". But if it's not like that, like someone gets you pissed off, then what's the point? Because either you deal with it with them and it gets sorted, or you just leave it and it doesn't, or it just sorts itself out, like, over time'.

(16-year-old boy)

'I'm a very independent person, I like to be on my own more than with friends. . . . I just like to be on my own most of the time. I keep things to myself . . . sometimes it just all builds up, but I think it's my own pressure, coming from me. . . . What do I do? I don't know, I just do things that help me to relax, like, I don't know, listening to music and stuff.'

(15-year-old girl)

Those who write about stress in adolescence, such as Compas (2004), are usually interested also in the process of coping. One good example which illustrates the links between stress and coping is the work of Seiffge-Krenke (1995). She proposes a schema which is illustrated in Figure 11.2. Here she shows a four-stage process, which includes the nature of the stressors, the internal resources of the individual, the type of social supports available, and finally the coping process itself. Seiffge-Krenke sees these four as being related sequentially, so that it is necessary to first consider the stressors, then the internal resources of the individual, and so on. Not everyone takes the same view, but this is a helpful way of approaching what is a complex area.

217

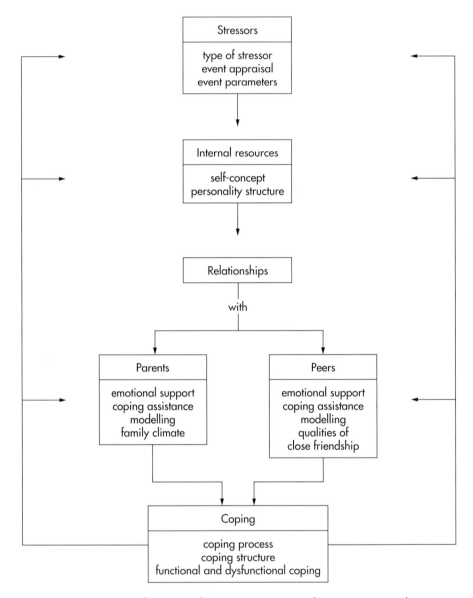

Figure 11.2 Conceptual issues and major questions in relation to stress and coping.
Source: Seiffge-Krenke (1995).

In terms of coping, here again there are different approaches, and there have been many attempts to classify coping strategies. One such attempt was first proposed by Lazarus (1966), and has been widely used by later commentators. This distinguishes between emotion-focussed and problem-focussed coping. The function of both types of coping is to modify the relation between the stressor and the individual, but in problem-focussed coping the individual attempts to alter, reduce or get rid of the stress, while in emotion-focussed coping there is an attempt to change the emotional state, such as anxiety, which is created by the stressor. Other writers have introduced different ideas, so that Frydenberg (2008) talks of productive and non-productive coping. Hampel and Peterman (2005), in their studies of German adolescents, use the distinction between emotion-focussed and problem-focussed coping, but they introduce a third category, that of maladaptive coping, by which they mean things like rumination, aggression, and denial.

Studies in this field indicate that three major factors have an influence on coping: these are age, gender and ethnicity. As far as age is concerned it is clear that emotion-focussed coping increases as adolescents become more mature. Frydenberg (2008) reports that the strongest age-related change is that older adolescents are more likely than younger ones to blame themselves if things go wrong, and to use tension-reduction strategies to deal with stress. These strategies can be adaptive, such as listening to music or doing some sporting activity, or they can be maladaptive, such as using drugs. However, age and gender are linked, and one of the most enduring findings in the research is that boys and girls have different styles of coping. As Frydenberg and Lewis (1993) put it in the title of one of their earlier papers on stress and coping in male and female adolescents: 'Boys play sport and girls turn to others'. Broadly speaking males make more use of active coping, being more inclined to go out and meet the problem head-on, and more often using aggressive or confrontational techniques to deal with interpersonal difficulties.

By contrast it is consistently reported that girls are more affected by stress than boys and are more likely to disclose a greater number of stressful events in their lives. Girls see setbacks and adversities as more threatening than boys do, and are more likely to expect the worst in stressful situations. In Seiffge-Krenke's (1995) study girls, in comparison with boys, see identical stressors as four times more threatening. In terms of coping females use social support far more than boys. Girls and young women are more likely to be dependent on parents and close friends for assistance, and are more sensitive to the expectations of others. In a study by Schonert-Reichl and Muller (1996), which compared help-seeking in boys and girls, results showed that females were far more likely to look for help from others than males were. This is of great significance, since it illustrates the different ways in which the two genders can be at risk. Boys and young men are at risk if they do not seek help, and bottle up their problems. Girls and young women, on the other hand, are at risk because they may be dependent on the very relationships that are at the heart of their difficulties.

Turning now to ethnicity, there are many fewer studies in this domain than there are where age and gender are concerned. There are some suggestions in the literature that particular ethnic groups may experience risk in different ways, so that, for example, Meltzer *et al.* (2000) report higher rates of mental disorder among Black African and Black Caribbean 11–15-year-olds in Britain, and Testa and Coleman (2006) found that Black Caribbean young men and young women were more likely to have unprotected sex and to become sexually active an earlier age than White young people. In terms of styles of coping, it is difficult to carry out research in this field because of the variety of ethnic groups and international contexts.

Alsaker and Flammer (1999) looked at coping among young people in 12 different countries across Europe, and concluded that one of the key variables affecting this was the context in which young people were growing up. Thus time spent in school, leisure activities, the role of the family and so on all varied across countries, and in turn influenced the style of coping adopted by the adolescents involved. To take one other example, D'Anastasi and Frydenberg (2005) investigated coping in Anglo-Australian and minority-group Australian adolescents, and one of their findings was that becoming involved in social action, and seeking spiritual support were two coping strategies used more frequently by minority-group Australians than by Anglo-Australians. This finding illustrates the importance of context, so that the background experiences as well as the sources of support available clearly determine the styles of coping adopted by different groups.

For some commentators the concepts of coping and resilience are very similar. However, as has been made clear here, the two originate from somewhat different literatures, with interest in stress and coping coming primarily from one group of writers and a focus on risk and resilience coming from another group. For the purposes of this chapter the two concepts have been kept separate, although it will be obvious that there is considerable overlap. In general it can be claimed that coping has to do with adaptation to normative everyday events, whilst resilience is about adjustment to adversity and disadvantage. With this in mind we will now turn to a consideration of resilience.

Resilience in adolescence

'It's good fun, going out, getting out, having a laugh. It's not particularly stressful, I don't think, because you don't have to worry about money, all you have to worry about is going to school, just getting through that. You've got it free to do what you want, to be honest. But then it's hard, like, you have to think about things like what your friends would think of you, and you've got your friends' issues going on and you've got some of your own, and it can build up, and when it's all happening at once it can be a bit like – Oh my God! But then you have to think, I'll sort out my issues and then I can sort out yours, or whatever.'

(15-year-old girl)

'I used to get really stressed about homework. I remember when I first came to secondary school, I was just like. . . . The idea that I hadn't done homework, or if I felt I couldn't do it, or couldn't do it well enough, I was just distraught. But now I've realised I don't need to fill out that survey, it's fine, or I can make excuses because I know I don't need to do that for my personal learning. I know how to manage things, or I'll just do it to make the teachers happy, but it doesn't need to be good, and I won't spend hours on it or something.'

(17-year-old girl)

The concept of resilience has become much more popular in recent years as a way of understanding how young people adapt to difficult circumstances. Yet there is a lot of confusion about what the term actually means. Is it a personality trait, or is it a process of adjustment? Does it continue over the lifespan, or is it limited to a response to particular circumstances? Is resilience always a positive thing, or can it have negative connotations? Olsson *et al.* (2003), in their review of resilience, make an important point when they indicate that resilience can apply both to processes and to outcomes, and that it is essential to keep these two things distinct. Thus the concept can be used to consider the types of behaviour, the psychosocial outcomes, seen in young people exposed to adversity. Here one might be looking at educational performance, avoidance of criminal behaviour or other measures of 'good' functioning. The problem with this is that there are many different possible outcomes, and therefore numerous possible criteria of resilience. On the other hand studies that look at processes are more likely to be interested in the way that risk and protective factors interact. Here there is less of a concern with outcome measures, and more of an interest in how the spectrum of risks and protective factors work together to produce adaptation in particular circumstances.

An example of such thinking can be found when looking at young people growing up in very disadvantaged communities (MacDonald, 2007). In such circumstances a commonly used outcome measure might be avoidance of substance misuse, or good school performance. However, in a situation where there is little motivation to achieve at school, and where substance misuse is common amongst teenagers, a better measure of resilience might be something like optimism or pro-social behaviour in relation to family or neighbourhood. For young people living in such environments it will be important to take into account not only the range of adversities, but also the potential strengths of the individual, and this will produce a more process-oriented view of resilience.

Another interesting question about resilience is whether it has any negative connotations. It is certainly the case that if resilience is seen as a personality attribute then the opportunity arises to perceive those who do not overcome adversity as somehow lacking in some essential quality. Luthar and Zelazo (2003) make the point that the resilience paradigm, as they call it, can foster a 'blame' perspective. They worry that, if some are able to survive serious adversity, those who do not manage to cope will be seen as lacking some personality characteristic or will be seen as not having made enough effort. This point links to the question of whether resilience is always a healthy response. Could there be such a thing as unhealthy coping?

Olsson *et al.* (2003) explore this question, and provide some useful examples. They ask: what is the most resilient response of a young person who experiences high levels of disadvantage over a long period? It could be argued that to display distressed emotions in response to this experience shows resilience, whilst to deny or avoid emotion would be a less 'healthy' response. As these authors put it: 'Considerable data exist suggesting that young people functioning well under high stress often show higher levels of emotional distress compared to their low stress peers' (Olsson *et al.*, 2003, p. 3).

In summary it can be stated that resilience is not a stable personality characteristic, but a process. It arises as a result of an interaction between risk and protective factors. It is often seen as an outcome, but this is misleading. Good school performance, or avoidance of crime, is an outcome. Resilience is not something that people have or do not have, but rather it is a response to difficult circumstances. There are many different types of resilience, depending on the particular individual. Some types of resilience may be considered more 'healthy' than others, but it will depend on the situation of the individual. Lastly resilience is not static, but it can change over the lifespan. It may not be apparent at one stage, but may then develop at another stage because of the availability of protective factors.

One of the key questions has to do with the interaction between risk and resilience. This is not a simple relation, but some conclusions from the research evidence can be outlined as follows.

- There is strong evidence from longitudinal studies that, where protective factors are present, most children and young people do recover from short-term adversity. In this sense it can be said that the majority have the capacity for resilience so long as the risk factors are limited, and protective factors are in place.
- Where risk factors are continuous and severe, only a minority manage to cope. The more serious the adversity, the stronger the protective factors need to be. Thus, under conditions of major risk, resilience is only apparent among a minority who can draw on the strengths gained from protective factors.
- The major risk factors for young people tend to lie within chronic and transitional events rather than in the acute risks. Thus adolescents show greater resilience when faced with acute adversities such as bereavement, or short-term illness, and less resilience when exposed to chronic risks such as continuing family conflict, long-term poverty, and multiple changes of home and school.
- Resilience can only develop in circumstances where there is risk or stress. Resilience is most likely to develop through gradual exposure to difficulties at a manageable level of intensity, and at points in the life cycle where protective factors can operate. Rutter (1985) calls these 'steeling experiences'.

One of the powerful attractions of the emphasis on resilience is that it reflects a positive approach, encouraging adults to keep the strengths and assets of the young person in mind at all times. The work of Luthar (2003) is a good example of such an approach. For this highly respected author it is essential to include positive predictors and outcomes in all models of change. Furthermore, in any assessment of an individual adolescent, it should be seen as mandatory that the capabilities and resources of the young person are identified alongside the risks.

A good way to conclude this discussion of risk and resilience is to briefly consider the work of Newman (2004), who suggests a number of strategies for the promotion of resilience in children and young people. The first strategy is to reduce the young person's exposure to risk. This sounds obvious, but is often difficult to achieve. One example given by Newman concerns the role of the school environment in combating low levels of parental care. Thus by providing breakfast clubs and after-school clubs the school can offer support to those who would have poor nutrition at the beginning of the day, who would struggle to find a safe space to do homework, and who might be unsupervised in the community at the end of the school day.

A second strategy is to find ways of interrupting the chain reaction of negative events. As has been noted the presence of one risk factor increases the likelihood that others will be present. As a result, if the impact of one risk factor can be diminished or reduced, then it may follow that other positive consequences flow from this. The provision of safe places for children and young people to meet with the non-residential parent following divorce is a good example. Many such parents find it hard to keep up regular contact with their sons and daughters if they live at a distance, or if there is nowhere for them to meet on neutral ground. Innovative schemes which provide contact centres make it possible for relationships to flourish despite adversity, and this may act to reduce the accumulation of negative experiences following parental separation.

The third strategy of note is to offer the young person positive experiences in order to enhance the strength of potential protective factors. Finding ways for young people to discover their strengths, to enhance self-esteem or to develop positive relationships with key adults can all contribute to the individual's capacity to overcome adversity. Results from the Christchurch study (Fergusson and Horwood, 2003) underline the role played by one significant adult in combating serious adversity, and a further example of this strategy may be taken from the literature on divorce. Where parental separation would initially appear to be a risk factor for a young person, new opportunities for growth can occur in such situations. The adolescent may have an opportunity to take on new roles, or to assume new responsibilities that would normally fall to the adults in the family. Research indicates that such experiences, so long as they are not too onerous, can give young people confidence, and assist them to develop new skills, thus bolstering protective factors for their development.

Conclusion

In looking back over the topics covered in this book it can be seen that a number of themes emerge. To begin with it is clear that adolescence cannot be understood without taking into account the social changes which occur in the societies in which young people grow up. In Western society the alterations in education and the labour market, the shifts in family functioning and the political and attitudinal changes that have been experienced over the past decades have all had a profound impact on the way young people develop. In addition it needs to be recognised that the adolescent transition has also altered, since it has become a much longer process. Those of 9 or 10 years of age are experiencing the beginnings of adolescence, whilst those in their early twenties remain economically dependent, and thus take longer to leave adolescence behind.

These factors are the background to any serious study of the adolescent stage of development. This stage is an extended one, and one in which a range of major emotional, physical and social transformations occur. In view of this it is right that the topics of coping and resilience are the subject of the final chapter in the book. The view has been advanced here that adolescence is not a stage of trauma or disorder. Theories which suggest such an idea do not accord with the empirical evidence. It seems that the majority of young people cope reasonably well with the normative risks and stresses which are inherent in the adolescent transition. Nonetheless there are, of course, those who experience difficulty, and an understanding of risk and adversity is equally important as recognising that most adapt to this development stage reasonably well.

There is general agreement among most commentators that the timing of stresses, the extent or number of changes experienced by the young person, and the synchronicity of changes all contribute to whether the adolescent will cope or not. These notions are inherent in the theories outlined in Chapter 1. In addition the role of social support is critical, and throughout the book the centrality of the family has been emphasised. The evidence is quite clear in showing that, of all the protective factors for adolescents, it is the family which plays the key role. The importance of the environment also needs to be underlined. It hardly needs to be pointed out that coping, when a young person is growing up in poverty or disadvantage, or living in a family with dysfunctional parents, or experiencing violence or racial harassment, will be quite different from coping in a supportive, settled and economically stable environment. It is here that the notions of developmental contextualism, noted in Chapter 1, can be seen to have an obvious contribution.

Three emergent themes have become evident in recent years in research on adolescence. These are:

- a more nuanced approach to some of the long-lasting questions about adolescent development;
- a stress on the reciprocal nature of relationships;
- an emphasis on adolescents as constructors or shapers of their own development.

As far as a nuanced approach is concerned, the example of autonomy is a useful one. Studies of autonomy have made it clear that this is not a yes or no question. It does not make sense to ask whether a young person has become autonomous or not. Rather within adolescent development there are different domains, with autonomy possibly being achieved in one domain (e.g. the choice of friends), whilst not in another domain (e.g. a decision about future educational choices). In addition of course there are different types of autonomy, with behavioural autonomy not necessarily following the same path as emotional autonomy.

In terms of reciprocal relationships, it has come to be recognised that early models in which it was assumed that certain types of parenting would lead to certain results are far too simplistic. It is now acknowledged that parents and young people influence each other. Parenting behaviour undoubtedly does impact on an adolescent's development, but parenting behaviour grows out of, and is changed by, the behaviour and characteristics of the young person. Recent research on information management (Chapter 5) highlights the way in which the behaviour of the young person influences parental behaviour.

The final, and perhaps the most important, idea to be emphasised here has to do with having an understanding of young people as agents in their own development. This has been noted as part of the discussion of the focal model in Chapter 1, and it links closely with a number of other concepts such as resilience, proactive coping and a strengths-based approach to this stage of development. The view proposed here is that the young person is an active rather than a passive agent in the coping process. Although some of the factors discussed in this book are outside the control of the individual, we cannot ignore the role the young person plays in adapting and adjusting to his or her own circumstances. To see the adolescent as constructing their own route through these years, to see an individual young person as someone who shapes the context in which they grow up, represents a profoundly important view of human development. It is argued here that the adolescent makes a personal contribution to managing the changes he or she experiences through the adolescent transition. In this sense it is possible, in many cases, for the young person to space things out and deal with one issue at a time. This book suggests that adolescents cope as well as they do by being active agents in their own development.

In Chapter 1 it was noted that historically there have been two ways of seeing this stage of development. For some commentators adolescence is a stage in which biology plays the key role, with puberty and the physical changes which follow from this being the primary determinants of development. For others the emphasis has been on the social construction of adolescence, with the primary focus being on the way in which the adult world shapes the young person as dependent child, pupil, citizen, consumer, or worker. A third perspective has been outlined in this book, one which is very much more adolescent-centred than either of the other two viewpoints. From this perspective it is argued that, for the most part, it is the young person rather than the adult who is constructing the adolescent environment and the adolescent course of development. Whilst this idea has been around for many years, it has existed very much on the periphery. It has rarely been at the heart of research investigations. It is only recently that it has started to influence the research agenda, with the work of Keijsers and Laird (2010) on information management being a good example. It can be predicted that this viewpoint will come to take centre stage in the years to come as a more productive way of understanding adolescent development. To illustrate this perspective, and to bring the book to an end, two examples will be given of young people taking an active role in shaping their adolescence.

'I think you sort of have to stop going to people and asking their opinions. You just have to think, like, "what do I actually want to do, and what would it turn out like if that did happen?" You need to isolate yourself from them, because you can get so easily influenced from what your friends are saying or what your parents are saying, and sometimes it can't really be right for you. You might not even consider either of their views.'

(17-year-old girl)

'I do sometimes think about who I am, and then you kind of think . . . like, you've got to be yourself. Because there are people who act differently just to be in different groups, like if they come late into school, and it's hard to find friends, so they just go with. . . . Like, to be a chav is easy, so you just get into that group. It's not easy to be yourself. I've seen people do that, they've come into school, had no friends, and they've changed their personality just to get into a group. Now that I know who I am , because before I thought I had to be someone else, but now that I know who I am it's easier to be, like, to kind of fit in, and to be more outgoing because you know who you are.'

(Interviewer) How did you figure out who you were?

'Well, seeing other people do stuff, doing stuff you didn't like, you could kind of come off of that [sic] and say who you are. So if someone was being mean to someone, like bullying or something, and you didn't like it, you could see you wouldn't be a bully or something. Yeah, learning from, like, what others are doing.'

(14-year-old boy)

Implications for practice

1. As might be expected, there are many implications for practice stemming from the material reviewed in this chapter. First, it is important to distinguish different meanings of the concept of risk. There are *risk factors* which might contribute to poor outcomes, such as poverty, illness, or abuse, and then there are young people who are *at risk*, referring to those who are vulnerable or who face significant adversity. There are also young people who are involved in *risk behaviour*, usually understood as behaviour that is potentially harmful or damaging, such as engaging in unsafe sex or binge drinking.
2. When considering young people under stress or faced with risk factors, there are four components to take into account. These are, first, the nature of the risk or stressor, then the internal resources of the individual, then the type of social support available, and then finally the coping process itself. From a different perspective, both risk and protective factors can be classified as being located in the individual, the family or the community.
3. Major studies of risk and resilience show that, in spite of significant adversity, there are those who are able to manage the risks and reach adulthood without being too badly affected. These studies show that the distinction between those who cope and those who do not has to do with whether there

are important protective factors in place. One of the most influential of these is the presence of one key adult during childhood and adolescence.

4. There are differences in coping processes according to age, gender and ethnicity. Emotion-focussed coping increases as young people move through adolescence, whilst boys and girls display very different coping strategies. Boys are more likely to use active coping, but they are also more likely to deny the problem, or to withdraw from stress. Girls, on the other hand, are more likely to use social support as a means of coping. In terms of ethnicity, it is clear that the context is critical in determining how coping skills develop. Different ethnic groups are very much influenced by the family and the environment in their choice of coping strategies.

5. Some of the central theoretical concepts represented by this book should be noted. How young people cope with development during adolescence will depend on the nature of the changes they experience, the timing and extent of these changes, and the synchronicity of their occurrence. The reciprocal nature of relationships has been emphasised, as has the importance of understanding that there are no simple yes or no answers to some of the key questions about this stage of development.

6. Finally, this book embraces a strengths-based perspective on adolescence. Young people take their development into their own hands. They make choices and select options all the time, and thus notions such as proactive coping, the development of competence, resilience and the building of connectedness are all central to our understanding of adolescence. Young people have skills, resources and enthusiasm to offer to the adult world. They are agents in their own development, a notion that is at the heart of 'The nature of adolescence'.

Further reading

Coleman, J and Hagell, A (2007) (Eds) *Adolescence, risk and resilience: against the odds*. John Wiley. Chichester.
A book which emphasises a resilience perspective, looking particularly at vulnerable groups of young people, including those in care, those with a disability, those socially excluded and so on. The book includes a review chapter on theoretical approaches to resilience.

Compas, B (2004) Processes of risk and resilience during adolescence. In Lerner, R and Steinberg, L (Eds) *Handbook of adolescent psychology*, 2nd edn. Wiley. New York.
Excellent coverage of the field from a North American perspective. Compas has been carrying out research on stress and resilience for many years, and is a noted expert on these topics.

Frydenberg, E (2008) *Adolescent coping: advances in theory, research and practice.* Routledge. London.
This is the second edition of a popular book in the '*Adolescence and society*' series. Frydenberg has been involved in developing research methods to study coping, as well as designing interventions to enhance coping skills. A comprehensive and useful book on the subject.

Luthar, S (Ed.) (2003) *Resilience and vulnerability: adaptation in the context of childhood adversities.* Cambridge University Press. Cambridge.
A landmark text by a leading developmental psychologist at Columbia University, New York. Suniya Luthar has an international reputation, and this book represents a major review of the field.

Appendix 1:

Interview questions

1 What sort of things do you like doing in your spare time?
2 It is said that during adolescence there is a change in the way people think, that they are able to think in more abstract terms. An example might be that it becomes easier to see both sides of an argument. Have you noticed this?
3 Another thing that is said to change is the way people decide what is right and wrong. Have you noticed a change in yourself as far as this is concerned?
4 A phrase that is often used when talking about teenagers is 'the generation gap'. Do you know what is meant by that? Do you think there is any truth in it?
5 Obviously parents are very important for adolescents. What do you think are the most important things that parents might provide?
6 It is assumed that young people see the world differently from the way adults see the world. What do you think are the main differences between the way adults and young people see the world?
7 Do you think adults provide role models for young people? If so, who would you say has been the main role model of how you want to be as an adult?
8 It is a well-known fact that teenagers are becoming physically more mature at a younger age these days. Do you think this makes things more difficult for young people today?
9 In early adolescence – usually around 11 or 12 – people experience something called the growth spurt, when their bodies change and grow quickly. Do you remember this? How did you feel at the time?
10 Another thing that is said to change at adolescence is the way young people think about themselves. It is said that adolescence can be a time of worries and identity problems, with young people asking themselves the question 'Who am I?' Does this ring any bells for you?

11   How about the question 'Who will I become?' 'What will I be in the future?'
12   Friends are often very important for teenagers. Why do you think this is so?
13   If there ever was a clash between what your friends wanted you to do and what your parents wanted you to do – which would you choose?
14   Do you feel that you are sometimes under pressure from people of your own age to do things that you would prefer not to do?
15   Obviously one important thing that has happened since the time your parents were teenagers is the existence of the internet. What do you think are the good things about the internet? Is it useful to you?
16   What about the bad things to do with the internet? What are these?
17   It is often said that we live in a permissive society today, with young people having much more sexual freedom than was the case twenty or thirty years ago. Do you think this is true?
18   As far as having boyfriends/girlfriends is concerned, what do you think are the problems that people of your age have to face?
19   People say adolescence is a time of 'storm and stress', a time of turmoil. Have you heard of this phrase? From your own experience would you agree with it?
20   There are different ways that teenagers cope when things don't go well. How do you cope when things are difficult? Where do you turn for support?
21   Now, finally, what do you think is the best thing that has happened to you in the last few years?

References

Adams, G and Berzonsky, M (Eds) (2003) *Blackwell handbook of adolescence*. Blackwell Publishing. Oxford.

Adams, G and Fitch, S (1982) Ego stage and identity status development: a cross-sequential analysis. *Journal of Personality and Social Psychology*. 43. 574–583.

Adelson, J (1971) The political imagination of the young adolescent. *Daedalus*. Fall. 1013–1050.

Adelson, J (1972) The political imagination of the young adolescent: 2. In Kagan, J and Coles, R (Eds) *Twelve to sixteen: early adolescence*. Norton. New York.

Adelson, J and O'Neill, R (1966) The development of political thought in adolescence. *Journal of Personality and Social Psychology*. 4. 295–308.

Adelson, J, Green, B and O'Neill, R (1969) Growth of the idea of law in adolescence. *Developmental Psychology*. 1. 327–332.

Alfermann, D and Stoll, O (2000) Effects of physical exercise on self-concept and well-being. *International Journal of Sport Psychology*. 30. 47–65.

Alsaker, F and Dick-Niederhauser, A (2006) Depression and suicide. In Jackson, S and Goossens, L (Eds) *Handbook of adolescent development*. Psychology Press. Hove.

Alsaker, F and Flammer, A (1999) Time use by adolescents in an international perspective. In Alsaker, F and Flammer, A (Eds) *The adolescent experience: European and American adolescents in the 1990s*. Lawrence Erlbaum. Hillsdale, NJ.

Alsaker, F and Flammer, A (2006) Pubertal maturation. In Jackson, S and Goossens, L (Eds) *Handbook of adolescent development*. Psychology Press. Hove.

Alsaker F and Kroger, J (2006) Self-concept, self-esteem and identity. In Jackson, S and Goossens, L (Eds) *Handbook of adolescent development*. Psychology Press. Hove.

Alsaker, F and Olweus, D (1992) Stability of self-evaluations in early adolescence: a cohort longitudinal study. *Journal of Research on Adolescence*. 2. 123–145.

Alsaker, F and Olweus, D (2002) Stability and change in global self-esteem and self-related affect. In Brinthaupt, T and Lipka, R (Eds) *Understanding the self of the early adolescent*. State University of New York Press. New York.

Anderson, S, Dallal, G and Must, A (2003) Relative weight and race influence average age at menarche: results from two nationally representative surveys of US girls studied 25 years apart. *Paediatrics.* 111. 844–850.

Andrews, R (1987) *Collins thematic dictionary of quotations.* Harper Collins. London.

Appleyard, K, Egeland, B, Van Dulmen, M and Sroufe, A (2005) When more is not better: the role of cumulative risk in child behaviour outcomes. *Journal of Child Psychology and Psychiatry.* 46. 235–245.

Archibald, A, Graber, J and Brooks-Gunn, J (2003) Pubertal processes and physiological growth in adolescence. In Adams, G and Berzonsky, M (Eds) *Blackwell handbook of adolescence.* Blackwell Publishing. Oxford.

Arnett, G (2004) *Emerging adulthood: the winding road from the late teens through the twenties.* Oxford University Press. Oxford.

Arnett, G and Taber, S (1994) Adolescence terminable and interminable: when does adolescence end? *Journal of Youth and Adolescence.* 23. 517–538.

Aspy, C, Vesely, S, Oman, R, Rodine, S, Marshall, L, Fluhr, J and McLeroy, K (2007) Parental communication and youth sexual behaviour. *Journal of Adolescence.* 30. 449–466.

Back, L (1997) Pale shadows, racisms, masculinity and multiculture. In Roche, J and Tucker, S (Eds) *Youth in society.* Sage. London.

Bailey, S and Shooter, M (Eds) (2009) *The young mind.* Bantam Press. London.

Balding, J (2006) *Young people in 2006.* Schools Health Education Unit. University of Exeter. Exeter.

Bancroft, J and Reinisch, J (1990) *Adolescence and puberty.* Oxford University Press. Oxford.

Barrett, H (2003) *Parenting programmes for families at risk.* National Family and Parenting Institute. London. www.familyandparenting.org.uk

Barter, C, McCarry, M, Berridge, D and Evans, K (2009) Partner exploitation and violence in teenage intimate relationships. NSPCC. London. www.nspcc.org.uk/inform

Baumrind, D (1971) Current patterns of parental authority. *Developmental Psychology Monographs.* 4. 1–102.

Benson, P, Mannes, M, Pitman, K and Ferber, T (2004) Youth development, developmental assets and public policy. In Lerner, R and Steinberg, L (Eds) *Handbook of adolescent psychology*, 2nd edn. Wiley. New York.

Berry, J (1990) Psychology of acculturation. In Berman, J (Ed.) *Cross-cultural perspectives: Nebraska Symposium on Motivation.* University of Nebraska Press. Lincoln, NB.

Berzonsky, M (2004) Identity style, parental authority, and identity commitment. *Journal of Youth and Adolescence.* 33. 213–220.

Beyers, W and Cok, F (2008) Adolescent self and identity development in context. *Special Issue of the Journal of Adolescence.* 31. 147–289.

Beyers, W and Goossens, L (1999) Emotional autonomy, psycho-social adjustment and parenting: interactions, moderating and mediating effects. *Journal of Adolescence.* 22. 753–769.

Bills, D (2009) Vocationalism. In Furlong, A (Ed.) *Handbook of youth and young adulthood.* Routledge. London.

Birman, D, Trickett, E and Vinokurov, A (2002) Acculturation and adaptation of Soviet Jewish refugee adolescents. *American Journal of Community Psychology.* 30. 585–607.

Blakemore, S-J and Choudhury, S (2006) Development of the adolescent brain: implications for executive function and social cognition. *Journal of Child Psychology and Psychiatry.* 47. 296–312.

Block, J and Robins, R (1993) A longitudinal study of consistency and change in self-esteem from early adolescence to early adulthood. *Child Development.* 64. 909–923.

Bois-Reymond, M (2009) Models of navigation and life management. In Furlong, A (Ed.) *Handbook of youth and young adulthood.* Routledge. London.

Bond, L, Patton, G, Glover, S, Carlin, J, Butler, H, Thomas, L and Bowes, G (2004) The Gatehouse Project: can a multi-level school intervention affect emotional well-being and health risk behaviours? *Journal of Epidemiology and Community Health.* 58. 997–1003.

Bonell, C, Fletcher, A and McCambridge, J (2007) Improving school ethos may reduce substance abuse and teenage pregnancy. *British Medical Journal*. 334 (March). 614–618.

Booth, A, Johnson, D, Granger, D, Crouter, A and McHale S (2003) Testosterone and child and adolescent adjustment: the moderating role of parent–child relationships. *Developmental Psychology*. 39. 85–98.

Botvin, G (1990) Substance abuse prevention: theory, practice and effectiveness. In Tonry, M and Wilson, J (Eds) *Drugs and crime*. University of Chicago Press. Chicago.

Bourdieu, P and Passeron, J-D (1977) *Reproduction in education, society and culture*. Sage. London.

Bridge, J, Goldstein, T and Brent, D (2006) Adolescent suicide and suicidal behaviour. *Journal of Child Psychology and Psychiatry*. 47. 372–394.

Bronfenbrenner, U (1979) *The ecology of human development: experiments by nature and design*. Harvard University Press. Cambridge, MA.

Brooks-Gunn, J and Warren, M (1985) The effects of delayed menarche in different contexts: dance and non-dance students. *Journal of Youth and Adolescence*. 14. 285–300.

Brown, B (1999) 'You're going out with who?' Peer group influences on adolescent romantic relationships. In Furman, W, Brown, B and Feiring, S (Eds) *Contemporary perspectives on adolescent romantic relationships*. Cambridge University Press. Cambridge.

Brown, B (2004) Adolescents' relationships with peers. In Lerner, R and Steinberg, L (Eds) *Handbook of adolescent psychology*, 2nd edn. Wiley. New York.

Brown, B, Lamborn, S and Newmann, F (1992) 'You live and you learn'. The place of school engagement in the lives of teenagers. In Newmann, F (Ed.) *Student engagement and achievement in American high schools*. Teachers' College Press. New York.

Brown, B, Larson, R and Saraswathi, T (Eds) (2002) *The world's youth: adolescence in eight regions of the globe*. Cambridge University Press. Cambridge.

Bryk, A, Lee, V and Holland, P (1993) *Catholic schools and the common goal*. Harvard University Press. Cambridge, MA.

Buchanan, C, Maccoby, E and Dornbusch, S (1996) *Adolescents after divorce*. Harvard University Press. London.

Buckingham, D (2007) *Beyond technology: children's learning in the age of digital culture*. Polity Press. Cambridge.

Bynner, J (2001) Childhood risks and protective factors in social exclusion. *Children and Society*. 15. 285–301.

Byrnes, J (2003) Cognitive development during adolescence. In Adams, G and Berzonsky, M (Eds) *Blackwell handbook of adolescence*. Blackwell Publishing. Oxford.

Cale, L and Harris, J (Eds) (2005) *Exercise and young people: issues, implications and initiatives*. Palgrave Macmillan. Basingstoke.

Call, C and Mortimer, J (2001) *Arenas of comfort in adolescence; a study of adjustment in context*. Lawrence Erlbaum. Mahwah, NJ.

Carlson, E, Sroufe, L and Byron, E (2004) The construction of experience: a longitudinal study of representation and behaviour. *Child Development*. 75. 66–83.

Carskadon, M and Acebo, C (2002) Regulation of sleepiness in adolescence: update, insights and speculation. *Sleep*. 25. 606–616.

Casteel, M (1993) Effects of inference necessity and reading goal on children's inferential generation. *Developmental Psychology*. 29. 346–357.

Catan, L (2004) Becoming adult: changing youth transitions in the 21st century. Economic and Social Research Council and Trust for the Study of Adolescence. Brighton. www.youngpeopleinfocus.org.uk

Cater, S and Coleman, L (2006) 'Planned' teenage pregnancy: perspectives of young parents from disadvantaged backgrounds. Policy Press. Bristol.

Caulfield, C, Hill, M and Shelton, A (2005) *The transition to secondary school: the experiences of Black and minority ethnic young people*. University of Glasgow. Glasgow.

Chao, R (2001) Extending research on the consequences of parenting style for Chinese Americans and European Americans. *Child Development*. 72. 1832–1843.

Chase, E, Maxwell, C, Knight, A and Aggleton, P (2006) Pregnancy and parenthood among young people in and leaving care. *Journal of Adolescence*. 29. 437–452.

Clarke, R (Ed.) (1992) *Situational crime prevention*. Harrow and Heston. New York.

Colby, A, Kohlberg, L, Gibbs, J and Lieberman, M (1983) A longitudinal study of moral judgements. *Monographs of the Society for Research in Child Development*. 48. Serial Number 200.

Cole, D, Maxwell, S, Martin, J *et al.* (2001) The development of multiple domains of child and adolescent self-concept: a cohort-sequential longitudinal design. *Child Development*. 72. 1723–1746.

Coleman, J (1974) *Relationships in adolescence*. Routledge and Kegan Paul. London.

Coleman, J (1978) Current contradictions in adolescent theory. *Journal of Youth and Adolescence*. 7. 1–11.

Coleman, J (1990) *Teenagers and divorce*. Trust for the Study of Adolescence. Brighton.

Coleman, J (2000) Young people in Britain at the beginning of a new century. *Children and Society*. 14. 230–242.

Coleman, J (2001) *Sex and your teenager*. Wiley. Chichester.

Coleman, J (2004) Suicide and self-harm: a training pack. Trust for the Study of Adolescence. Brighton. www.youngpeopleinfocus.org.uk

Coleman, J (2007) Emotional health and well-being. In Coleman, J, Hendry, L and Kloep, M (Eds) *Adolescence and health*. John Wiley. Chichester.

Coleman, J (2009) Well-being in schools: empirical measure or politician's dream? *Oxford Review of Education*. 35. 281–292.

Coleman, J and Brooks, F (2009) *Key data on adolescence*, 7th edn. Young People in Focus. Brighton. www.youngpeopleinfocus.org.uk

Coleman, J and Hagell, A (Eds) (2007) *Adolescence, risk and resilience*. Wiley Blackwell. Oxford.

Coleman, J and Roker, D (Eds) (1998) *Teenage sexuality: health, risk and education*. Harwood Academic Press. London.

Coleman, J and Roker, D (Eds) (2001) *Supporting parents of teenagers: a handbook for professionals*. Jessica Kingsley. London.

Coleman, J and Schofield, J (2007) *Key data on adolescence*, 6th edn. Trust for the Study of Adolescence. Brighton.

Coleman, J, Catan, L and Dennison, C (2004) 'You're the last person I'd talk to' In Roche, J, Tucker, S, Thomson, R and Flynn, R (Eds) *Youth in society*, 2nd edn. Sage. London.

Coleman, J, Hendry, L and Kloep, M (Eds) (2007) *Adolescence and health*. John Wiley. Chichester.

Coleman, JS (1961) *The adolescent society*. The Free Press. New York.

Coleman, L and Coleman, J (2002) The measurement of puberty: a review. *Journal of Adolescence*. 25. 535–550.

Coles, B (1996) *Youth and social policy*. UCL Press. London.

Collins, A (1990) Parent–child relationships in the transition to adolescence. In Montemayor, R, Adams, G and Gullotta, T (Eds) *Advances in adolescent development*, Vol. 2. Sage. Beverley Hills, CA.

Collins, A and Laursen, B (2004) Parent–adolescent relationships and influences. In Lerner, R and Steinberg, L (Eds) *Handbook of adolescent psychology*, 2nd edn. Wiley. New York.

Collishaw, S, Goodman, R, Pickles, A and Maughan, B (2007) Modelling the contribution of changes in family life to time trends in adolescent conduct problems. *Social Science and Medicine*. 65. 2576–2587.

Collishaw, S, Maughan, B, Goodman, R and Pickles, A (2004) Time trends in adolescent mental health. *Journal of Child Psychology and Psychiatry*. 45. 1350–1362.

Compas, B (2004) Processes of risk and resilience during adolescence. In Lerner, R and Steinberg, L (Eds) *Handbook of adolescent psychology*, 2nd edn. Wiley. New York.

Connolly, J and McIsaac, C (2009) Adolescents' explanations for romantic dissolutions: a developmental perspective. *Journal of Adolescence*. 32. 1209–1224.

Cooper, C (1994) Cultural perspectives on continuity and change in adolescent relationships. In Montemayor, R, Adams, G and Gullotta, T (Eds) *Personal relationships during adolescence*. Sage. London.

Costello, J, Erkanli, A and Angold, A (2006) Is there an epidemic of child or adolescent depression? *Journal of Child Psychology and Psychiatry*. 47. 1263–1271.

Cote, J (2000) *Arrested adulthood: the changing nature of maturity and identity*. New York University Press. New York.

Cotterell, J (2007) *Social networks in youth and adolescence*. Routledge. London.

Cowie, H, Boardman, C, Dawkins, J and Jennifer, D (2004) *Emotional health and well-being: a practical guide for schools*. Paul Chapman Publishing. London.

Coyle, A (1993) A study of psychological well-being among gay men using the GHQ-30. *British Journal of Clinical Psychology*. 32. 218–220.

Coyle, A (1998) Developing lesbian and gay identity in adolescence. In Coleman, J and Roker, D (Eds) *Teenage sexuality: health, risk and education*. Harwood Academic Press. London.

Craig, R and Mindell, J (Eds) (2008) *Health survey for England, 2006. Vol. 2: Obesity and other risk factors in children*. The Information Centre. London.

Crick, N (1996) The role of overt aggression, relational aggression and pro-social behaviour in the prediction of children's future social adjustment. *Child Development*. 67. 2317–2327.

Crick, N and Dodge, K (1994) A review and reformulation of social information processing mechanisms in children's social adjustment. *Psychological Bulletin*. 115. 74–101.

Crick, N and Dodge, K (1996) Social information processing mechanisms in reactive and proactive aggression. *Child Development*. 67. 993–1002.

Crockett, L, Raffaelli, M and Moilanen, K (2003) Adolescent sexuality: behaviour and meaning. In Adams, G and Berzonsky, M (Eds) *Blackwell handbook of adolescence*. Blackwell Publishing. Chichester.

Crockett, L, Bingham, C, Chopak, J and Vicary, J (1996) Timing of first sexual intercourse: the role of social control, social learning, and problem behaviour. *Journal of Youth and Adolescence*. 25. 89–111.

Crosnoe, R and Needham, B (2004) Holism, contextual variability and the study of friendships in adolescent development. *Child Development*. 75. 264–279.

Crosnoe, R, Erickson, K and Dornbusch, S (2002) Protective function of family relationships and school factors on the deviant behaviour of adolescent boys and girls: reducing the impact of risky friendships. *Youth and Society*. 33. 515–544.

Currie, C (Ed.) (2004) *Health behaviour in school-aged children: report from the 2001/2002 study*. World Health Organisation. Copenhagen.

Currie, C, Morgan, A and Roberts, C (2000) *Health and health-behaviour among young people*. World Health Organisation. Copenhagen.

Currie, C, Roberts, C and Morgan, A (2008) *Health behaviour in school-aged children. International report from the 2005/06 study*. World Health Organisation. Geneva.

Daddis, C and Randolph, D (2010) Dating and disclosure: adolescent management of information regarding romantic involvement. *Journal of Adolescence*. 33. 309–320.

D'Anastasi, T and Frydenberg, E (2005) Ethnicity and coping: what young people do and what young people learn. *Australian Journal of Guidance and Counselling*. 15. 43–59.

Davis, E and Friel, L (2001) Adolescent sexuality: disentangling the effects of family structure and family context. *Journal of Marriage and Family*. 63. 669–681.

De Goede, I, Branje, S and Meeus, W (2009) Developmental changes and gender differences in adolescents' perceptions of friendships. *Journal of Adolescence*. 32. 1105–1124.

REFERENCES

Demetriou, A, Christou, C, Spanoudis, G and Platsidou, M (2002) The development of mental processing: efficiency, working memory and thinking. *Monographs of the Society for Research in Child Development*. 67. Serial number 268.

Dennison, C and Coleman, J (1998) Teenage motherhood: experiences and relationships. In Clement, S (Ed.) *Psychological perspectives on pregnancy and childbirth*. Churchill Livingstone. Edinburgh.

Dishion, T and Andrews, D (1995) Preventing escalation in problem behaviours with high risk young adolescents. *Journal of Consulting and Clinical Psychology*. 63. 538–548.

Dishion, T and Patterson, G (2006) The development and ecology of antisocial behaviour in children and adolescents. In Cicchetti, D and Cohen, D (Eds) *Developmental psychopathology. Vol. 3: Risk, disorder and adaptation*. Wiley. New York.

Dishion, T, Patterson, G and Kavanagh, K (1992) An experimental test of the coercion model: linking theory, measurement and intervention. In McCord, J and Tremblay, R (Eds) *Preventing anti-social behaviour*. Guilford. New York.

Dornbusch, S, Ritter, P, Liederman, P and Fraleigh, M (1987) The relation of parenting style to adolescent school performance. *Child Development*. 58. 1244–1257.

Douvan, E and Adelson, J (1966) *The adolescent experience*. John Wiley. New York.

Drapeau, S, St-Jacques, M, Lepine, R, Begin, G and Bernard, M (2007) Processes that contribute to resilience among youth in foster care. *Journal of Adolescence*. 30. 977–1000.

Dunn, J and Deater-Deckard, K (2001) *Children's views of their changing families*. Joseph Rowntree Foundation. York.

Dunn, J, O'Connor, T and Cheng, H (2005) Children's responses to conflict between their different parents: mothers, stepfathers, non-resident fathers, and non-resident stepmothers. *Journal of Clinical Child and Adolescent Psychology*. 34. 223–234.

Dunphy, D (1972) Peer group socialisation. In Hunt, F (Ed.) *Socialisation in Australia*. Angus and Robertson. Sydney.

Durbin, D, Darling, N and Steinberg, L (1993) Parenting styles and peer group membership. *Journal of Research on Adolescence*. 3. 87–100.

Dusek, J and McIntyre, J (2003) Self-concept and self-esteem development. In Adams, G and Berzonsky, M (Eds) *Blackwell handbook of adolescence*. Blackwell Publishing. Oxford.

East, P and Rook, K (1992) Compensatory patterns of support among children's peer relationships: a test using school friends, non-school friends and siblings. *Developmental Psychology*. 28. 163–172.

Eccles, J (2004) Schools, academic motivation, and stage–environment fit. In Lerner, R and Steinberg, L (Eds) *Handbook of adolescent psychology*: 2nd edn. Wiley. New York.

Eccles, J and Roeser, R (2003) Schools as developmental contexts. In Adams, G and Berzonsky, M (Eds) *Blackwell handbook of adolescence*. Blackwell Publishing. Oxford.

Eccles, J, Lord, S and Roeser, R (1996) Round holes, square pegs, rocky roads and sore feet: the impact of stage–environment fit on young adolescents' experiences in schools and families. In Cicchetti, D and Toth, S (Eds) *Rochester symposium on developmental psychopathology. Vol. 8: Adolescence: opportunities and challenges*. University of Rochester Press. Rochester, NY.

Eden, K and Roker, D (2002) *'Doing something': young people as social actors*. National Youth Agency. Leicester.

Eisenberg, N and Morris, A (2004) Moral cognitions and prosocial responding in adolescence. In Lerner, R and Steinberg, L (Eds) *Handbook of adolescent psychology*, 2nd edn. Wiley. New York.

Eisenberg, N, Miller, P, Shell, R, McNalley, S and Shed, C (1991) Prosocial development in adolescence: a longitudinal study. *Developmental Psychology*. 27. 849–857.

Eisenberg, N, Carlo, G, Murphy, B and Van Court, B (1995) Prosocial development in late adolescence: a longitudinal study. *Child Development*. 66. 1179–1197.

Elder, G (1998) The life course as developmental theory. *Child Development*. 69. 1–12.

Elkind, D (1966) Conceptual orientation shifts in children and adolescents. *Child Development*. 37. 493–498.

Elkind, D (1967) Egocentrism in adolescence. *Child Development*. 38. 1025–1034.

Elkind, D and Bowen, R (1979) Imaginary audience behaviour in children and adolescents. *Developmental Psychology*. 15. 38–44.

Emler, N and Reicher, S (1995) *Adolescence and delinquency*. Blackwell. Oxford.

Engels, R and van den Einjden, R (2007) Substance use in adolescence. In Coleman, J, Hendry, L and Kloep, M (Eds) *Adolescence and health*. John Wiley. Chichester.

Ennett, S, Bauman, K, Hussong, K and Du Rant, R (2006) The peer context of adolescent substance use: findings from social network analysis. *Journal of Research on Adolescence*. 16. 159–186.

Enright, R, Shukla, D and Lapsley, D (1980) Adolescent egocentrism – sociocentrism and self-consciousness. *Journal of Youth and Adolescence*. 9. 101–116.

Erikson, E (1968) *Identity, youth and crisis*. Norton. New York.

Eslea, M, Menesini, E, Morita, Y, O'Moore, M, Mora-Merchán, J, Pereira, B and Smith P (2003) Friendship and loneliness among bullies and victims: data from seven countries. *Aggressive Behaviour*. 30. 71–83.

Euridyce (1997) *Secondary education in the European Union: structures, organisation and administration*. European Unit of Euridyce. Brussels.

Evangelou, M, Taggart, B, Sylva, K, Melhuish, E, Sammons, P and Siraj-Blatchford, I (2008) *What makes a successful transition from primary to secondary school?* Department for Children, Schools and Families. London.

Eveleth, P and Tanner, J (1977) *Worldwide variation in human growth*. Cambridge University Press. Cambridge.

Eveleth, P and Tanner, J (1990) *Worldwide variation in human growth*, 2nd edn. Cambridge University Press. Cambridge.

Facio, A and Batistuta, M (1998) Latins, Catholics and those from the far south: Argentinian adolescents and their parents. *Journal of Adolescence*. 21. 49–68.

Fadjukoff, P, Pulkinnen, L and Kokko, A (2005) Identity processes in adulthood: diverging domains. *Identity. An International Journal of Theory and Research*. 5. 1–20.

Farrell, C (1978) *My mother said . . .* Routledge. London.

Farrington, D (1995) The challenge of teenage anti-social behaviour. In Rutter, M (Ed.) *Psychosocial disturbances in young people: challenges for prevention*. Cambridge University Press. Cambridge.

Faulkner, S (2007) Eating disorders, diet and body image. In Coleman, J, Hendry, L and Kloep, M (Eds) *Adolescence and health*. John Wiley. Chichester.

Feiring, C (1996) Concepts of romance in 15 year-old adolescents. *Journal of Research on Adolescence*. 6. 181–200.

Ferguson, R (1998) Teachers' perceptions and expectations and the Black–White test score gap. In Jencks, C and Phillips, M (Eds) *The Black–White test score gap*. Brookings Institute Press. Washington, DC.

Fergusson, D and Horwood, L (2003) Resilient children in adversity: results of a 21 year study. In Luthar, S (Ed.) *Resilience and vulnerability*. Cambridge University Press. Cambridge.

Fergusson, D and Lynskey, J (1996) Adolescent resiliency to family adversity. *Journal of Child Psychology and Psychiatry*. 37. 281–292.

Fergusson, D, Lynskey, M and Horwood, J (1997) The effects of unemployment on juvenile offending. *Criminal Behaviour and Mental Health*. 7. 49–68.

Finkelhor, D (2008) *Childhood victimisation: violence, crime and abuse in the lives of young people*. Oxford University Press. Oxford.

Flammer, A and Alsaker, F (2006) Adolescents in school. In Jackson, S and Goossens, L (Eds) *Handbook of adolescent development*. Psychology Press. Hove.

Flanagan, C (2004) Volunteerism, leadership, political socialisation and civic engagement. In Lerner, R and Steinberg, L (Eds) *Handbook of adolescent psychology*, 2nd edn. Wiley. New York.

Flanagan, C and Tucker, C (1999) Adolescents' explanations for political issues: concordance with their views of self and society. *Developmental Psychology*. 35. 1198–1209.

Fletcher, A, Darling, N, Steinberg, L and Dornbusch, S (1995) The company they keep: relation of adolescents' adjustment and behaviour to their friends' perceptions of authoritative parenting. *Developmental Psychology*. 31. 300–310.

Flouri, E (2006) Non-resident fathers' relationships with their secondary school age children. *Journal of Adolescence*. 29. 525–538.

Flouri, E and Buchanan, A (2003) The role of father involvement in children's later mental health. *Journal of Adolescence*. 26. 63–78.

Fogelman, K (1976) *Britain's 16 year-olds*. National Children's Bureau. London.

Fonagy, P, Target, M, Cottrell, D, Phillips, J and Kurtz, Z (2005) *What works for whom? A critical review of treatments for children and adolescents*. Guilford Press. London.

Fontaine, N, Carbonneau, R, Vitaro, F and Tremblay, R (2009) Research review: a critical review of studies on the developmental trajectories of anti-social behaviour in females. *Journal of Child Psychology and Psychiatry*. 50. 363–385.

Fortner, M, Crouter, A and McHale, S (2004) Is parents' work involvement responsive to the quality of relationships with adolescent offspring? *Journal of Family Psychology*. 19. 530–538.

France, A (2009) Young people and anti-social behaviour. In Furlong, A (Ed.) *Handbook of youth and young adulthood*. Routledge. London.

Frank, A (1993) *The diary of a young girl*. Bantam. New York.

Frankel, R (1998) *The adolescent psyche*. Routledge. London.

Fredriksen, K, Rhodes, J, Reddy, R and Way, N (2004) Sleepless in Chicago: tracking the effects of adolescent sleep loss during the middle school years. *Child Development*. 75. 84–95.

Freud, A (1937) *The ego and the mechanisms of defence*. Hogarth Press. London.

Frosh, S, Phoenix, A and Pattman, R (2002) *Young masculinities*. Palgrave. London.

Frydenberg, E (2008) *Adolescent coping: advances in theory, research and practice*. Routledge. London.

Frydenberg, E and Lewis, R (1993) Boys play sport and girls turn to others: gender and ethnicity as determinants of coping. *Journal of Adolescence*. 16. 253–266.

Furlong, A (Ed.) (2009) *Handbook of youth and young adulthood*. Routledge. London.

Furlong, A and Cartmel, F (2009) Mass higher education. In Furlong, A (Ed.) *Handbook of youth and young adulthood*. Routledge. London.

Galambos, N (2004) Gender and gender role development in adolescence. In Lerner, R and Steinberg, L (Eds) *Handbook of adolescent psychology*, 2nd edn. Wiley. New York.

Galambos, N, Leadbetter, B and Barker, E (2004) Gender differences in and risk factors for depression in adolescence: a 4-year longitudinal study. *International Journal of Behavioural Development*. 28. 16–25.

Galton, M and Wilcocks, J (1983) *Moving from the primary classroom*. Routledge and Kegan Paul. London.

Galton, M, Comber, C and Pell, T (2002) The consequences of transition for pupils: attitudes and attainment. In Hargreaves, L and Galton, M (Eds) *Transfer from the primary classroom: 20 years on*. Routledge/Falmer. London.

Galton, M, Hargreaves, L and Pell, T (2003) Progress in the middle years of schooling: continuities and discontinuities at transfer. *Education 3–13*. 31. 9–19.

Garmezy, N and Rutter, M (Eds) (1983) *Stress, coping and development in children*. McGraw-Hill. New York.

Gau, S, Soong, W and Merikangas, K (2004) Correlates of sleep–wake patterns among children and young adolescents in Taiwan. *Sleep*. 27. 512–519.

Gauze, C, Bukowski, W and Sippola, L (1996) Interactions between family environment and friendship and associations with self-perceived well-being during early adolescence. *Child Development*. 67. 2201–2216.

Ge, X, Brody, G, Conger, R, Simons, R and Murry, V (2002) Contextual amplification of pubertal transition effects on deviant peer affiliation and externalising behaviour among African-American children. *Developmental Psychology.* 38. 42–54.

Ghate, D and Hazell, N (2002) *Parenting in poor environments: stress, support and coping.* Jessica Kingsley. London.

Giannotta, F, Settanni, M, Kliewer, W and Ciairano, S (2009) Results of an Italian school-based expressive writing intervention trial focussed on peer problems. *Journal of Adolescence.* 32. 1377–1390.

Gilani, N (1999) Conflict management of mothers and daughters belonging to individualistic and collectivistic cultural backgrounds. *Journal of Adolescence.* 22. 853–866.

Gilligan, C, Lyons, N and Hanmer, T (1990) *Making connections: the relational worlds of adolescent girls at Emma Willard School.* Harvard University Press. Cambridge, MA.

Gjerde, P and Shimizu, H (1995) Family relationships and adolescent development in Japan. *Journal of Research on Adolescence.* 5. 218–318.

Goleman, D (1996) *Emotional intelligence.* Bloomsbury. London.

Goodman, R and Scott, S (2005) *Child psychiatry,* 2nd edn. Blackwell. Oxford.

Goossens, L (2006a) Theories of adolescence. In Jackson, S and Goossens, L (Eds) *Handbook of adolescent development.* Psychology Press. Hove.

Goossens, L (2006b) Emotion, affect and loneliness in adolescence. In Jackson, S and Goossens, L (Eds) *Handbook of adolescent development.* Psychology Press. Hove.

Goossens, L (2006c) The many faces of adolescent autonomy. In Jackson, S and Goossens, L (Eds) *Handbook of adolescent development.* Psychology Press. Hove.

Goossens, L and Marcoen, A (1999) Relationships during adolescence: constructive versus negative themes and relational dissatisfaction. *Journal of Adolescence.* 22. 65–79.

Gowers, S and Bryant-Waugh, R (2004) Management of child and adolescent eating disorders: the current evidence base and future directions. *Journal of Child Psychology and Psychiatry.* 45. 63–83.

Graber, J and Brooks-Gunn, J (1996) Transitions and turning points: navigating the passage from childhood to adolescence. *Developmental Psychology.* 32. 768–776.

Graber, J, Brooks-Gunn, J and Warren, M (2006) Pubertal effects on adjustment. *Journal of Youth and Adolescence.* 35. 391–401.

Graham, J and Bowling, B (1995) *Young people and crime.* Home Office Research Study No. 145. Home Office. London.

Graham, P (2004) *The end of adolescence.* Oxford University Press. Oxford.

Graham, S and Juvonen, J (1998) Self-blame and peer victimisation in middle school: an attributional analysis. *Developmental Psychology.* 34. 587–599.

Green, H, McGinnity, A, Meltzer, H, Ford, T and Goodman, R (2005) *Mental health of children and adolescents in Great Britain, 2004.* Office for National Statistics. Stationery Office. London.

Grolnick, W, Beiswenger, K and Price, C (2008) Stepping up without over-stepping: disentangling parenting dimensions and their implications for adolescent adjustment. In Kerr, M, Stattin, H and Engels, R (Eds) *What can parents do?* Wiley. Chichester.

Grotevant, H and Cooper, C (1986) Individuation in family relationships: a perspective on individual differences in the development of identity and role-taking in adolescence. *Human Development.* 29. 82–100.

Grotevant, H and Cooper, C (1998) Individuality and connectedness in adolescent development: review and prospects for research on identity, relationships and context. In Skoe, E and von der Lippe, A (Eds) *Personality development in adolescence: a cross-sectional and lifespan perspective.* Routledge. London.

Gunnell, D (2000) The epidemiology of suicide. *International Review of Psychiatry.* 12. 21–26.

Gutman, L and Feinstein, L (2008) *Children's well-being in primary school: pupil and school effects.* The Wider Benefits of Learning Research Report 25. Institute of Education. London.

Haase, C, Silbereisen, R and Reitzle, M (2008) Adolescents' transitions to behavioural autonomy after German reunification. *Journal of Adolescence.* 31. 337–354.

Hagell, A (2007) Anti-social behaviour. In Coleman, J and Hagell, A (Eds) *Adolescence, risk and resilience.* John Wiley. Chichester.

Hagell, A and Newburn, T (1996) Family and social contexts of adolescent re-offenders. *Journal of Adolescence.* 19. 5–18.

Hagerdorn, J (2009) Youth in a world of gangs. In Furlong, A (Ed.) *Handbook of youth and young adulthood.* Routledge. London.

Hale, S (1990) A global developmental trend in cognitive processing speed. *Child Development.* 61. 653–663.

Hall, GS (1904) *Adolescence: its relation to physiology, anthropology, sociology, sex, crime, religion and education.* Appleton. New York.

Hall, W (2006) Cannabis use and the mental health of young people. *Australian and New Zealand Journal of Psychiatry.* 40. 105–113.

Halpern-Meekin, S and Tach, L (2008) Heterogeneity in two-parent families and adolescent well-being. *Journal of Marriage and the Family.* 70. 435–451.

Hampel, P and Peterman, F (2005) Age and gender effects on coping in children and adolescents. *Journal of Youth and Adolescence.* 34. 73–83.

Hansen, M, Jansen, I and Schiff, A (2005) The impact of school daily schedule on adolescent sleep. *Paediatrics.* 115. 1555–1661.

Hargreaves, L and Galton, M (Eds) (2002) *Transfer from the primary classroom: 20 years on.* Routledge/Falmer. London.

Harris, J (1998) *The nurture assumption: why children turn out the way they do.* Free Press. New York.

Hart, R (1997) *Children's participation: the theory and practice of involving young citizens in community development and community care.* UNICEF. Earthscan.

Harter, S (1988) The construction and conservation of the self: James and Cooley revisited. In Lapsley, D and Power, F (Eds) *Self, ego and identity.* Springer-Verlag. New York.

Harter, S (1989) Causes, correlates, and the functional role of global self-worth: a life-span perspective. In Kolligan, J and Sternberg, R (Eds) *Perceptions of competence and incompetence across the life-span.* Yale University Press. New Haven, CT.

Harter, S (1990) Self and identity development. In Feldman, S and Elliott, G (Eds) *At the threshold: the developing adolescent.* Harvard University Press. Cambridge, MA.

Harter, S and Monsour, A (1992) Developmental analysis of conflict caused by opposing attributes in the adolescent self-portrait. *Developmental Psychology.* 28. 251–260.

Hasebe, Y, Nucci, L and Nucci, M (2004) Parental control of the personal domain and adolescent symptoms of psychopathology: a cross-national study in the United States and Japan. *Child Development.* 75. 815–828.

Hawker, D and Boulton, M (2000) Twenty years research on peer victimisation and psychosocial maladjustment. *Journal of Child Psychology and Psychiatry.* 41. 441–455.

Hawton, K, Hall, S, Simkin, S, Bale, L, Bond, A, Codd, S and Stewart, A (2003) Deliberate self-harm in adolescents: a study of characteristics and trends in Oxford. *Journal of Child Psychology and Psychiatry.* 44. 1191–1198.

Haynie, D, Nansel, T and Eitel, P (2001) Bullies, victims and bully/victims: distinct groups of at-risk youth. *Journal of Early Adolescence.* 21. 29–49.

Heaven, P (1996) *Adolescent health: the role of individual differences.* Routledge. London.

Heinz, W (2009) Youth transitions in an age of uncertainty. In Furlong, A (Ed.) *Handbook of youth and young adulthood.* Routledge. London.

Henderson, M, Wight, D, Raab, G, Abraham, C, Buston, K, Hart, G and Scott, S (2002) Heterosexual risk behaviour among young teenagers in Scotland. *Journal of Adolescence.* 25. 483–494.

Henderson, S, Holland, J, McGrellis, S, Sharpe, S and Thomson, R (2007) *Inventing adulthoods: a biographical approach to youth transitions.* Sage. London.

Hendry, L, Shucksmith, J and Glendinning, A (1993) *Young people's leisure and lifestyles.* Routledge. London.

Henggeler, S, Schoenwald, S, Bourdin, C, Rowland, M and Cunningham, P (1998) *Multisystemic treatment of anti-social behaviour in children and adolescents.* Guilford Press. New York.

Herman-Giddens, M, Kaplowitz, P and Wasserman, R (2004) Navigating the recent articles on girls' puberty in paediatrics: what do we know and where do we go from here? *Paediatrics.* 113. 911–917.

Hill, J and Maughan, B (Eds) (2001) *Conduct disorders in childhood and adolescence.* Cambridge University Press. Cambridge.

Hill, J and Palmquist, W (1978) Social cognition and social relations in early adolescence. *Journal of Behavioural Development.* 1. 1–36.

Hillier, L and Harrison, L (2004) Homophobia and the production of shame: young people discovering the fault lines in discourse about same-sex attraction. *Culture, Health and Sexuality.* 6. 79–91.

Hillier, L, Harrison, L and Warr, D (1998) 'When you carry condoms all the boys think you want it': negotiating competing discourses about safe sex. *Journal of Adolescence.* 21. 15–30.

Hillier, L, Warr, D and Haste, B (1996) *The rural mural: sexuality and diversity in rural youth.* National Centre for HIV Research, La Trobe University. Melbourne.

Hirsch, B and Dubois, D (1991) Self-esteem in early adolescence: the identification and prediction of contrasting longitudinal trajectories. *Journal of Youth and Adolescence.* 20. 53–72.

Hobcraft, J and Kiernan, K (2001) Childhood poverty, early motherhood and adult social exclusion. *British Journal of Sociology.* 52. 495–517.

Hofstede, G (1983) Dimensions of national cultures in 50 countries and 3 regions. In Deregowski, J, Dzurnwiecz, S and Annis, R (Eds) *Explications in cross-cultural psychology.* Swets and Zietlinger. Lisse, The Netherlands.

Hoge, D, Smit, E and Crist, J (1995) Reciprocal effects of self-concept and academic achievement in sixth and seventh grade. *Journal of Youth and Adolescence.* 24. 295–314.

Honess, T, Charman, E and Zani, B (1997) Conflict between parents and adolescents: variation by family constitution. *British Journal of Developmental Psychology.* 15. 367–385.

Hoskin, C and Lindfield, S (2007) Involving young people in parenting programmes. In Roker, D and Coleman, J (Eds) *Working with parents of young people: research, policy and practice.* Jessica Kingsley. London.

Inhelder, B and Piaget, J (1958) *The growth of logical thinking.* Routledge and Kegan Paul. London.

Jackson, A and Davies, G (2000) *Turning points 2000: educating adolescents in the 21st century.* Teachers' College Press. New York.

Jackson, S, Bijstra, J, Oostra, L and Bosma, H (1998) Adolescents' perceptions of communication with parents relative to specific aspects of relationships with parents and personal development. *Journal of Adolescence.* 21. 305–322.

Jeffs, T and Smith, M (1990) *Young people, inequality and youth work.* Macmillan. London.

Jenkins, J, Simpson, A, Dunn, J, Rasbash, J and O'Connor, T (2005) Mutual influence of marital conflict and children's behaviour problems: shared and non-shared family risks. *Child Development.* 76. 24–39.

Johnson, A, Wadsworth, K, Wellings, K and Field, J (1994) *Sexual attitudes and lifestyles.* Blackwell. Oxford.

Jones, G (1995) *Leaving home.* Open University Press. Milton Keynes.

Julkunen, I (2009) Youth unemployment and marginalisation. In Furlong, A (Ed.) *Handbook of youth and young adulthood.* Routledge. London.

Jussim, L, Eccles, J and Madon, S (1996) Social perception, social stereotypes and teacher expectations: accuracy and the quest for the powerful self-fulfilling prophecy. In

Berkowitz, L (Ed.) *Advances in experimental social psychology*. Academic Press. New York.

Kaffman, M (1993) Kibbutz youth: recent past and present. *Journal of Youth and Adolescence*. 22. 573–604.

Kail, R (1991) Developmental change in speed of processing during childhood and adolescence. *Psychological Bulletin*. 109. 490–501.

Keating, D (2004) Cognitive and brain development. In Lerner, R and Steinberg, L (Eds) *Handbook of adolescent development*, 2nd edn. John Wiley. Chichester.

Keijsers, L and Laird, R (2010) Introduction to special issue. Careful conversations: adolescents managing their parents' access to information. *Journal of Adolescence*. 33. 255–260.

Kelly, J (2000) Children's adjustment in conflicted marriage and divorce: a decade review of research. *Journal of the American Academy of Child and Adolescent Psychiatry*. 39. 963–973.

Kerr, M and Stattin, H (2000) What parents know, how they know it, and several forms of adolescent adjustment. *Developmental Psychology*. 36. 366–380.

Kerr, M, Stattin, H and Engels, R (2008) *What can parents do? New insights into the role of parents in adolescent problem behaviour*. Wiley. Chichester.

Kiesner, J, Poulin, F and Nicotra, E (2003) Peer relations across contexts: individual–network homophily and network inclusion in and after school. *Child Development*. 74. 1328–1343.

Kloep, M (1999) Love is all you need? Focussing on adolescents' life concerns from an ecological perspective. *Journal of Adolescence*. 22. 49–64.

Kohlberg, L (Ed.) (1981) *The philosophy of moral development*, Vol. 1. Harper and Row. San Francisco, CA.

Kohlberg, L (Ed.) (1984) *The philosophy of moral development*, Vol. 2. Harper and Row. San Francisco, CA.

Kohlberg, L and Gilligan, C (1971) Twelve to sixteen: early adolescence. *Daedalus*. 100, No. 4. 1068–1072.

Kolvin, I, Miller, F, Scott, D and Fleeting, M (1990) *Continuities of deprivation*. Avebury. Aldershot.

Koops, W and Castro, B (2006) Development of aggression and its linkages with violence and juvenile delinquency. In Jackson, S and Goossens, L (Eds) *Handbook of adolescent development*. Psychology Press. Hove.

Kracke, B and Noack, P (1998) Continuity and change in family interactions across adolescence. In Hofer, M, Youniss, J and Noack, P (Eds) *Verbal interactions and development in families with adolescents*. Ablex Publishing. Norwood, NJ.

Kremer, J, Trew, K and Ogle, S (1997) *Young people's involvement in sport*. Routledge. London.

Kroger, J (1985) Relationships during adolescence: a cross-national comparison of New Zealand and United States teenagers. *Journal of Youth and Adolescence*. 8. 47–56.

Kroger, J (2004) *Identity in adolescence*, 3rd edn. Routledge. London.

Lahey, B, Moffitt, T and Caspi, A (2003) (Eds) *Causes of conduct disorder and juvenile delinquency*. Guilford Press. New York.

Laird, R, Pettit, G, Bates, J and Dodge, K (2003) Parents' monitoring – relevant knowledge and adolescents' delinquent behaviour: evidence of correlated developmental changes and reciprocal influences. *Child Development*. 74. 752–768.

Lamborn, S, Dornburg, S and Steinberg, L (1996) Ethnicity and community context as moderators of the relation between family decision-making and adolescent adjustment. *Child Development*. 66. 283–301.

Larson, R and Wilson, S (2004) Adolescence across time and place: globalisation and the changing pathways to adulthood. In Lerner, R and Steinberg, L (Eds) *Handbook of adolescent psychology*. John Wiley. Chichester.

Larson, R, Richards, M, Moneta, G, Holmbeck, G and Duckett, E (1996) Changes in adolescents' daily interactions with their families from age 10 to 18: disengagement and transformation. *Developmental Psychology*. 32. 744–754.

Layard, R and Dunn, J (2008) *A good childhood*. Penguin Books. London.

Lazarus, R (1966) *Psychological stress and the coping process*. McGraw-Hill. New York.

Lee, V and Smith, J (2001) *Restructuring high schools for equity and excellence*. Teachers' College Press. New York.

Lees, S (1993) *Sugar and spice: sexuality and adolescent girls*. Penguin. London.

Lehalle, H (2006) Cognitive development in adolescence: thinking freed from concrete restraints. In Jackson, S and Goossens, L (Eds) *Handbook of adolescent development*. Psychology Press. Hove.

Liebkind, K, Jasinkaja-Lahti, I and Solheim, E (2004) Cultural identity, perceived discrimination and parental support as determinants of immigrants' school adjustment. *Journal of Adolescent Research*. 19. 635–656.

Lila, M, van Aken, M, Musitu, G and Buelga, S (2006) Families and adolescents. In Jackson, S and Goossens, L (Eds) *Handbook of adolescent development*. Psychology Press. Hove.

Livingstone, S (2009) *Children and the internet*. Polity Press. Cambridge.

Livingstone, S and Bober, M (2004) *UK children go on-line: surveying the experiences of young people and their parents*. London School of Economics. London.

Lloyd, B and Lucas, K (1998) *Smoking in adolescence: images and identities*. Routledge. London.

Loeber, R and Stouthamer-Loeber, M (1986) Family factors as correlates and predictors of juvenile conduct problems and delinquency. In Morris, M and Tonry, M (Eds) *Crime and justice*, Vol. 7. University of Chicago Press. Chicago.

Lowry, R, Kremer, J and Trew, K (2007) Young people: physical health, exercise and recreation. In Coleman, J, Hendry, L and Kloep, M (Eds) *Adolescence and health*. John Wiley. Chichester.

Luthar, S (2003) (Ed.) *Resilience and vulnerability*. Cambridge University Press. Cambridge.

Luthar, S and Zelazo, L (2003) Research on resilience: an integrative view. In Luthar, S (Ed.) *Resilience and vulnerability*. Cambridge University Press. Cambridge.

Luyckx, K and Goossens, L (2006) Unpacking commitment and exploration: preliminary validation of an integrative model of late adolescent identity formation. *Journal of Adolescence*. 29. 361–378.

Maccoby, E (1998) *The two sexes: growing up apart, coming together*. Harvard University Press. Cambridge, MA.

Maccoby, E and Martin, J (1983) Socialization in the context of the family: parent–child interaction. In Hetherington, E (Ed.) *Handbook of child psychology*. Wiley. New York.

MacDonald, R (2007) Social exclusion, risk and young adulthood. In Coleman, J and Hagell, A (Eds) *Adolescence, risk and resilience*. John Wiley. Chichester.

Macfarlane, A and McPherson, A (2007) Getting it right in health services for young people. In Coleman, J, Hendry, L and Kloep, M (Eds) *Adolescence and health*. John Wiley. Chichester.

Mackinnon, D (2007) Health promotion and health education. In Coleman, J, Hendry, L and Kloep, M (Eds) *Adolescence and health*. John Wiley. Chichester.

Malmberg, L and Trempala, J (1997) Anticipated transitions to adulthood: the effect of educational track, gender and self-evaluation on Polish and Finnish adolescents. *Journal of Youth and Adolescence*. 26. 517–538.

Marcia, J (1966) Development and validation of ego-identity status. *Journal of Personality and Social Psychology*. 3. 551–558.

Marcia, J (1993) The relational roots of identity. In Kroger, J (Ed.) *Discussions on ego-identity*. Lawrence Erlbaum. Hillsdale, NJ.

Marsh, H, Byrne, B and Shavelson, R (1988) A multi-faceted academic self-concept: its hierarchical structure and its relation to academic achievement. *Journal of Educational Psychology*. 80. 366–380.

Marshall, S (1995) Ethnic socialisation of African-American children. *Journal of Youth and Adolescence*. 24. 377–396.

Marshall, S, Tilton-Weaver, L and Bosdet, L (2005) Information management: considering adolescents' regulation of parental knowledge. *Journal of Adolescence*. 28. 633–648.

Marsland, D (1987) *Education and youth*. Falmer Press. London.

Martinez, R and Dukes, R (1997) The effects of ethnic identity, ethnicity, and gender on adolescent well-being. *Journal of Youth and Adolescence*. 26. 503–516.

Marwick, A (2005) 'I'm a lot more interesting than a friendster profile': identity presentation, authenticity and power in social networking. Paper presented at the Association of Internet Researchers, Chicago. Retrieved from http//www.tiara.org/blog/?page_id=299

Mason, D (2003) (Ed.) *Explaining ethnic differences: changing patterns of disadvantage in Britain*. Policy Press. Bristol.

Masten, A and Powell, J (2003) A resilience framework for research, policy and practice. In Luthar, S (Ed.) *Resilience and vulnerability*. Cambridge University Press. Cambridge.

Mazor, A (Ed.) (1993) Kibbutz adolescents. Special Issue of the *Journal of Youth and Adolescence*. 22. 569–714.

Measor, L and Woods, P (1984) *Changing schools*. Open University Press. Milton Keynes.

Meeus, W, Iedema, J, Helsen, M and Vollerbergh, W (1999) Patterns of adolescent identity development: review of the literature and longitudinal analysis. *Developmental Review*. 19. 419–461.

Meltzer, H, Gatward, R, Goodman, R and Ford, T (2000) *The mental health of children and adolescents in Great Britain*. HMSO. London.

Mendelson, M and Aboud, F (1999) Measuring friendship quality in late adolescents and young adults: McGill friendship questionnaires. *Canadian Journal of Behavioural Science*. 31. 130–132.

Mesch, G and Talmud, I (2007) Similarity and the quality of on-line and off-line social relationships among adolescents in Israel. *Journal of Research on Adolescence*. 17. 455–466.

Mesch, G and Talmud, I (2010) *Wired youth: the social world of adolescence in the information age*. Routledge. London.

Michaud, P-A (2006) Adolescents and risk: why not change our paradigm? *Journal of Adolescent Health*. 38. 481–483.

Michaud, P-A, Chossis, I and Suris, J-C (2006) Health-related behaviour: current situation, trends and prevention. In Jackson, S and Goossens, L (Eds) *Handbook of adolescent development*. Psychology Press. Hove.

Midgley, C (2002) *Goals, goal structures and patterns of adaptive learning*. Erlbaum. Mahwah, NJ.

Milburn, K (1995) A critical review of peer education with young people with special reference to sexual health. *Health Education Research*. 10. 407–420.

Miller, B, Bayley, B, Christensen, M and Coyl, D (2003) Adolescent pregnancy and child-bearing. In Adams, G and Berzonsky, M (Eds) *Blackwell handbook of adolescence*. Blackwell Publishing. Oxford.

Millar, F (2008) *The secret world of the working mother*. Vermillion. London.

Mirzah, H (1992) *Young, female and black*. Routledge. London.

Moffitt, T (1993) Adolescence-limited and life-course-persistent anti-social behaviour: a developmental taxonomy. *Psychological Review*. 100. 674–701.

Moffitt, T (2006) Life-course-persistent versus adolescence-limited anti-social behaviour. In Cicchetti, D and Cohen, D (Eds) *Developmental psychopathology*, Vol. 2. Wiley. New York.

Montagna, W and Sadler, W (Eds) (1974) *Reproductive behaviour*. Plenum. New York.

Montemayor, R (1983) Parents and adolescents in conflict: all families some of the time and some families most of the time. *Journal of Early Adolescence*. 3. 83–103.

Montgomery, M and Cote, J (2003) College as a transition to adulthood. In Adams, G and Berzonsky, M (Eds) *Blackwell handbook of adolescence*. Blackwell Publishing, Oxford.

Moore, L (1994) *Who will run the frog hospital?* Faber. London.

Moore, S (1995) Girls' understanding and construction of menarche. *Journal of Adolescence*. 18. 87–104.

Moore, S and Rosenthal, D (2006) *Sexuality in adolescence: current trends*. Routledge. London.

Moore, T, Zemmit, A, Lingford-Hughes, T, Barnes, T, Jones, P, Burke, M and Lewis, G (2007) Cannabis use and the risk of psychotic or affective mental health outcomes: a systematic review. *Lancet*. 370 (9584). 319–328.

Mortimer, J (2009) Changing experiences of work. In Furlong, A (Ed.) *Handbook of youth and young adulthood*: Routledge. London.

Mortimer, J and Larson, R (Eds) (2002) *The changing adolescent experience*. Cambridge University Press. Cambridge.

Mounts, N (2002) Parental management of adolescent peer relationships in context. *Journal of Family Psychology*. 16. 58–69.

Mounts, N (2004) Adolescents' perceptions of parental management of peer relationships in an ethnically diverse sample. *Journal of Adolescent Research*. 19. 446–467.

Mulder, C (2009) Leaving the parental home in young adulthood. In Furlong, A (Ed.) *Handbook of youth and young adulthood*. Routledge. London.

Murray, F (1990) The conversion of truth into necessity. In Overton, W (Ed.) *Reasoning, necessity and logic: developmental perspectives*. Erlbaum. Hillsdale, NJ.

Mustanski, B, Viken, R, Kaprio, J, Pulkinnen, L and Rose, RJ (2004) Genetic and environmental influences on pubertal development: longitudinal data from Finnish twins. *Developmental Psychology*. 40. 1188–1198.

Muuss, R (1996) *Theories of adolescence*, 6th edn. McGraw-Hill. New York.

Nakkula, M and Selman, R (1991) How people treat each other: pair therapy as a context for the development of interpersonal ethics. In Kurtines, W and Gewirtz, J (Eds) *Handbook of moral behaviour and development*. Erlbaum. Hillsdale, NJ.

Nathanson, V (Ed.) (2003) *Adolescent health*. British Medical Association. London.

Newman, T (2004) *What works in building resilience?* Barnado's. Essex.

NHS Information Centre (2008) *Smoking, drinking and drug use among young people in England in 2007*. The NHS Information Centre. London.

Noack, P, Hoffer, M, Kracke, B and Klein-Allerman, E (1995) Adolescents and their parents facing social change: families in East and West Germany after re-unification. In Noack, P, Hoffer, M and Youniss, J (Eds) *Psychological responses to social change*. Walter de Gruyter. Berlin.

Noller, P and Callan, V (1991) *The adolescent in the family*. Routledge. London.

Nuffield Foundation (2009) *Time trends in parenting and outcomes for young people*. Nuffield Foundation. London.

Nurmi, J-E (2004) Socialization and self-development. In Lerner, R and Steinberg, L (Eds) *Handbook of adolescent psychology*, 2nd edn. Wiley. New York.

O'Connor, T, Dunn, J, Jenkins, J and Pickering, K (2001) Family settings and children's adjustment: differential adjustment within and across families. *British Journal of Psychiatry*. 179. 110–115.

Offer, D (1969) *The psychological world of the teenager*. Basic Books. New York.

Offer, D, Ostrov, D, Howard, K and Dolin, S (1992) *The Offer Self-Image Questionnaire for Adolescents – revised*. Western Psychological Services. Los Angeles, CA.

Ogden, T and Hagen, K (2009) What works for whom? Gender differences in intake characteristics and treatment outcomes following Multisystemic Therapy. *Journal of Adolescence*. 32. 1425–1436.

Ogden, T, Beyers, W and Ciairano, S (2009) Intervention and prevention with adolescents. Special Issue of the *Journal of Adolescence*. 32. 1343–1442.

Ohida, T, Osaki, Y, Doi, Y and Tanahata, T (2004) An epidemiological study of self-reported sleep problems among Japanese adolescents. *Sleep*. 27. 978–985.

Olsson, C, Bond, L, Burns, J, Vella-Brodrick, D and Sawyer, S (2003) Adolescent resilience: a concept analysis. *Journal of Adolescence*. 26. 1–11.

Olweus, D (1993) *Bullying at school: what we know and what we can do*. Blackwell Publishing. Oxford.

Osgood, D, Wilson, J, O'Malley, P and Johnson, L (1996) Routine activities and individual deviant behaviour. *American Sociological Review*. 61. 635–655.

Paikoff, R, Brooks-Gunn, J and Carlton-Ford, S (1991) Effect of reproductive status changes on family functioning and well-being of mothers and daughters. *Journal of Early Adolescence*. 11. 201–220.

Palmer, S (2007) *Toxic childhood: how the modern world is damaging our children and what we can do about it*. Orion Publishing. London.

Papini, D and Sebby, R (1987) Adolescent pubertal status and affective family relationships: a multivariate assessment. *Journal of Youth and Adolescence*. 16. 1–16.

Papini, D, Clark, S, Barnett, J and Savage, C (1989) Grade, pubertal status and gender-related variations in conflictual issues among adolescents. *Adolescence*. 24. 977–987.

Parent, A-S, Teilman, G, Juul, A, Skakkebaek, N, Toppari, J and Bourguignon, J (2003) The timing of normal puberty and the age limits of sexual precocity: variations around the world. *Endocrine Review*. 24. 668–693.

Patchin, J and Hinduja, S (2006) Bullies move beyond the school-yard: a preliminary look at cyber-bullying. *Youth Violence and Juvenile Justice*. 4. 148–169.

Patterson, G and Stouthamer-Loeber, M (1984) The correlation of family management practices and delinquency. *Child Development*. 55. 1299–1307.

Pearce, J (2007) Sex and risk. In Coleman, J and Hagell, A (Eds) *Adolescence, risk and resilience*. John Wiley. Chichester.

Pearce, JJ (2009) *Young people and sexual exploitation: hard to reach and hard to hear*. Routledge. London.

Pellegrini, A and Long, J (2002) A longitudinal study of bullying, dominance and victimisation during the transition from primary to secondary school. *British Journal of Developmental Psychology*. 20. 259–280.

Petersen, A, Leffert, N and Hurrelmann, K (1993) Adolescence and schooling in Germany and the United States: a comparison of peer socialisation for adulthood. *Teachers College Record*. 94. 611–628.

Pflieger, J and Vazsonyi, A (2006) Parenting processes and dating violence: the mediating role of self-esteem in low and high SES adolescents. *Journal of Adolescence*. 29. 495–512.

Phinney, J (1992) The multi-group ethnic identity measure: a new scale for use with adolescents and adults from diverse groups. *Journal of Adolescent Research*. 7. 156–176.

Phinney, J (1993) A three-stage model of ethnic identity development. In Bernal, M and Knight, G (Eds) *Ethnic identity: formation and transmission among Hispanics and other minorities*. State University of New York Press. Albany, NY.

Phinney, J and Chavira, V (1995) Parental ethnic socialisation and adolescent coping with problems related to ethnicity. *Journal of Research on Adolescence*. 5. 31–53.

Phinney, J and Devich-Navarro, M (1997) Variations in bicultural identification among African American and Mexican American adolescents. *Journal of Research on Adolescence*. 7. 3–32.

Phinney, J and Goossens, L (Eds) (1996) Identity development in context. Special Issue of the *Journal of Adolescence*. 19. 401–500.

Phinney, J and Rosenthal, D (1992) Ethnic identity in adolescence: process, context and outcome. In Adams, G, Gullotta, T and Montemayor, R (Eds) *Adolescent identity formation*. Sage. London.

Phoenix, A (1991) *Young mothers?* Polity Press. London.

Piaget, J (1932) *The moral judgement of the child*. Routledge and Kegan Paul. London.

Pitts, J (2008) *Reluctant gangsters: the changing face of youth crime*. Willan Publishing. Cullompton, Devon.

Pratt, M, Skoe, E and Arnold, M (2004) Care reasoning development and family socialisation patterns in later adolescence: a longitudinal analysis. *International Journal of Behavioural Development*. 28. 139–147.

Pring, R, Hayward, G, Hodgson, A and Johnson, J (2009) *Education for all: the future of education and training for 14–19 year-olds*. Routledge. London.

Pulkinnen, L and Koko, A (2000) Identity development in adulthood: a longitudinal study. *Journal of Personality*. 34. 445–470.

Punamaki, R, Wallenius, M, Nygard, C and Rimpela, A (2007) Use of information and communication technology and perceived health in adolescence: the role of sleeping habits and waking time tiredness. *Journal of Adolescence*. 30. 569–586.

Quadrel, M, Fishoff, B and Davis, W (1993) Adolescent (in)vulnerability. *American Psychologist*. 48. 102–116.

Raffe, D (2009) Explaining cross-national differences in education-to-work transitions. In Furlong, A (Ed.) *Handbook of youth and young adulthood*. Routledge. London.

Rankin, J, Lane, D and Gibbons, F (2004) Adolescent self-consciousness: longitudinal age changes and gender differences in two cohorts. *Journal of Research on Adolescence*. 14. 1–21.

Reicher, H (1993) Family and peer relations and social-emotional problems in adolescence. *Studia Psychologica*. 35. 403–408.

Reitz, E, Dekovic, M and Meijer, A (2006) Relations between parenting and externalising and internalizing problem behaviour: child behaviour as moderator and predictor. *Journal of Adolescence*. 29. 419–436.

Rest, J (1973) The hierarchical nature of moral judgement. *Journal of Personality*. 41. 86–109.

Rice, K, Herman, M and Petersen, A (1993) Coping with challenge in adolescence: a conceptual model and psycho-educational intervention. *Journal of Adolescence*. 16. 235–252.

Riley, T, Adams, G and Nielsen, G (1984). Adolescent egocentrism: the association among imaginary audience behaviour, cognitive development and parental support and rejection. *Journal of Youth and Adolescence*. 13. 401–438.

Rippl, S and Boehnke, K (1995) Authoritarianism: adolescents from East and West Germany and the United States compared. In Youniss, J (Ed.) *After the wall: family adaptation in East and West Germany*. New Directions for Child Development. No. 70. Winter. Jossey-Bass. San Francisco, CA.

Roberts, R, Roberts, C and Duong, H (2009) Sleeplessness in adolescence: prospective data on sleep deprivation, health and functioning. *Journal of Adolescence*. 32. 1045–1058.

Roche, J, Tucker, S, Thomson, R and Flynn, R (2004) *Youth in society*, 2nd edn. Sage Publications. London.

Rodham, K, Brewer, H, Mistral, W and Stallard, P (2006) Adolescents' perceptions of risk and challenge: a qualitative study. *Journal of Adolescence*. 29. 261–272.

Rodkin, P, Farmer, T, Pearl, R and Van Aker, R (2000) Heterogeneity of popular boys: anti-social and pro-social configurations. *Developmental Psychology*. 36. 14–24.

Roeser, R, Eccles, J and Sameroff, J (1998) Academic and emotional functioning in early adolescence: longitudinal relations, patterns, and prediction by experience in middle school. *Development and Psychopathology*. 10. 321–352.

Roker, D (2007) Getting information and support from websites. In Roker, D and Coleman, J (Eds) *Working with parents of young people: research, policy and practice*. Jessica Kingsley. London.

Roker, D and Coleman, J (Eds) (2007) *Working with parents of young people: research, policy and practice*. Jessica Kingsley. London.

REFERENCES

Roker, D and Foster, H (2007) Working with schools to support parents: lessons from two evaluations. In Roker, D and Coleman, J (Eds) *Working with parents of young people: research, policy and practice.* Jessica Kingsley. London.

Rolfe, A (2005) 'There's helping and there's hindering': young mothers, support and control. In Barry, M (Ed.) *Youth policy and social inclusion.* Routledge. London.

Ronka, A, Oravala, S and Pulkinnen, L (2002) 'I met this wife of mine and things got on a better track'. Turning points in risk development. *Journal of Adolescence.* 25. 47–64.

Rosenberg, M (1965) *Society and the adolescent self-image.* Princeton University Press. Princeton, NJ.

Rosenberg, M (1979) *Concerning the self.* Basic Books. New York.

Rosenthal, R and Jacobsen, L (1968) *Pygmalion in the classroom.* Holt, Rinehart and Winston. New York.

Rotheram-Borus, M, Hunter, J and Rosario, M (1994) Suicidal behaviour and gay-related stress among gay and bisexual male adolescents. *Journal of Adolescent Research.* 9. 498–508.

Ruiz, S, Roosa, M and Gonzalez, M (2002) Predictors of self-esteem for Mexican-American and European American youths: a re-examination of the influence of parenting. *Journal of Family Psychology.* 16. 70–80.

Russell, S and Joyner, K (2001) Adolescent sexual orientation and suicide risk: evidence from a national study. *American Journal of Public Health.* 91. 1276–1281.

Rutter, M (1985) Resilience in the face of adversity: protective factors and resistance to psychiatric disorders. *British Journal of Psychiatry.* 147. 589–611.

Rutter, M (2003) Genetic influences on risk and protection: implications for understanding resilience. In Luthar, S (Ed.) *Resilience and vulnerability.* Cambridge University Press. Cambridge.

Rutter, M (2006) Is Sure Start an effective intervention? *Child and Adolescent Mental Health.* 11. 135–141.

Rutter, M and Smith, D (Eds) (1995) *Psychosocial disorders in young people.* John Wiley. Chichester.

Rutter, M, Giller, H and Hagell, A (1998) *Anti-social behaviour by young people.* Cambridge University Press. Cambridge.

Rutter, M, Maughan, B, Mortimore, P, Ouston, J and Smith, A (1979) *Fifteen thousand hours: secondary schools and their effects on children.* Open Books. London.

Ryan, A (2001) The peer group as a context for the development of young adolescent motivation and achievement. *Child Development.* 72. 1135–1150.

Ryan, R and Lynch, J (1989) Emotional autonomy versus detachment: revisiting the vicissitudes of adolescence and young adulthood. *Child Development.* 60. 340–356.

Sabatier, C (2008) Ethnic and national identity among second-generation immigrant adolescents in France: the role of social context and family. *Journal of Adolescence.* 31. 185–206.

Salinger, J (1994) *The catcher in the rye.* Penguin. Harmondsworth, Middlesex.

Sampson, R and Laub, J (1993) *Crime in the making: pathways and turning points through life.* Harvard University Press. Cambridge, MA.

Sampson, R and Laub, J (1994) Urban poverty and the family context of delinquency: a new look at structure and process in a classic study. *Child Development.* 65. 523–540.

Savage, J (2007) *Teenage: the creation of youth 1875–1945.* Chatto and Windus. London.

Savin-Williams, R and Diamond, L (2004) Sex. In Lerner, R and Steinberg, L (Eds) *Handbook of adolescent psychology.* Wiley. New York.

Sawyer, M, Pfeiffer, S, Spence, S *et al.* (2010) School-based prevention of depression: a randomised control study of the *beyondblue* schools research initiative. *Journal of Child Psychology and Psychiatry.* 51. 199–209.

Schaefer, S and Uggen, C (2009) Juvenile delinquency and desistance. In Furlong, A (Ed.) *Handbook of youth and young adulthood*. Routledge. London.

Schaffer, R (2006) *Key concepts in developmental psychology*. Sage. London.

Schofield, M (1965) The sexual behaviour of young people. Longmans. London.

Scholte, R and van Aken, M (2006) Peer relations in adolescence. In Jackson, S and Goossens, L (Eds) *Handbook of adolescent development*. Psychology Press. Hove.

Scholte, R, van Lieshout, C and van Aken, M (2001) Perceived relational support in adolescence: dimensions, configurations and adolescent adjustment. *Journal of Research on Adolescence*. 11. 71–94.

Schonert-Reichl, K and Muller, J (1996) Correlates of help-seeking in adolescence. *Journal of Youth and Adolescence*. 25. 705–732.

Schwartz, S, Cote, J and Arnett, J (2005) Identity and agency in emerging adulthood: two developmental routes in the individualisation process. *Youth and Society*. 37. 201–229.

Schweinhart, L and Weikart, D (1980) *Young children grow up*. High/Scope. Ypsilanti, MI.

Scott, J (2004) Children's families. In Scott, J, Treas, J and Richards, M (Eds) *The Blackwell companion to the sociology of the families*. Wiley Blackwell. Oxford.

Scott, J (2007) The role of the family. In Coleman, J and Hagell, A (Eds) *Adolescence, risk and resilience*. John Wiley. Chichester.

Sears, H, Byers, E and Price, E (2007) The co-occurrence of adolescent boys' and girls' use of psychologically, physically and sexually abusive behaviours in their dating relationships. *Journal of Adolescence*. 30. 487–504.

Seiffge-Krenke, I (1995) *Stress, coping and relationships in adolescence*. Lawrence Erlbaum. Mahwah, NJ.

Seiffge-Krenke, I (2003) Testing theories of romantic development from adolescence to young adulthood: evidence of a developmental sequence. *International Journal of Behavioural Development*. 27. 519–531.

Selfhout, M, Branje, S, Delsing, M and Meeus, W (2009) Different types of internet use, depression and social anxiety: the role of perceived friendship quality. *Journal of Adolescence*. 32. 819–834.

Seligman, M, Ernst, R, Gillham, J and Linkins, M (2009) Positive education: positive psychology and classroom interventions. *Oxford Review of Education*. 35. 293–311.

Selman, R (1980) *The growth of interpersonal understanding: developmental and clinical analyses*. Academic Press. London.

Selman, R and Schultz, L (1990) *Making a friend in youth: developmental theory and pair therapy*. University of Chicago Press. Chicago.

Selman, R, Beardslee, W, Schultz, L, Krupa, M and Podorefsky, D (1986) Assessing adolescent interpersonal negotiation strategies. *Developmental Psychology*. 22. 450–459.

Sessa, F and Steinberg, L (1991) Family structure and the development of autonomy in adolescence. *Journal of Early Adolescence*. 11. 38–55.

Shavelson, R, Hubner, J and Stanton, G (1976) Self-concept: validation of construct interpretations. *Review of Educational Research*. 46. 407–441.

Shayer, M (1979) *Science reasoning tasks*. National Foundation for Educational Research. Slough.

Shayer, M and Adey, P (2002) *Cognitive acceleration across the curriculum*. Open University Press. Milton Keynes.

Shayer, M and Wylam, H (1978) The distribution of Piagetian stages of thinking in British middle and secondary school children: 2. *British Journal of Educational Psychology*. 48. 62–70.

Shayer, M, Kuchemann, D and Wylam, H (1976) The distribution of Piagetian stages of thinking in British middle and secondary school children. *British Journal of Educational Psychology*. 46. 164–173.

Shih, M, Pittinsky, T and Ambady, M (1999) Stereotype susceptibility: identity salience and shifts in quantitative performance. *Psychological Science*. 10. 80–83.

Shorter-Gooden, K and Washington, N (1996) Young, Black and female: the challenge of weaving an identity. *Journal of Adolescence*. 19. 465–476.

Shucksmith, J and Hendry, L (1998) *Health issues and adolescents: growing up and speaking out*. Routledge. London.

Shulman, S and Seiffge-Krenke, I (1997) *Fathers and adolescents*. Routledge. London.

Siddique, C and D'Arcy, C (1984) Adolescence, stress and psychological well-being. *Journal of Youth and Adolescence*. 13. 459–474.

Siegler, R (1988) Individual differences in strategy choices: good students, not-so-good students, and perfectionists. *Child Development*. 59. 833–851.

Silbereisen, R and Kracke, B (1997) Self-reported maturational timing and adaptation in adolescence. In Schulenberg, J, Maggs, J and Hurrelmann, K (Eds) *Health risks and developmental transitions during adolescence*. Cambridge University Press. Cambridge.

Simmons, R and Blyth, D (1987) *Moving into adolescence: the impact of pubertal change and school context*. Aldine de Gruyter. New York.

Simmons, R and Rosenberg, M (1975) Sex, sex-roles and self-image. *Journal of Youth and Adolescence*. 4. 229–236.

Smetana, J (1988) Adolescents' and parents' conceptions of parental authority. *Child Development*. 59. 321–335.

Smetana, J (2002) Culture, autonomy and personal jurisdiction in parent–adolescent relationships. *Advances in Child Development and Behaviour*. 29. 51–87.

Smetana, J and Asquith, P (1994) Adolescents' and parents' conceptions of parental authority and personal autonomy. *Child Development*. 65. 1147–1162.

Smetana, J and Chuang, S (2001) Middle-class African-American parents' conceptions of parenting in the transition to adolescence. *Journal of Research on Adolescence*. 11. 177–198.

Smetana, J and Daddis, C (2002) Domain-specific antecedents of parental psychological control and monitoring: the role of parenting beliefs and practices. *Child Development*. 73. 631–650.

Smetana, J, Metzger, A and Campion-Barr, N (2004) African-American late adolescents' relationships with parents: developmental transitions and longitudinal patterns. *Child Development*. 75. 932–947.

Smith, A, Agius, P, Dyson, S and Mitchell, A (2003) *Secondary students and sexual health: results of the 3rd national survey of Australian secondary school students*. Australian Research Centre in Sex, Health and Society. La Trobe University. Melbourne.

Smith, D (1995) Towards explaining patterns and trends in youth crime. In Rutter, M (Ed.) *Psychosocial disturbances in young people: challenges for prevention*. Cambridge University Press. Cambridge.

Smith, D (2005) Ethnic differences in inter-generational crime patterns. In Tonry, M (Ed.) *Crime and justice: a review of research*, Vol. 32. University of Chicago Press. Chicago, IL.

Smith, P, Morita, Y, Junger-Tas, J, Olweus, D and Slee, P (Eds) (1999) *The nature of school bullying: a cross-national perspective*. Routledge. London.

Social Exclusion Unit (1999) *Teenage pregnancy*. HMSO. London.

Solomon, Y, Warin, J, Lewis, C and Langford, W (2002) Intimate talk between parents and their teenage children. *Sociology*. 36. 965–983.

Speak, S (1997) *Young single fathers: participation in fatherhood*. Joseph Rowntree Foundation. York.

Stattin, H and Kerr, M (2000) Parental monitoring: a reinterpretation. *Child Development*. 71. 1070–1083.

Stattin, H and Kerr, M (2009) Challenges in intervention research on adolescent development. *Journal of Adolescence*. 32. 1437–1442.

Stattin, H and Magnusson, D (1990) *Pubertal maturation in female development*. Erlbaum. Hillsdale, NJ.

Stattin, H and Magnusson, D (1996) Anti-social development: a holistic approach. *Development and Psychopathology*. 8. 617–645.

Stein, J and Reiser, L (1994) A study of white middle-class boys' responses to semenarche (the first ejaculation). *Journal of Youth and Adolescence*. 23. 373–384.

Steinberg, L (2007) Risk-taking in adolescence: new perspectives from brain and behavioural science. *Current Directions in Psychological Science*. 16. 55–59.

Steinberg, L (2008) *Adolescence*, 8th edn. McGraw-Hill. New York.

Steinberg, L and Silverberg, S (Eds) (1986) The vicissitudes of autonomy in early adolescence. *Child Development*. 57. 841–851.

Steinberg, L and Silverberg, S (1987) Influences on marital satisfaction during the middle stages of the family life cycle. *Journal of Marriage and the Family*. 49. 751–760.

Stevens, E and Prinstein, M (2005) Peer contagion of depressogenic attributional styles among adolescents: a longitudinal study. *Journal of Abnormal Child Psychology*. 33. 25–38.

Susman, E (1997) Modelling developmental complexity in adolescence: capturing the future of biology and behaviour in context. *Journal of Research in Adolescence*. 7. 283–306.

Susman, E and Rogol, A (2004) Puberty and psychological development. In Lerner, R and Steinberg, L (Eds) *Handbook of adolescent psychology*, 2nd edn. John Wiley. Chichester.

Susman, E, Dorn, L and Schiefelbien, V (2003) Puberty, sexuality and health. In Lerner, R, Easterbrooks, M and Mistry, J (Eds). *The comprehensive handbook of psychology*. Wiley. New York.

Tajfel, H (1978) Social categorisation, social identity and social comparison. In Tajfel, H (Ed.) *Differentiation between social groups*. Academic Press. London.

Tanner, J (1962) *Growth at adolescence*. Blackwell Scientific Publications. Oxford.

Tanner, J (1973) Growing up. *Scientific American*. 229. 35–42.

Tanner, J (1978) *Foetus into man*. Open Books. London.

Tanner, J and Arnett, G (2009) The emergence of 'emerging adulthood': the new life stage between adolescence and adulthood. In Furlong, A (Ed.) *Handbook of youth and young adulthood*. Routledge. London.

Tanner, J, Whitehouse, R and Takaishi, M (1966) Standards from birth to maturity for British children. *Archives of Disease in Childhood*. 41. 455–471.

Tate, D, Reppucci, N and Mulvey, E (1995) Violent juvenile delinquents: treatment effectiveness and implications for future action. *American Psychologist*. 50. 777–781.

Testa, A and Coleman, L (2006) *Sexual health knowledge, attitudes and behaviours among black and minority youth in London*. Trust for the Study of Adolescence, Brighton and the Naz Project. www.youngpeopleinfocus.org.uk

Thomson, R and Holland, J (1998) Sexual relationships, negotiation and decision-making. In Coleman, J and Roker, D (Eds) *Teenage sexuality: health, risk and education*. Harwood Academic Press. London.

Tilleczek, K and Hine, D (2006) The meaning of smoking as health and social risk in adolescence. *Journal of Adolescence*. 29. 273–288.

Tilton-Weaver, L, Kerr, M, Salihovic, S and Stattin, H (2010) Open up or close down: how do parental reactions affect youth information management? *Journal of Adolescence*. 33. 333–346.

Tizard, B and Phoenix, A (2002) *Black, white or mixed race? Race and racism in the lives of young people*, 2nd edn. Routledge. London.

Tobler, N (1986) Meta-analysis of 143 drug treatment programmes: quantitative outcome results. *Journal of Drug Issues*. 16. 537–567.

Torney-Purta, J (1990) Youth in relation to social institutions. In Feldman, S and Elliott, G (Eds) *At the threshold: the developing adolescent*. Harvard University Press. Cambridge, MA.

REFERENCES

Torsheim, T and Wold, B (2001) School-related stress, support, and subjective health complaints among early adolescents. *Journal of Adolescence*. 24. 701–713.

Tremain, R (1997) *The way I found her*. Sinclair-Stevenson. London.

Troiden, R (1989) The formation of homosexual identities. In Herdt, G (Ed.) *Gay and lesbian youth*. Haworth Press. New York.

Tucker, S and Walker, S (2004) Education and training provision for young people: a new era? In Roche, R, Tucker, S, Thomson, R and Flynn, R (Eds) *Youth in society*, 2nd edn. Sage. London.

Udry, J (1990) Hormonal and social determinants of adolescent sexual initiation. In Bancroft, J and Reinisch, J (Eds) *Adolescence and puberty*. Oxford University Press. Oxford.

Udry, J and Billy, J (1987) Initiation of coitus in early adolescence. *American Sociological Review*. 52. 841–855.

UNICEF (2007) UNICEF Report Card 7. Child poverty in perspective: an overview of child well-being in rich countries. February. Available online at www.unicef.org

Upchurch, D, Lillard, L, Aneschensel, D and Li, N (2002) Inconsistencies in reporting the occurrence and timing of first intercourse among adolescents. *Journal of Sex Research*. 39. 197–206.

Valkenberg, P and Peter, J (2007) Internet communication and its relation to well-being. *Media Psychology*. 9. 43–58.

Van den Bulck, J (2004) Television viewing, computer game playing and Internet use and self-reported time to bed and time out of bed in secondary school children. *Sleep*. 27. 101–104.

Van Hoof, A (1999) The identity status approach: in need of fundamental revision and qualitative change. *Developmental Review*. 19. 497–556.

Verkuyten, M (1993) Self-esteem among ethnic minorities and three principles of self-esteem formation. *International Journal of Psychology*. 28. 307–321.

Verkuyten, M (1995) Self-esteem, self-concept stability, and aspects of ethnic identity among minority and majority youth in the Netherlands. *Journal of Youth and Adolescence*. 24. 155–176.

Viner, R and Barker, M (2005) Young people's health: the need for action. *British Medical Journal*. 330. 901–903.

Vostanis, P (2007) Mental health and mental disorders. In Coleman, J and Hagell, A (Eds) *Adolescence, risk and resilience*. John Wiley. Chichester.

Walker, L and Hennig, K (1999) Parenting style and the development of moral reasoning. *Journal of Moral Education*. 28. 359–374.

Walker, L, Gustafson, P and Hennig, K (2001) The consolidation/transition model in moral reasoning development. *Developmental Psychology*. 37. 187–197.

Walker, L, Hennig, K and Krettenauer, T (2000) Parent and peer contexts for children's moral reasoning development. *Child Development*. 71. 1033–1048.

Walker, L, Pitts, R, Hennig, K and Matsuba, M (1995) Reasoning about morality and real-life moral problems. In Killen, M and Hart, D (Eds) *Morality in everyday life*. Cambridge University Press. Cambridge.

Walker-Barnes, C and Mason, C (2004) Delinquency and substance use among gang-involved youth: the moderating role of parenting practices. *American Journal of Community Psychology*. 34. 235–250.

Ward, S and Overton, W (1990) Semantic familiarity, relevance and the development of deductive reasoning. *Developmental Psychology*. 26. 488–493.

Warren, C, Jones, M and Eriksen, S (2006) Patterns of global tobacco use in young people and implications for future chronic disease burden in adults. *Lancet*. 367 (9512). 749–753.

Waterman, A and Goldman, J (1976) A longitudinal study of ego identity development at a liberal arts college. *Journal of Youth and Adolescence*. 5. 361–369.

Weare, K (2004) *Developing the emotionally literate school*. Paul Chapman Publishing. London.

Webb, R, Vulliamy, G, Sarja, A and Poikonen, P-L (2009) Professional learning communities and teacher well-being? A comparative analysis of primary schools in England and Finland. *Oxford Review of Education*. 35. 405–422.

Webster, C (2009) Young people, race and ethnicity. In Furlong, A (Ed.) *Handbook of youth and young adulthood*. Routledge. London.

Wellings, K, Field, J, Johnson, A and Wadsworth, J (2001) Sexual behaviour in Britain: early heterosexual experience. *Lancet*. 358. 1843–1850.

Wenzel, V, Weichold, K and Silbereisen, R (2009) The life skills programme IPSY: positive influences on school bonding and prevention of substance abuse. *Journal of Adolescence*. 32. 1391–1402.

Werner, E and Smith, R (1982) *Vulnerable but invincible: a study of resilient children*. McGraw-Hill. New York.

Werner, E and Smith, R (1992) *Overcoming the odds: high risk children from birth to adulthood*. Cornell University Press. New York.

Werner, N and Silbereisen, R (2003) Family relationship quality and contact with deviant peers as predictors of adolescent problem behaviour: the moderating role of gender. *Journal of Adolescent Research*. 18. 454–480.

West, D and Farrington, D (1977) *The delinquent way of life*. Heinemann. London.

West, P (2009) Health in youth: changing times and changing influences. In Furlong, A (Ed.) *Handbook of youth and young adulthood*. Routledge. London.

West, P and Sweeting, H (2003) Fifteen, female and stressed: changing patterns of psychological distress over time. *Journal of Child Psychology and Psychiatry*. 44. 399–411.

West, P, Sweeting, H and Leyland, A (2004) School effects on pupils' health behaviours: evidence in support of the health-promoting school. *Research Papers in Education*. 19. 261–292.

White, R (2009) Young people, crime and justice. In Furlong, A (Ed.) *Handbook of youth and young adulthood*. Routledge. London.

Wight, D, Williamson, L and Henderson, M (2006) Parental influences on young people's sexual behaviour: a longitudinal analysis. *Journal of Adolescence*. 29. 473–494.

Windfuhr, K, While, D, Hunt, I *et al*. (2008) Suicide in juveniles and adolescents in the United Kingdom. *Journal of Child Psychology and Psychiatry*. 49. 1155–1165.

Wissink, I, Dekovic, M, Yagmur, S, Stams, G and de Haan, M (2008) Ethnic identity, externalizing problem behaviour and the mediating role of self-esteem among Dutch, Turkish-Dutch and Moroccan-Dutch adolescents. *Journal of Adolescence*. 31. 223–240.

Wolak, J, Mitchell, K and Finkelhor, D (2003) Escaping or connecting? Characteristics of youth who form close on-line relationships. *Journal of Adolescence*. 26. 105–120.

Wolfson, A and Carskadon, M (1998) Sleep schedules and daytime functioning in adolescence. *Child Development*. 69. 875–887.

Wu, L, Mendola, P and Buck, G (2002) Ethnic differences in the presence of secondary sex characteristics and menarche among US girls. *Paediatrics*. 110. 47–63.

Wyn, J (2006) Youth transitions to work and further education in Australia. In Cartwright, P, Chapman, J and McGilp, E (Eds) *Lifelong learning: participation and equity*. Springer. Dordrecht.

Wyn, J (2009) Educating for late modernity. In Furlong, A (Ed.) *Handbook of youth and young adulthood*. Routledge. London.

Yau, J and Smetana, J (1966) Adolescent–parent conflict among Chinese adolescents in Hong Kong. *Child Development*. 67. 1262–1275.

Yau, J and Smetana, J (2003) Adolescent–parent conflict in Hong Kong and Shenzen: a comparison of youth in two cultural contexts. *International Journal of Behavioural Development*. 27. 201–211.

Young, I (2004) Exploring the role of schools in sexual health promotion. In Burtney, E and Duffy, M (Eds) *Young people and sexual health: individual, social and policy contexts*. Palgrave Macmillan. Basingstoke.

REFERENCES

Youngman, L and Lunzer, E (1977) *Adjustment to secondary schooling*. School of Education, University of Nottingham. Nottingham.

Youniss, J and Smollar, J (1985) *Adolescent relations with mothers, fathers and friends*. University of Chicago Press. Chicago.

Zani, B and Cicognani, E (2006) Sexuality and intimate relationships in adolescence. In Jackson, S and Goossens, L (Eds) *Handbook of adolescent development*. Psychology Press. Hove.

Zimmer-Gembeck, M, Chipuer, H, Hanisch, M, Creed, P and McGregor, L (2006) Relationships at school and stage–environment fit as resources for adolescent engagement and achievement. *Journal of Adolescence*. 29. 911–934.

Zimmerman, M, Copeland, L, Shope, J and Dielman, T (1997) A longitudinal study of self-esteem: implications for adolescent development. *Journal of Youth and Adolescence*. 26. 117–142.

Zinzow, H, Ruggiero, K, Hanson, R, Smith, D, Saunders, B and Kilpatrick, DG (2009) Witnessed community and parental violence in relation to substance abuse and delinquency in a national sample of adolescents. *Journal of Traumatic Stress*. 22. 523–533.

Author index

Subject index

academic achievement: school ethos 167; self-esteem 63, 64; transition to secondary school 164

active agents 17, 20, 225–6

adolescence: age boundaries 2, 10; constructing own adolescence 3, 20, 93, 225–6, 227; sub-stages 10; theories 13–21; transition 10–13

African-Americans: ethnic identity 73–4, 75; puberty 26, 31; sexual behaviour 137

age: anti-social behaviour 197, 198; attitude to science at school 164; autonomy 84; boundaries of adolescence 2, 10; control 100; coping 219; growth spurt 28–9; identity achievement 70; loneliness 185; menarche 30, 31; peer influence 180; political thought 52–3; puberty 26; self-consciousness 46; sexual behaviour 134–6; smoking 112; social perspective taking 47–8; sports involvement 109; time spent with family 86

agency 16–17, 20, 71, 225–6

aggression 185

AIDS/HIV 143–4, 154

alcohol use 112, 114–15, 202, 214

anal sex 136

androgen 140

anger management 204

anorexia 118–19

anthropology 163

anti-social behaviour 55, 193–208; age 197, 198; environmental factors 202, 205–6; family factors 200–1; gender 194–5, 196, 197, 199–200, 207; interventions 204–7; parenting style 91; peer influences 181, 201–2, 205; prevalence 195–9; risk factors 199–203; social factors 202; trajectories 198–9, 200, 207

anxiety 63, 84, 190

arenas of comfort 20

Argentina, family life 94

Aristotle 14

Asians: parents and ethnic identity 74; sexual behaviour 137; social capital 96; teacher expectations 165–6

asset framework 210

at risk 211, 214, 226

attachment representations 177

attachment theory 177

attention 44

Australia: Chlamydia infections 144; coping 220; ethnicity and sexual behaviour 137; school ethos 167; secondary education 160; sexual orientation 148

Austria, education 161

authoritarian parents 90, 95

authoritarianism 52–4